THE
One & Only
salads
Cookbook

THE One & Only salads Cookbook

All the recipes you will ever need

With a foreword by
Jenny Linford

WELDONOWEN
PUBLISHING

WELDONOWEN
PUBLISHING

First published in the UK by
Weldon Owen Ltd., an imprint of the Bonnier Group
The Plaza
535 King's Road
London
SW10 0SZ
www.weldonowen.co.uk
www.bonnierpublishing.com

ISBN-13: 978 1 78342 223 4

A catalogue record for this book is available from the
British Library

Printed and bound by Interak, Poland
10 9 8 7 6 5 4 3 2 1

"To make a good salad is to be a brilliant diplomat — the problem is entirely the same in both cases. To know exactly how much oil one must put with one's vinegar."

Oscar Wilde

Contents

Foreword

By Jenny Linford

Salads offer the creative cook lots of scope. While for many a simple assortment of green leaves remains the iconic salad, the reality is far more varied and interesting. Salads come in numerous forms: savoury, sweet, hot, warm or cold. They range from hearty concoctions, based on pasta, potatoes or pulses, to light, elegant, leaf-based creations, favoured by those watching their waistlines. Salads can be created using meat, fish and seafood, vegetables, fruit, grains and pulses.

The secret to great dressings

A good dressing has a wonderfully transformative effect on even the simplest salad, lifting it from the dull to the enjoyable. It acts as a pick-me-up, giving zest and zing to ingredients from earthy lentils to noodles.

A classic French-style vinaigrette consists of olive oil to wine vinegar used in a ratio of three to five parts oil to one part vinegar. Place the wine vinegar in a bowl, season with salt and pepper, whisking until the salt has dissolved, then add in the olive oil and whisk until well-combined. Alternatively, place all the ingredients in a clean-lidded jar and shake until thoroughly mixed.

Olive oil, with its distinctive, sophisticated flavour, is a classic choice for making salad dressings. Do, however, try experimenting with other oils, such as walnut oil or hazelnut oil, with their distinctive toasted nutty flavour, to achieve different results. Similarly, vary the acidic element of the dressing by substituting lemon juice, lime juice, grapefruit juice, orange juice or verjus for the vinegar. Vinegars, too, offer scope for variation. A dressing made with a good quality, mellow balsamic vinegar will taste very different from one made with a more restrained Spanish sherry vinegar or delicate rice vinegar. The vinaigrette can be further tweaked by adding in flavourings such as a touch of mustard, a little sugar or honey, crushed garlic or chopped fresh herbs.

When making your salad dressing, match it to the contents of your salad. Delicate fresh salad leaves require a lightly flavoured dressing, while more robustly flavourful ingredients can take a bigger hitting dressing, flavoured say with crushed garlic and balsamic vinegar.

One simple but golden rule to bear in mind with many salads, especially leaf-based ones, is to dress them at the last minute, that is **just before serving**, in order to prevent them becoming limp and sodden.

Making Mayonnaise

Another traditional salad dressing is mayonnaise, which adds a luxurious creaminess to salads such as potato or coleslaw. Although it has an intimidating reputation, in fact, making your own mayonnaise is very simple, although patience is required.

It's very important to have all the ingredients, including the eggs, at **room temperature**. Use 1 egg yolk for 150ml oil. Light-flavoured oils such as sunflower are recommended for mayonnaise rather than strongly flavoured olive oil, although a combination of sunflower and olive oil works well.

Whisk the egg yolk with a pinch of salt, add in 1 tsp of vinegar or lemon juice and whisk again. Now gradually add in your oil, at first just a drop at a time, whisking thoroughly all the time. As the mixture begins to emulsify and thicken you can add the oil in a thin, steady trickle, still whisking continuously. The finished mayonnaise should have a thick,

but smooth texture. Once made, the mayonnaise can be flavoured to taste, for example, with crushed garlic, ground saffron soaked in a little water or chopped fresh herbs.

Putting together your salad

When creating a salad, do bear in mind you want combinations that work either by harmonising or contrasting nicely. While variety has a part to play, using too many disparate ingredients can simply result in a salad that lacks clarity and impact.

Using good-quality ingredients is key, especially for raw salads. Look for the freshest and tastiest, seasonal vegetables, fruits and herbs that you can find, so, for example, ripe, sweet tomatoes rather than dull, insipid ones.

Make sure your salad leaves are thoroughly dried before you toss them with the dressing. Salad spinners are an effective way of drying them; alternately place them between layers of kitchen paper.

Vary the textures within your salad. Combine crisp, firm-textured ingredients such as red pepper or cucumber, croutons, fried or lightly toasted nuts with soft ingredients such as lettuce leaves, tomatoes or avocado chunks.

Use colourful ingredients to make your salad visually appealing. Sprinkling in sprigs of fresh herbs, edible flowers such as nasturtiums or chive flowers or chopped fruit are all simple ways of adding vibrancy.

Warm Jerusalem artichoke and mackerel salad

1. Cook the artichokes until easily pierced with the tip of a knife; this should take around 15 minutes. When they are cooked, drain and cut into quarters.

2. Place the artichokes in a large salad bowl along with the flatleaf parsley.

3. Whisk together the dressing ingredients and pour over the artichokes. Toss the artichokes to coat with the dressing.

4. Flake over the mackerel fillets and serve.

Preparation time: 5 min
Cooking time: 15 min
Serves 4

650g peeled Jerusalem artichokes
small bunch of flat leaf parsley
   roughly chopped
4 smoked mackerel fillets

For the dressing:
1 shallot, finely chopped
1 tbsp chopped tarragon
80ml rapeseed oil
40ml sherry vinegar
2 tbsp mayonnaise (preferably
   rapeseed)

Beetroot carpaccio salad with smoked salmon and baby capers

1. Cook 2 of the beetroots in boiling salted water until cooked through and easily pierced with the tip of a knife, this should take around 30 to 40 minutes. When cooked, chop into quarters. Whilst the beetroot is cooking, peel the other beetroots and thinly slice using a mandoline.

2. Layer the raw sliced beetroots over 2 plates to fill the surface area of both.

3. Whisk together the dressing ingredients and toss the cooked quartered beetroots in half of the dressing and arrange over your 2 plates.

4. Sprinkle each plate with capers and the purple radish sprouts. Divide the salmon between the 2 plates, draping the slices over the beetroot.

5. Finish by drizzling over the remaining dressing.

Preparation time: 5 min
Cooking time: 40 min
Serves 2

4 small beetroots
10g alfalfa sprouts
2 tsp baby capers
100g smoked salmon

For the dressing:
40ml extra virgin olive oil
20ml red wine vinegar
1 tbsp honey
½ grated red onion
2 drops of Valencian orange extract

Broad bean, pea and smoked trout salad

1. Cook the broad beans and peas in a pan of boiling water for 5 minutes before draining and removing the skin from the broad beans. Place the podded broad beans and peas in a large salad bowl along with the dill, pea shoots and shaved courgettes.

2. Whisk together the dressing ingredients and pour over the salad, tossing to combine.

3. Flake in the smoked trout and serve.

Preparation time: 10 min
Cooking time: 5 min
Serves 4

400g broad beans
200g peas or petit pois
1 small bunch of dill,
  roughly chopped
20g pea shoots
4 baby courgettes, shaved
  into ribbons
250g smoked trout fillets

For the dressing:
60ml extra virgin olive oil
2 tsp Dijon mustard
juice of 1 lemon
¼ tsp sugar

Baby courgette, fennel and chorizo salad

Preparation time: 5 min
Cooking time: 5 min
Serves 4

2 bulb of fennel
12 baby courgettes
olive oil
150g chorizo
4 tsp fennel seeds

For the dressing:
60ml extra virgin olive oil
30ml balsamic vinegar

1. Slice the fennel into ½ cm thick diagonal slices, then slice the courgettes into 3 diagonally. Toss the vegetables in a little olive oil.

2. Add the chorizo to a hot griddle pan and cook for 1 to 2 minutes, allowing the oils to be released. Add in the fennel seeds and the vegetables and griddle until dark lines appear, then flip over and repeat on the other side.

3. Whisk together the dressing ingredients and toss over the vegetable mixture.

4. Serve immediately.

Crab and avocado salad

1. Lay the salad leaves out on a large plate. Peel and chop the avocadoes and scatter on top of the leaves.

2. Whisk together all the dressing ingredients and season to taste.

3. Drizzle the dressing over the leaves, making sure they all get an even coating of the dressing. Finish by scattering over the picked crab.

Preparation time: 5 min
Serves 4

70g mixed leafs such as baby gem,
  rocket, green oak leaf
2 ripe avocado
300g picked white crabmeat

For the dressing:
2 tbsp crème fraiche
40ml lime juice
80ml rapeseed oil
2 heaped tsp Dijon mustard

Coleslaw

1. Mix the cabbage with the carrots.

2. Mix together the mayonnaise, vinegar and soured cream. Season to taste with salt and pepper.

3. Stir into the cabbage and carrots. Cover and chill overnight.

Preparation time: 10 min
   plus 12 h chilling
Serves 4

300g white cabbage leaves,
   finely sliced
150g carrots, cut into strips
70ml mayonnaise
1 tbsp white wine vinegar
100ml soured cream
salt and pepper to taste

Beef and vegetable salad with peanuts

1. Heat the oven to 200°C (400°F). Heat the oil in a roasting tin and brown the meat on all sides. Cook for 20 minutes. Remove from the oven, wrap in foil and leave to rest in the turned-off oven.

2. Blanch the carrots, beans and broccoli in a pan of boiling salted water for 5 minutes. Drain and rinse in cold water and drain again.

3. For the dressing: whisk together all the ingredients and season to taste. Mix the blanched vegetables and spring onions with half of the dressing.

4. Slice the beef thinly across the grain and mix lightly with the dressing and vegetables. Arrange on a large plate, drizzle with the remaining dressing and scatter with peanuts and chilli.

Preparation time: 25 min
Cooking time: 25 min
Serves 4

1 tbsp oil
500g piece beef sirloin
250g carrots, cut into matchsticks
250g green beans
200g broccoli florets
2 spring onions, sliced

For the dressing:
6 tbsp lemon juice
6 tbsp sunflower oil
1 tsp sesame oil
1 tsp sugar
1 tsp ginger, finely chopped
1 garlic clove, finely chopped
100g roasted peanuts, to serve
1 green chilli, very thinly sliced,
  to serve

Rice salad with green asparagus, peppers and sweetcorn

Preparation time: 5 min
Cooking time: 6 min
Serves 4

12 green asparagus spears
1 green pepper, diced
1 red pepper, diced
juice of 1 lemon
6 tbsp olive oil
salt and pepper to taste
400g cooked long grain rice
2 tomatoes, diced
½ bunch spring onions, sliced
150g tinned sweetcorn
basil leaves and lemon wedges,
  to serve

1. Cook the asparagus in boiling salted water for 6 minutes. Add the peppers for the last 3 minutes. Drain and rinse in cold water. Drain again.

2. Whisk together the lemon juice and olive oil. Season to taste with salt and pepper.

3. Stir into the rice, then stir in all the vegetables.

4. Divide the salad among the serving plates and garnish with basil and lemon wedges.

Rice noodle salad with ground meat and nuts

1. Cook the rice noodles in boiling, salted water for 4 minutes. Drain and rinse in cold water and leave to drain.

2. Heat the oil in a wok or frying pan and brown the meat. Add the shallots and the garlic and cook for a few minutes, then season with salt and pepper. Remove from the wok and set aside.

3. Whisk the egg and fry in the hot wok. Chop and set aside.

4. For the dressing: whisk together all the ingredients.

5. Toss the noodles, meat, egg and vegetables with the dressing. Divide the salad between 4 plates, scatter with coriander and cashew nuts and serve with a wedge of lime.

Preparation time: 15 min
Cooking time: 10 min
Serves 4

250g thin rice noodles
1 tbsp oil
300g minced beef
2 shallots, finely chopped
3 garlic clove, finely chopped
salt and pepper to taste
1 egg
3–4 leaves Chinese cabbage, shredded
1 tomato, chopped
1 red pepper, chopped

For the dressing:
2 tbsp peanut oil
2 tbsp fish sauce
1 tbsp lime juice
2 tbsp vinegar
½ tsp sambal oelek
½ tbsp sugar

To garnish:
½ bunch coriander, shredded
40g chopped cashew nuts
1 lime, cut into wedges

Asparagus and orange salad

1. Heat the olive oil and quickly cook the asparagus and shallot. Deglaze with Noilly Prat and orange juice.

2. Stir in the sugar, salt and pepper to taste and bring to the boil. Simmer gently to reduce slightly. Leave to cool.

3. Arrange the chicory leaves and orange segments on serving plates with the asparagus and olives and sprinkle with pine nuts.

Preparation time: 10 min
Cooking time: 10 min
Serves 4

4 tbsp olive oil
400g asparagus spears
1 shallot, chopped
40ml Noilly Prat
2 tbsp orange juice
pinch sugar
salt and pepper to taste
chicory, leaves, torn
2 large oranges, peeled and
  segmented
70g black olives, pitted
2 tbsp chopped pine nuts, toasted,
  to serve

Grilled tuna steaks with kidney beans and tomato salad

1. Drain the kidney beans and rinse under running water.

2. Mix together the beans, red onion, peppers, tomatoes, 1 tablespoon olive oil and lime juice in a bowl and set aside.

3. Mix the garlic with the remaining olive oil and add the lime zest. Season with salt and pepper.

4. Brush the fish with the lime oil and grill for about 3 minutes each side or according to taste.

5. Mix the parsley and mint into the bean salad and season to taste.

6. Arrange the tuna and salad on plates. Garnish with the mint leaves and lime wedges.

Preparation time: 5 min
Cooking time: 25 min
Serves 4

200g tinned red kidney beans
1 red onion, finely chopped
1 green pepper, finely chopped
1 red pepper, finely chopped
3 tomatoes, deseeded and finely
 chopped
3 tbsp olive oil
salt and pepper to taste
juice and zest of 1 lime
1 garlic clove, finely chopped
4 tuna steaks
1 tbsp finely chopped parsley
1 tbsp finely chopped mint
mint leaves and 4 lime wedges,
 to serve

Rocket salad with citrus fruits

1. Peel the citrus fruits with a sharp knife, removing all the white pith. Separate the segments by cutting down inside the segment skin and catching any juice into a bowl.

2. Squeeze the fruit scraps by hand. Mix the juices with the honey, olive oil and salt and pepper to taste.

3. Mix together the fruit segments and rocket.

4. Arrange on serving plates and drizzle with the vinaigrette. Sprinkle with sesame seeds.

Preparation time: 5 min
Cooking time: 10 min
Serves 4

1 orange
1 pink grapefruit
1 lemon
1 tbsp honey
1 tbsp olive oil
salt and pepper to taste
200g rocket
1 tbsp sesame seeds

Aubergine and tomato salad with minted yoghurt dressing

1. Heat 2 tablespoons oil in a frying pan and fry the aubergine slices on both sides until golden. Drain on kitchen towel.

2. Slice 2 tomatoes and dice the remaining 2.

3. Mix the chopped tomatoes with a sprinkling of salt and pepper, the remaining oil and the garlic.

4. Mix together the yoghurt, a little salt and pepper and the mint.

5. Place a tomato slice on a slice of aubergine. Place a teaspoon of the yoghurt mixture on top and finish with a slice of aubergine. Repeat with the remaining slices.

6. Arrange on a serving plate and spoon the chopped tomatoes in the centre. Drizzle with the remaining dressing. Scatter over the mint to garnish.

Preparation time: 15 min
Cooking time: 5 min
Serves 4

3 tbsp olive oil
2 aubergines, sliced
4 large tomatoes
salt and pepper to taste
1 garlic clove, finely chopped
150ml plain yoghurt
2 tbsp chopped mint
mint leaves, to serve

Spinach chicken salad with sesame

Preparation time: 10 min
    plus 20 min marinating
Cooking time: 5 min
Serves 4

4 chicken breasts, cut into bite
    size pieces
2 tbsp light soy sauce
4 tbsp sesame oil
2 tbsp rice wine vinegar
salt and pepper to taste
2 tbsp sunflower oil
1 red pepper, deseeded and
    finely sliced
400g baby spinach, washed
100g cooked ham, shredded
2 nori leaves, shredded
2 tbsp sesame seeds

1. Mix the chicken pieces with the soy sauce and allow to marinate for 20 minutes.

2. Mix the sesame oil and rice wine vinegar, season with salt and pepper and set aside.

3. Heat the sunflower oil in a wok or frying pan and stir-fry the chicken for 3 minutes or until lightly browned.

4. Mix the spinach with the pepper and toss in the dressing. Add more seasoning if desired.

5. Carefully toss the chicken with the spinach. Arrange the salad on plates.

6. Garnish with the ham and seaweed strips, sprinkle with the sesame seeds and serve immediately.

Beetroot salad with onions and goat's cheese

1. Heat the oven to 180°C (350°F).

2. Brush the beetroot and onions with the oil. Sprinkle with the crushed peppercorns, coriander and mustard seeds and season to taste with salt and pepper.

3. Put into a roasting bag and add the stock. Cook for 1 hour, until tender. Remove from the bag and leave to cool.

4. Place on serving plates and scatter with the shaved cheese. Garnish with beetroot leaves.

Preparation time: 20 min
Cooking time: 1 h
Serves 4

1kg small young beetroot
3 red onions, quartered
3 tbsp olive oil
1 tsp peppercorns, crushed
1 tsp coriander seeds, crushed
salt and pepper to taste
2 tsp mustard seeds, crushed
50ml vegetable stock
1 mature Crottin de Chavignol
   cheese, shaved
beetroot leaves, to serve

Tuna with sesame crust on glass noodle and sugarsnap pea salad

1. Marinate the tuna in the soy sauce for 30 minutes.

2. For the dressing: whisk together all the ingredients.

3. For the salad: put the glass noodles into a bowl, pour boiling water over and stand for 5 minutes. Drain and rinse in cold water. Drain well.

4. Blanch the peas in boiling salted water for 4 minutes. Drain and rinse in cold water and drain again.

5. Toss the noodles and salad vegetables in the dressing.

6. Heat the sesame oil in a wok or frying pan and sear the tuna quickly on both sides. Roll in the sesame seeds and slice thickly.

7. Divide the salad between serving plates. Add a few slices of tuna and garnish with coriander.

Preparation time: 15 min
  plus 30 min marinating
Cooking time: 10 min
Serves 4

800g tuna fillet
3 tbsp soy sauce

For the dressing:
3 tbsp sesame oil
1 tbsp fish sauce
3 tbsp soy sauce
pinch sugar
juice of 2 limes

For the salad:
150g glass noodles
400g sugarsnap peas, halved
4 red chillies, finely sliced
1 bunch spring onions, sliced
1 tbsp sesame oil
2 tbsp white sesame seeds
2 tbsp black sesame seeds

To garnish:
1 bunch coriander, chopped

Fruit salad brulee with grated lemon peel

1. Heat the oven to 180°C (350°F). Butter a baking dish.

2. Put the fruit into the baking dish and sprinkle with lemon juice.

3. Beat the egg yolks with the sugar, vanilla, lemon zest and liqueur until smooth.

4. Whisk the egg white until stiff and gently fold into the egg yolk mixture until combined.

5. Pour on top of the fruit and bake for 15–20 minutes until the topping has set. Serve warm or cold decorated with lemon zest.

Preparation time: 20 min
Cooking time: 20 min
Serves 4

1kg fruit, e. g. raspberries, apricots, blueberries
1 tbsp lemon juice
2 eggs, separated
3 tbsp sugar
1 tsp vanilla extract
1 tsp grated lemon zest
2 tbsp orange liqueur
finely grated lemon zest, to serve

Smoked salmon salad

Preparation time: 15 min
Serves 4

1 tbsp white wine vinegar
1 tbsp sunflower oil
pinch sugar
salt and pepper to taste
1 onion, sliced
1 small head iceberg
 lettuce leaves
50g cress or watercress
1 lime, sliced
100g capers
400g smoked salmon, thinly
 sliced
parsley, to serve

1. Whisk together the vinegar, oil and sugar and season to taste with salt and pepper.

2. Toss the onion, lettuce and watercress in the dressing.

3. Arrange on 4 serving plates and put a slice of lime on each plate. Scatter with the capers.

4. Place the smoked salmon on top of the salad and sprinkle with the pepper. Garnish with parsley.

Winter salad with quail's eggs and croutons

1. For the croutons: heat the oil in a frying pan and fry the bread cubes until crisp and golden. Drain on kitchen paper.

2. For the dressing: whisk together the olive oil, vinegar and mustard.

3. Simmer the quail's eggs in boiling water for 2 ½ minutes. Rinse in cold water to cool.

4. Toss the bacon and salad leaves with a little dressing. Peel the eggs.

5. Divide the bacon and leaves between serving plates. Top with the croutons and eggs. Drizzle with the remaining dressing.

Preparation time: 10 min
Cooking time: 10 min
Serves 4

For the croutons:
3 tbsp olive oil
½ ciabatta loaf, cubed

For the dressing:
6 tbsp olive oil
2 tbsp white wine vinegar
2 tsp wholegrain mustard

For the salad:
12 quail's eggs
12 rashers cooked bacon,
  cut into pieces
4 handfuls mixed salad leaves

Radicchio salad with gorgonzola, grapes and croutons

1. Mix the salad leaves and red onion in a bowl.

2. Mix together the oil, vinegar and mustard and season to taste with salt and pepper.

3. Add to the salad leaves and onion and toss to combine.

4. Put onto serving plates and crumble over the cheese.

5. Halve some of the grapes and leave some whole. Scatter over the salad.

6. For the croutons: heat the oil in a frying pan and fry the bread cubes until crisp and golden. Drain on kitchen paper. Scatter over the salad.

Preparation time: 15 min
Cooking time: 5 min
Serves 4

1 head radicchio, leaves torn
handful of lamb's lettuce leaves
1 red onion, finely diced
4 tbsp extra virgin olive oil
1 tbsp red wine vinegar
1 tsp Dijon mustard
salt and pepper to taste
250g Gorgonzola cheese
225g green grapes, peeled

For the croutons:
3 tbsp olive oil
½ ciabatta herb loaf, cubed

Preparing asparagus

Asparagus are utterly delicious when steamed or lightly cooked and added to salads. They need only a little preparation to get the best flavour and texture.

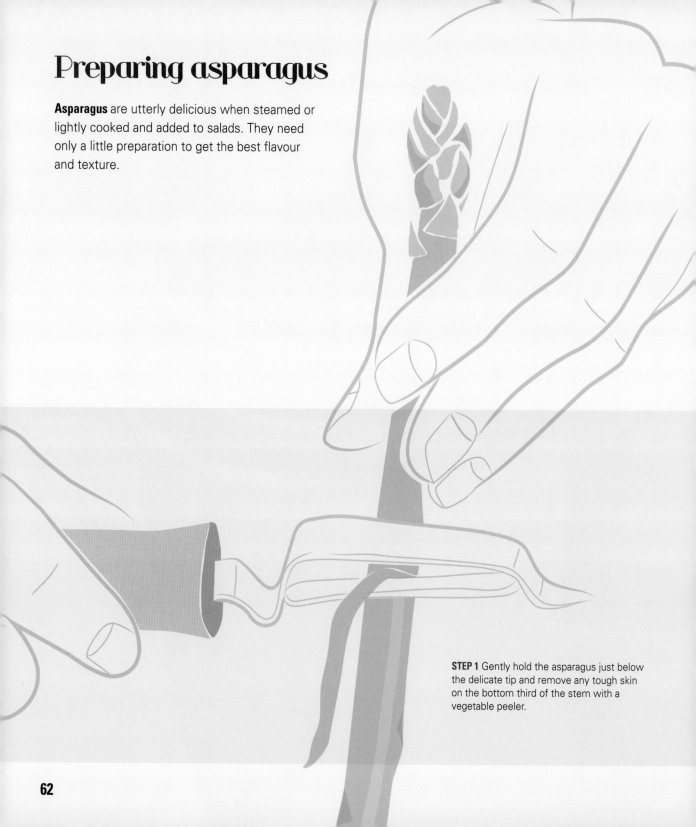

STEP 1 Gently hold the asparagus just below the delicate tip and remove any tough skin on the bottom third of the stem with a vegetable peeler.

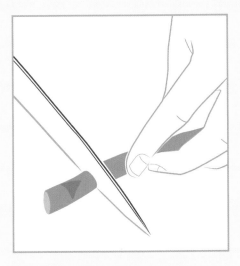

STEP 2 With a sharp knife, cut away the hard ends, or hold the stems in two hands and bend until it snaps.

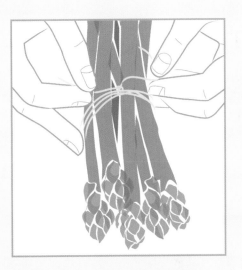

STEP 3 For ease of cooking, tie together the asparagus stems with a little kitchen string to make a bundle.

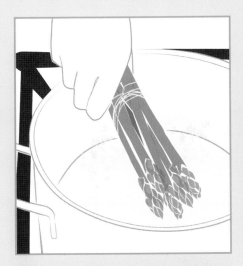

STEP 4 Put the stems into a large pan of boiling water. Cook for 3–5 minutes or until tender when pierced with a knife.

STEP 5 With a slotted spoon, remove the asparagus and transfer to a plate lined with kitchen paper and pat dry.

Salad with blue cheese, bacon-wrapped plums and apricots

1. Cook the bacon in a dry frying pan until cooked but not crisp.

2. Thread a prune and apricot onto 12 wooden skewers. Wrap 2 slices of bacon around each skewer.

3. For the dressing: whisk all the ingredients together until thickened.

4. Toss with the salad leaves and arrange on serving plates. Place the skewers and cheese on top.

Preparation time: 15 min
Cooking time: 5 min
Serves 4

24 slices bacon
12 ready to eat prunes
12 ready to eat dried apricots
200g mixed salad leaves
200g blue cheese, cubed

For the dressing:
1 shallot, finely chopped
1 tbsp white wine vinegar
1 tsp apricot jam
1 tsp grainy mustard

Rice salad with smoked trout and sesame

1. Put the rice and salt into a pan and cover with water. Bring to a boil and cook for 10 minutes.

2. Add the asparagus and cook for a further 3–4 minutes, until the rice is completely cooked and the asparagus is slightly crunchy. Drain, rinse in cold water and drain again.

3. Stir the oil, lemon zest and juice, mint and sesame seeds into the rice and asparagus. Season well with salt and pepper and leave to cool.

4. Spoon the rice mixture into serving bowls and top with the smoked trout.

Preparation time: 15 min
Cooking time: 15 min
Serves 4

250g long grain rice
1 tsp salt
250g asparagus, cut in bite-size
   pieces
3 tbsp olive oil
1 lemon, finely grated zest and
   juice
4 tbsp chopped mint
2 tbsp white sesame seeds
2 tbsp black sesame seeds
salt and pepper to taste
4 smoked trout fillets, cut
   into pieces

Pasta salad with vegetables and chicken

1. Put the chicken breast fillets into a shallow dish. Mix 2 tablespoons teriyaki sauce with 2 tablespoons oil and brush the chicken with the mixture. Cover and leave to marinate for 1 hour.

2. Cook the noodles in boiling, salted water for 5 minutes, then drain thoroughly and rinse in cold water. Drain and set aside.

3. Heat the remaining oil in a frying pan and toast the sesame seeds, then stir in the curry paste, vinegar and the remaining teriyaki sauce.

4. Put the noodles, onion, carrot and cucumber into a bowl, add the sauce and mix well.

5. Heat a frying pan and cook the chicken for about 10 minutes, turning once, until cooked through. Slice the chicken breasts at an angle.

6. Mix the salad leaves and bean sprouts into the noodle salad and serve in glasses, topped with slices of chicken breast.

Preparation time: 15 min
   plus 1 h marinating
Cooking time: 15 min
Serves 4

3 chicken breast fillets
3 tbsp teriyaki sauce
3 tbsp oil
100g thin rice noodles
2 tbsp sesame seeds
1 tsp red curry paste
1 tbsp rice vinegar
½ red onion, thinly sliced
1 carrot, cut into sticks
1/3 cucumber, cut into thin sticks
50g mixed leaves, spinach, rocket
   and watercress
100g bean sprouts

Green salad of kiwi fruits, cucumber and avocados

Preparation time: 15 min
Serves 4

2 ripe avocados
4 ripe kiwi fruit
1 cucumber, cut into sticks
1 lime, juice
parsley and cucumber slices,
* to serve*

1. Slice the avocados and remove the stones.

2. Slice the kiwi fruit.

3. Mix these with the cucumber and toss in the lime juice and some black pepper to taste.

4. Put into serving bowls and garnish with parsley and cucumber slices.

Savoury orange salad with onions and olives

1. Stir together the lemon juice and olive oil.

2. Peel the oranges and remove all the white pith. Slice the flesh, catching the juice in a bowl.

3. Add the juice to the olive oil mixture and season to taste with salt and pepper.

4. Stir the onion, oranges and olives into the marinade and leave to stand for 20 minutes before serving, garnished with mint.

Preparation time: 15 min
  plus 20 min resting
Serves 4

3 tbsp lemon juice
4 tbsp olive oil
4 oranges
salt and pepper to taste
1 large red onion, sliced
125g black olives, pitted
chopped mint leaves, to serve

Salad leaves with pears, walnuts and gorgonzola

1. Place the salad leaves, chives and pear slices on serving plates.

2. Scatter over the walnuts and cheese.

3. Whisk together the vinegar, walnut and sunflower oils and honey. Season to taste with salt.

4. Drizzle the dressing over the salad.

Preparation time: 15 min
Serves 4

200g baby spinach leaves
100g rocket leaves
½ radicchio, leaves
½ bunch chives
2 pears, cored and sliced
50g chopped walnuts
100g cheese, crumbled
3 tbsp cider vinegar
1 tbsp walnut oil
2 tbsp sunflower oil
1 tbsp honey

Aubergine and bean salad with capers

1. Mix together the anchovies, capers, onion, vinegar, 3 tablespoons oil and horseradish and season to taste with salt and pepper.

2. Heat the remaining oil in a frying pan and cook the aubergine and peppers for 4 minutes.

3. Cook the beans in salted boiling water for 10 minutes. Drain and mix with the aubergines and peppers.

4. Mix the vegetables with the anchovy mixture. Gently stir in the avocado slices.

5. Arrange the radicchio leaves in serving bowls. Spoon in the vegetable and anchovy mixture. Sprinkle with the bacon. Serve with bread.

Preparation time: 15 min
Cooking time: 15 min
Serves 4

3 pickled anchovy fillets, drained
2 tbsp capers
1 red onion, chopped
4 tbsp white wine vinegar
5 tbsp olive oil
2 tsp grated horseradish
salt and pepper to taste
400g green beans, halved
300g aubergine, sliced
1 red pepper, cut into strips
1 avocado, peeled, pitted and
  sliced
1 small head radicchio
5 slices cooked bacon, diced

Duck breast with pears, watercress and walnuts

Preparation time: 15 min
Cooking time: 30 min
Serves 4

4 duck breasts
salt and pepper to taste
100g chopped walnuts
1 tbsp oil
3 pears, thickly sliced
1 tbsp honey
4 tbsp balsamic vinegar
1 bunch watercress

1. Slash the duck breasts with a sharp knife and rub in salt and pepper to taste.

2. Cook in a dry frying pan over a low heat for 6–8 minutes on each side, until cooked through. Pour off the fat and set aside.

3. Add the walnuts to the pan and cook for a few minutes until lightly toasted. Remove and set aside.

4. Add the oil to the pan and cook the pears until just golden. Add the honey and balsamic vinegar to the pan and warm through.

5. Slice the duck breasts and arrange on serving plates with the watercress, walnuts and pears. Drizzle over the honey mixture and serve immediately.

Salad nicoise

1. For the dressing: mix the ingredients together, season with salt and pepper and set aside.

2. Heat the oven to 200°C (400°F).

3. Bring a large pan of salted water to a boil and cook the potatoes until tender. Drain well and set aside. Cut the potatoes in half if they are large.

4. Rub the tomatoes with a little oil, put in a roasting tin and roast in the oven for 10 minutes.

5. Blanch the beans in boiling water for 5 minutes, drain and refresh in cold water. Pat dry with kitchen paper.

6. While the potatoes are still slightly warm, combine all the ingredients and toss in the dressing. Garnish with mint leaves.

Preparation time: 15 min
Cooking time: 30 min
Serves 4

For the dressing:
2 shallots, very finely chopped
3 tbsp white wine vinegar
1 tbsp grain mustard
7 tbsp olive oil
salt and pepper to taste

For the salad:
400g new potatoes
200g cherry tomatoes
200g green beans
200g tinned tuna, drained of oil
100g pitted black olives
4 tinned anchovies, sliced thinly
*   into strips*
1 handful rocket, washed
mint, to garnish

Savoury melon salad in hollowed-out melon

1. Halve the melons and remove the seeds. Hollow out the melons with a spoon, scooping the flesh into a bowl.

2. Mix the melon flesh with the cress and diced pepper.

3. Heat the butter in a frying pan and cook the turkey cubes until golden. Remove and drain on kitchen paper. Set aside to cool.

4. Stir the turkey into the melon mixture and season to taste with salt and pepper.

5. Whisk together the vinegar and olive oil.

6. Spoon the melon mixutre into the hollowed-out melon shells. Drizzle with the dressing and garnish with rocket.

Preparation time: 15 min
Cooking time: 15 min
Serves 4

2 Galia melons
1 punnet salad cress
1 large red pepper, diced
1 tbsp butter
300g boneless turkey breast, cut
   into small cubes
salt and pepper to taste
8 tbsp balsamic vinegar
4 tbsp olive oil
rocket, to serve

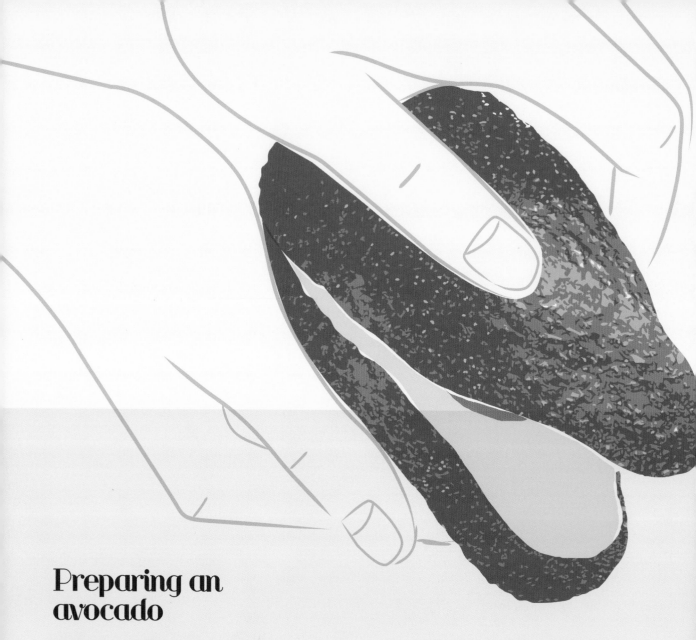

Preparing an avocado

Avocado adds a soft, creamy texture to salads, but it must be prepared as close to serving as possible as the flesh turns brown when exposed to the air.

STEP 1 Using a sharp knife, cut all the way around the avocado through to the stone, then carefully pull the two halves away from each other to separate.

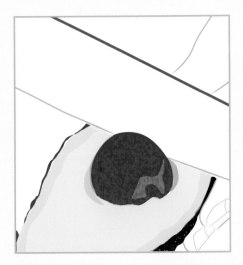

STEP 2 Strike the stone with the knife blade until it embeds. Pull away the knife and the stone should come with it.

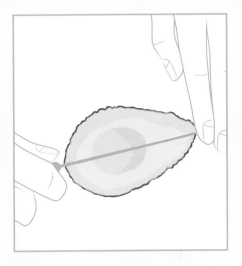

STEP 3 Once the stone has been removed, take each avocado half and cut it in half again lengthways.

STEP 4 Carefully peel away the skin from each avocado quarter, starting at the top.

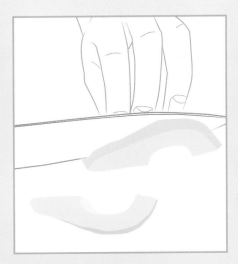

STEP 5 Once all the quarters are peeled, slice the avocado lengthways or cut into chunks.

Fried goat's cheese with dates

1. Coat the goats' cheese in flour, then dip in the egg. Coat in flour again.

2. Heat 2 tablespoons oil in a frying pan and fry the cheese for 2–3 minutes on each side, until golden. Remove and set aside.

3. Heat the remaining oil in the pan and cook the dates until golden.

4. For the dressing: whisk all the ingredients together. Stir in the almonds and peppercorns and season to taste with salt and pepper.

5. Place the cheese and dates on serving plates with the radicchio leaves. Drizzle over the dressing.

Preparation time: 10 min
Cooking time: 10 min
Serves 4

450g goats' cheese, thickly sliced
110g flour
2 eggs, beaten
4 tbsp oil
12 dates, pitted and halved

For the dressing:
3 tbsp cider vinegar
110ml apple juice
50ml olive oil
4 tsp Dijon mustard
1 tbsp honey
1 tbsp chopped almonds, toasted
1 tsp black peppercorns
salt and pepper to taste
radicchio leaves, to serve

Warm salad of broad beans, pancetta and feta with lemon and herb dressing

1. Cook the broad beans in boiling water until just tender, then drain well.

2. Heat the oil in a frying pan and cook the pancetta until crisp and golden. Drain on kitchen paper.

3. Add the garlic to the pan and cook for 2–3 minutes until softened.

4. For the dressing: whisk together all the ingredients and season to taste with salt and pepper.

5. Stir the dressing into the warm beans and add the pancetta and garlic. Season to taste with ground black pepper.

6. Stir in the salad leaves and divide between serving plates. Scatter the cheese over the salad.

Preparation time: 15 min
Cooking time: 15 min
Serves 4

450g broad beans
2 tbsp olive oil
110g pancetta, diced
2 garlic cloves, crushed
2 handfuls mixed salad leaves
200g feta cheese, crumbled

For the dressing:
5 tbsp olive oil
2 tbsp white wine vinegar
1 tbsp Dijon mustard
2 tbsp chopped mixed herbs
salt and pepper to taste

Apple salad with spinach and cheese

1. Mix the spinach, apples, dates and cheese in a large bowl.

2. Whisk together the walnut oil, vinegar, salt and pepper to taste, until thickened.

3. Toss the dressing with the salad and garnish with fresh herbs.

Preparation time: 15 min
Serves 4

*200g baby spinach
4 red apples, cored and sliced
  into matchsticks
8 dried dates, pitted and sliced
175g Cheddar cheese,
  thinly sliced
100ml walnut oil
50ml cider vinegar
salt and pepper to taste
fresh herbs, to serve*

Chickpea salad with orange and peppers

Preparation time: 15 min
Cooking time: 1 h 30 min
Serves 4

500g dried chickpeas, soaked
* overnight*
2 red peppers, diced
4 spring onions, sliced
2 oranges, juice
1 orange, segmented
4 tbsp white wine vinegar
2 tbsp lemon juice
6 tbsp olive oil
parsley sprigs, to serve

1. Put the chickpeas into a large pan and cover with water. Bring to a boil and simmer for 1½ hours until tender. Drain and set aside.

2. Mix together the remaining ingredients and stir in the chickpeas.

3. Divide between serving bowls and garnish with parsley.

Chard salad with pine nuts and raisins

1. Whisk together the mustard, vinegar, oil, salt and pepper until thickened.

2. Toss the chard leaves and beansprouts in the dressing and arrange in a serving bowl.

3. Scatter over the pine nuts and raisins.

Preparation time: 15 min
Serves 4

2 tsp Dijon mustard
2 tsp red wine vinegar
2 tbsp extra virgin olive oil
salt and pepper to taste
4–5 handfuls chard leaves, torn
75g beansprouts
60g pine nuts, toasted
60g raisins

Mixed salad with egg and herbs

1. Boil the eggs for 10 minutes, them immediately cover with cold water. Set aside.

2. Whisk the vinegar and oil until thickened. Season to taste with salt and pepper.

3. Peel the eggs and cut into quarters.

4. Toss the vegetables and eggs gently in the dressing and divide between serving bowls. Garnish with parsley and thyme.

Preparation time: 10 min
Cooking time: 10 min
Serves 4

4 eggs
2 tbsp white wine vinegar
4 tbsp olive oil
200g lettuce leaves
1 handful beansprouts
1 red onion, thinly sliced
salt and pepper to taste
parsley and thyme sprigs, to serve

Redfish with mint and corn salad

1. Heat the sherry and 5cm water in a frying pan. Add the fish and bring to a simmer. Cook for 3–5 minutes until the fish flakes easily when tested with a fork. Remove the fish and drain on kitchen paper. Chill for about 30 minutes.

2. For the dressing: whisk together all the ingredients and season to taste with salt and pepper.

3. Divide the lettuce leaves between 4 serving bowls. Place the fish on top and scatter over the smoked salmon and mint leaves. Serve with the dressing separately.

Preparation time: 10 min
  plus 30 min chilling
Cooking time: 10 min
Serves 4

4 fish fillets
2 tbsp dry sherry
1 lamb's lettuce

For the dressing:
1 tsp sugar
1 tsp mustard
1 lemon, juice
2 garlic cloves, crushed
5 tbsp olive oil
2 tbsp sherry vinegar
1 tsp cumin seeds, toasted in a
  hot pan
salt and pepper to taste

To garnish:
110g smoked salmon, finely
  chopped
mint leaves

Chicory salad with Roquefort, apple and walnuts

Preparation time: 5 min
Serves 4

*4 heads chicory, outer leaves
  removed and sliced in half
  lengthways*
1 green apple, cored and sliced
1 stalk celery, sliced
100g Roquefort, crumbled
50g walnut halves
salt and pepper to taste
6 chives, chopped

1. Arrange the chicory, apple, celery, Roquefort and walnuts on a plate, season with salt and pepper and garnish with the chopped chives.

Warm apple and red cabbage salad

1. Heat the oil in a large frying pan and cook the shallot until soft.

2. Add the honey and cumin and pour in the wine, vinegar, apple juice and lemon juice. Add the cabbage, cover and simmer for 20 minutes, stirring occasionally, until the cabbage is tender.

3. Add the apple slices and cook for a further 5 minutes. Season to taste with salt and pepper. Serve warm.

Preparation time: 10 min
Cooking time: 40 min
Serves 4

2 tbsp oil
1 shallot, diced
1 tsp honey
1 tsp ground cumin
100ml red wine
2 tbsp red wine vinegar
100ml apple juice
½ lemon, juice
½ head red cabbage, cut into strips
2 apples, peeled, cored and sliced
salt and pepper to taste

Lentil salad with fried pumpkin and goat cheese

1. Blanch the pumpkin in boiling salted water for about 5 minutes. Drain and pat dry.

2. Heat 2 tablespoons oil in a large pan and gently fry the garlic. Add the pumpkin and cook until tender and starting to brown.

3. Arrange the lentils on plates with the pumpkin, rocket and cheese.

4. Mix together the remaining oil, cider vinegar and balsamic vinegar. Season with salt and pepper and drizzle over the salad.

Preparation time: 15 min
   plus 12 h soaking
Cooking time: 30 min
Serves 4

*800g pumpkin, skinned, seeds
   removed and cubed*
6 tbsp olive oil
2 garlic cloves, crushed
*400g tinned lentils, drained
   and rinsed*
1 bunch rocket
150g chopped hard goat's cheese
2 tbsp cider vinegar
1 tsp balsamic vinegar
salt and pepper to taste

Baked fruit salad

1. Place all the fruits in a bowl. Add the sherry, sugar and orange juice and toss to combine. Cover and stand overnight.

2. Heat the oven to 180°C (350°F). Butter a baking dish.

3. Put the fruit and liquid into the baking dish. Add the star anise.

4. Cover and cook for 30–40 minutes, until the liquid is bubbling and the fruits are very soft. Remove from the oven and cool slightly.

5. Spoon onto a serving plate and serve warm.

Preparation time: 20 min
  plus 12 h soaking
Cooking time: 40 min
Serves 4

375g mixed fruits, e. g. apricots,
  apples, peaches, figs, grapes
300ml sherry
1 tbsp light brown sugar
250ml orange juice
3 star anise

Greek salad

1. Mix together all the ingredients, seasoning to taste with salt and pepper.

2. Put into a serving bowl and garnish with parsley.

Preparation time: 10 min
Serves 4

2 onions, sliced
5 tbsp black olives, pitted
200g feta cheese, cubed
4 tomatoes, quartered
½ iceberg lettuce, torn
1 cucumber, peeled and sliced
1 green pepper, sliced
5 tbsp extra virgin olive oil
2–3 tbsp lemon juice
salt and pepper to taste
parsley sprigs, to serve

Roast pumpkin and Gorgonzola salad

1. Heat the oven to 200°C (400°F).

2. Cut the pumpkin into slim wedges and cut each in half. Brush with a little of the oil and place on a baking tray. Bake for 20–30 minutes or until tender. Remove from the oven and let cool.

3. Mix the remaining oil with the balsamic vinegar, season with salt and pepper and set aside.

4. Arrange the spinach on serving plates, add the cooked pumpkin and Gorgonzola and drizzle over the balsamic dressing.

Preparation time: 15 min
Cooking time: 30 min
Serves 4

*1 medium pumpkin, peeled and
   seeds removed*
150ml olive oil
2 tbsp balsamic vinegar
200g baby spinach
salt and pepper to taste
325g Gorgonzola cheese, crumbled

Beetroot salad with apple and chives

Preparation time: 10 min
Serves 4

4 pickled cucumbers, thinly sliced
50ml pickled cucumber liquor
2 red apples, thinly sliced
350–400g cooked beetroot, sliced
2–3 tsp finely grated horseradish
2 tbsp chopped chives
salt and pepper to taste

1. Toss all the ingredients together in a bowl, seasoning with salt and pepper to taste.

Beef salad with mixed vegetables

1. Heat the oil in a frying pan. Season the meat with salt and pepper and cook for 2 minutes. Remove from the pan and set aside.

2. Deglaze the frying juices with soy sauce and stock and season to taste.

3. Arrange the salad vegetables on serving plates and place the meat on top, while still hot. Drizzle with the sauce and serve immediately.

Preparation time: 15 min
Cooking time: 5 min
Serves 4

1 tbsp oil
400g beef fillet steaks,
  thickly sliced
salt and pepper to taste
4 tbsp soy sauce
4 tbsp beef stock
½ cucumber, sliced into
  thin ribbons
100g Swiss chard leaves
100g beetroot leaves
1 carrot, sliced into thin ribbons
1 chilli, very finely chopped
1 red onion, sliced

Warm chorizo and potato salad

1. Cook the potatoes in salted boiling water for 20–30 minutes until tender. Drain and halve.

2. Heat the oil in a pan and fry the potatoes and chorizo until golden brown.

3. Place the radicchio in a bowl and add the potatoes and chorizo. Add a little water to the liquid in the pan and pour over the salad.

4. Stir in the vinegar and the herbs and season with salt and ground black pepper to taste. Serve immediately.

Preparation time: 5 min
Cooking time: 40 min
Serves 4

800g small potatoes
2 tbsp olive oil
400g chorizo sausage, thinly sliced
1 radicchio, torn into bite-sized
* pieces*
4 tbsp white wine vinegar
4 tbsp mixed herbs, e.g. chives,
* cress, oregano, basil*

Pepper salad with sesame

1. Put the peppers in a pan and cover with water. Bring to a boil and cook for 5–6 minutes, until partially softened. Drain, sprinkle with salt and allow to cool for 20 minutes.

2. Slice the peppers, discarding the seeds and pith.

3. Mix together the garlic, oil and vinegar in a bowl. Season to taste with salt and pepper. Add the sliced peppers, cover and leave to stand for 1 hour.

4. Put the peppers and dressing in a serving bowl and sprinkle the sesame seeds over the top.

Preparation time: 15 min
  plus 20 min standing,
  1 h marinating
Cooking time: 15 min
Serves 4

2 yellow peppers
2 green peppers
2 garlic cloves, finely chopped
70ml extra virgin olive oil
50ml white wine vinegar
3 tbsp sesame seeds

Asparagus and vegetable salad with fried Norway lobster

Preparation time: 15 min
Cooking time: 20 min
Serves 4

2 x 1 kg cooked lobsters, shells
   removed, cut into serving pieces
1 tbsp ginger wine
1 tbsp cornflour
salt and pepper to taste
oil, for frying
4 courgettes, sliced
12 asparagus spears
parsley, to serve

For the dressing:
1 tsp Dijon mustard
½ tsp salt
½ tsp ground black pepper
2 tbsp lemon juice
2 tbsp white wine vinegar
60ml olive oil

1. Mix together the lobster, ginger wine, cornflour, salt and pepper.

2. Heat the oil in a wok to come 5cm up the sides. Cook the lobster in batches for 2 minutes. Drain on kitchen paper.

3. Cook the courgette slices for a few minutes until softened.

4. Cook the asparagus in a pan of salted boiling water for 5–8 minutes until tender. Drain and rinse in cold water. Drain well.

5. For the dressing: whisk all the ingredients together.

6. Toss the asparagus and courgettes in the dressing.

7. Place the vegetables on serving plates with the lobster. Garnish with parsley.

Red rice salad with red kidney beans, feta and dill

1. Cook the rice according to the pack instructions. Drain and rinse in cold water. Tip into a bowl and toss with the vinegar, oil and seasoning to taste.

2. Add the remaining ingredients and toss again.

3. Divide between serving plates and garnish with dill flowers.

Preparation time: 15 min
Cooking time: 25 min
Serves 4

300g Camargue red rice
2 tbsp red wine vinegar
4 tbsp extra virgin olive oil
100g feta cheese, cut into cubes
2 tbsp pine nuts, toasted
2 red onions, sliced
2 tbsp chopped dill
400g tinned kidney beans, drained
dill flowers, to serve

Thai salad with lime, shrimps and peanuts

1. Toast the peanuts in a dry frying pan and set aside.

2. Heat the oil and gently cook the chilli, garlic and ginger for 3–4 minutes until softened.

3. Increase the heat and add the shrimps, then pour in the fish stock and simmer for 4 minutes. Season with salt, pepper and add the chilli powder, soy sauce, oyster sauce and lime juice.

4. Pour boiling water over the glass noodles and leave to stand for 5 minutes. Drain, rinse with boiling water and drain again.

5. Stir the noodles into the shrimp sauce. Garnish with the chopped coriander and toasted peanuts.

Preparation time: 15 min
Cooking time: 20 min
Serves 4

4 tbsp chopped peanuts
4 tbsp oil
1 red chilli, finely chopped
2 garlic cloves, finely chopped
1 piece ginger, 4cm
200g shrimps
150ml fish stock
2 pinches chilli powder
2 tbsp soy sauce
1 tbsp oyster sauce
juice of 1 lime
200g glass noodles
3 tbsp chopped coriander, to serve

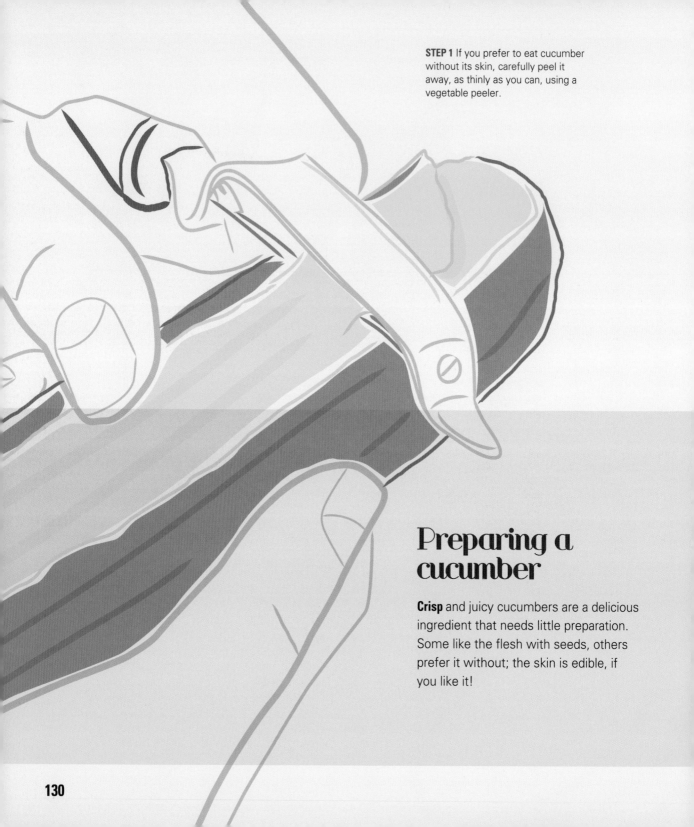

STEP 1 If you prefer to eat cucumber without its skin, carefully peel it away, as thinly as you can, using a vegetable peeler.

Preparing a cucumber

Crisp and juicy cucumbers are a delicious ingredient that needs little preparation. Some like the flesh with seeds, others prefer it without; the skin is edible, if you like it!

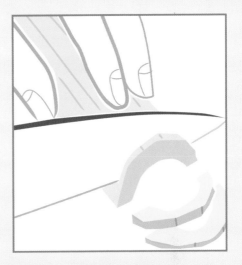

STEP 2 Cut the cucumber in half lengthways and place the halves seed-side up on a chopping board. Scoop out the seeds using a teaspoon.

STEP 3 Turn over each scooped-out cucumber half, so that the curved side is uppermost, then cut into chunky slices using a sharp knife.

STEP 4 For a decorative effect, score the cucumber skin. This is best done with a channel knife, but if you don't have one, use the prongs of a fork.

STEP 5 Leaving the cucumber whole, and using a very sharp knife, cut along the length of the cucumber to make very thin slices.

Artichoke and orange salad with rosemary

1. Sprinkle the artichokes with lemon juice to prevent them turning black.

2. Heat the oil in a pan and cook the artichokes and garlic for a few minutes until softened. Season to taste with salt and pepper and pour in the water.

3. Add the rosemary to the pan, cover and bring to a boil. Simmer gently for 15 minutes. Drain and leave to cool.

4. Peel the oranges, removing the white pith and divide into segments, over a bowl to catch the juice.

5. Put the juice in a pan with the butter and honey and bring to a boil. Simmer for 2 minutes.

6. Pour the orange juice mixture over the artichokes and stir in the orange segments.

7. Put into a serving bowl and garnish with rosemary and thyme.

Preparation time: 20 min
Cooking time: 20 min
Serves 4

12–16 baby artichokes
2 lemons, juice
4 tbsp olive oil
2 garlic cloves, crushed
salt and pepper to taste
150ml water
4 sprigs rosemary
4 oranges
2 tbsp butter
1 tbsp honey
rosemary and thyme sprigs, to
  serve

French bean salad with shallots and pine nuts

1. Cook the beans in plenty of boiling salted water for about 8 minutes, until al dente.

2. Heat the oil and butter in a pan and fry the shallots over a medium heat. Add the pine nuts and toast quickly. Add the sugar and cook until slightly caramelised.

3. Stir in the vinegar. Drain the beans and add to the pan. Stir well and season to taste with salt and ground black pepper. Serve warm or cold.

Preparation time: 15 min
Cooking time: 15 min
Serves 4

600g French beans
2 tbsp oil
2 tbsp butter
250g shallots, quartered
100g pine nuts
1 tsp sugar
6 tbsp white wine vinegar

Warm beef salad with carrots and tamarind

1. Heat the oven to 200°C (400°F). Heat the oil in a roasting tin and brown the meat on all sides. Cook for 10–20 minutes, depending on how rare you like your meat. Remove from the oven, wrap in foil and leave to rest in the turned-off oven.

2. Arrange the vegetables on serving plates. Slice the beef and put on the plates.

3. For the dressing: whisk together all the ingredients until the sugar has dissolved. Drizzle the dressing over the salad.

Preparation time: 15 min
Cooking time: 20 min
Serves 4

1 tbsp oil
500g piece beef sirloin
175g beansprouts
110g cherry tomatoes, halved
2 shallots, finely chopped
4 carrots, sliced into ribbons

For the dressing:
2 tbsp tamarind paste
2 tbsp fish sauce
2 tbsp soy sauce
1 lime, juice
2 tbsp palm sugar

Potato salad with chives and mustard

Preparation time: 5 min
Cooking time: 35 min
Serves 4

1kg small, waxy potatoes
200g mayonnaise or soured cream
  (or more, depending on taste)
salt and pepper to taste
1 large red onion, sliced
½ bunch chives, snipped
3–4 tbsp wholegrain mustard

1. Cook the potatoes in boiling salted water for about 20 minutes, until tender. Drain well.

2. Mix the warm potatoes with the mayonnaise or soured cream and season with salt and pepper.

3. Divide between serving bowls and scatter with onion and chives. Add small dabs of mustard and leave to cool.

Fish salad in a smoked salmon basket

1. Mix all the ingredients together, except for the smoked salmon and melba toast. Season to taste with salt and pepper.

2. Divide the mixture among the salmon slices, placing it onto the middle of each slice. Fold the salmon around the filling to make a neat parcel.

3. Serve with melba toast.

Preparation time: 5 min
Cooking time: 10 min
Serves 4

1 smoked trout fillet, flaked
110g soft cream cheese
juice of 1 lemon
10 chives, snipped
1 tsp horseradish sauce
1 tbsp double cream
4 slices smoked salmon, each about
   13cm square
salt and pepper to taste
melba toast, to serve

Green pasta salad

1. Cook the pasta according to the pack instructions.

2. Heat the butter and oil in a frying pan and cook the leek, celery and pepper until soft. Remove from the pan and drain on kitchen paper.

3. Cook the mangetout in boiling water for about 5 minutes until tender.

4. Drain the pasta and mix with the vegetables, stock, vinegar and celery leaves. Season to taste with salt and pepper and leave to stand for 10 minutes.

5. Transfer to a serving bowl and garnish with basil. Serve warm or cold.

Preparation time: 15 min
    plus 10 min standing
Cooking time: 20 min
Serves 4

250g small pasta shapes
2 tbsp butter
2 tbsp oil
1 leek, sliced
1 stick celery, sliced
1 red pepper, diced
200g mangetout
50ml vegetable stock
6 tbsp white wine vinegar
2 tbsp chopped celery leaves
salt and pepper to taste
basil leaves, to serve

Shrimp salad

1. Whisk together the oil, vinegar and lemon juice and season to taste with salt and pepper.

2. Mix with the shrimps, crab and vegetables and season with salt and cayenne pepper.

3. Divide between 4 serving bowls and garnish with coriander.

Preparation time: 10 min
Serves 4

4 tbsp sunflower oil
3 tbsp white wine vinegar
1 tbsp lemon juice
salt and pepper to taste
300g cooked shrimps
300g cooked crab meat
2 tomatoes, skinned and
  quartered
2 red peppers, diced
2 shallots, diced
150g celery, thinly sliced
cayenne pepper
1 tbsp chopped coriander, to
  serve

Autumn salad with baked pumpkin

Preparation time: 15 min
Cooking time: 55 min
Serves 4

1 pumpkin, cut into thick slices
olive oil
salt and pepper to taste
2 red onions, cut into wedges
1 bulb fennel, quartered
1 tbsp capers
4 tbsp extra virgin olive oil
2 tbsp fresh lemon juice
chicory and mint leaves, to serve

1. Heat the oven to 200°C (400°F).

2. Put the pumpkin slices into a roasting tin and season with salt and pepper. Drizzle with oil and cook for 30 minutes.

3. Add the onions and fennel to the roasting tin and drizzle with oil. Cook for a further 20–25 minutes, until the vegetables are tender. Remove from the tin and leave to cool.

4. Stir together the capers, extra virgin oil and lemon juice. Season to taste with salt and pepper. Pour over the vegetables and toss gently.

5. Put onto serving plates and garnish with chicory and mint leaves.

Sauteed strawberries and cherries with pine nuts

1. Toast the pine nuts in a dry frying pan until lightly browned. Set aside to cool.

2. Melt the butter in the frying pan. Add the sugar and vanilla pod and stir until the sugar has dissolved.

3. Add the cherries and strawberries and cook for 3–5 minutes, stirring occasionally, until the fruits are tender and heated through. Add a squeeze of lemon juice, stir, then remove from the heat. Stir in the cinnamon, if using.

4. Remove the fruit with a slotted spoon and place on a serving plate. Sprinkle with the pine nuts.

5. Add the wine to the juices in the pan and bring to a boil. Cook until the liquid is reduced and syrupy. Allow to cool and pour over the fruit. Decorate with the vanilla pod and strawberry leaves.

Preparation time: 15 min
Cooking time: 20 min
Serves 4

75g pine nuts
4 tbsp unsalted butter
4 tbsp light brown sugar
1 vanilla pod
900g yellow and red cherries, pitted
450g strawberries
juice of 1 lemon
1 tsp ground cinnamon (optional)
200ml red wine
strawberry leaves, to serve

Lentil and onion salad with fresh herbs

1. Put the lentils in a pan with 1 sliced onion and the bouquet garni. Cover with water and bring to a boil. Cover and simmer for 25 minutes. Leave to stand for 5 minutes, until the water is almost completely absorbed.

2. Remove the bouquet garni and tip the lentils into a bowl.

3. Whisk together the vinegar and olive oil. Stir in the herbs and season to taste with salt and pepper.

4. Add half the dressing to the warm lentils and onions and mix well.

5. Divide between serving dishes and drizzle over the remaining dressing.

6. Heat the butter in a frying pan and cook the onions until soft and just golden. Drain and place on top of the lentil salad.

Preparation time: 15 min
Cooking time: 35 min
Serves 4

225g Puy lentils
2 onions, sliced
1 bouquet garni
2 tbsp balsamic vinegar
6 tbsp extra virgin olive oil
2 tbsp chopped mixed herbs
salt and pepper to taste
1 tbsp butter

Penne with prawns and peas

1. Cook the penne according to the instructions on the packet.

2. Heat the butter in a frying pan and cook the prawns for a few minutes until cooked through. Remove and set aside.

3. Add the garlic to the pan and cook for 3 minutes. Stir in the peas and cream and bring to a boil. Season to taste with salt and pepper.

4. Mix the cornflour with a little water and stir into the pan until thickened. Add the prawns to the pan.

5. Drain the pasta and mix with the contents of the pan and season with salt and pepper.

6. Divide between 4 serving bowls and garnish with the dill.

Preparation time: 10 min
Cooking time: 20 min
Serves 4

300g penne
2 tbsp butter
300g prawns
1 garlic clove, finely chopped
100–150g peas
200ml double cream
salt and pepper to taste
1 tbsp cornflour
2 sprigs dill, to serve

Asian egg noodle salad with chicken and vegetables

1. Heat 2 tablespoons sesame oil in a frying pan and cook the chicken and squid for a few minutes until cooked through. Set aside to cool.

2. Cook the green beans in a pan of boiling salted water for 5 minutes. Drain and cool.

3. Heat the remaining oil in the pan and cook the peppers and onion until soft. Drain and set aside to cool.

4. Cook the noodles according to the instructions on the pack. Drain and mix with the soy sauce, fish sauce and hoisin sauce.

5. Toss all the ingredients together and season to taste with salt and pepper. Serve warm or cold.

Preparation time: 10 min
Cooking time: 15 min
Serves 4

3 tbsp sesame oil
200g chicken breast, thickly sliced
200g squid, cut into rings
1 handful green beans
1–2 red peppers, cut into strips
1 onion, sliced
½ small Chinese cabbage, shredded
1 handful young spinach
250g egg noodles
2 tbsp light soy sauce
1 tbsp fish sauce
1 tbsp hoisin sauce
salt and pepper to taste

Spinach and avocado salad, with bacon

1. Divide the spinach, avocados and onion between 4 plates and season with salt and pepper.

2. Fry the bacon in a dry frying pan until crisp and brown. Add the walnuts to the pan and toast until lightly browned.

3. Spoon off most of the bacon fat from the pan, reduce the heat and add the olive oil until warmed through.

4. Remove from the heat, add the vinegar and mustard and whisk until thickened.

5. Chop the bacon and scatter over the salad with the walnuts. Drizzle with the warm dressing.

Preparation time: 15 min
Cooking time: 10 min
Serves 4

200g young spinach
2 avocados, sliced
1 small onion, thinly sliced
salt and pepper to taste
10 rashers lean bacon
100g chopped walnuts
3–4 tbsp olive oil
2 tbsp white wine vinegar
3 tsp Dijon mustard

Raw tuna with basil on glass noodles

Preparation time: 20 min
  plus 1 h marinating
Cooking time: 5 min
Serves 4

4 lemons, juice and zest
2 garlic cloves, crushed
1 onion, diced
4 tbsp olive oil
450g very fresh tuna loin, thinly
  sliced
salt and pepper to taste
250g glass noodles
juice of 2 limes
1 tbsp finely grated ginger
3 tbsp shredded mint leaves
2–3 tbsp beansprouts
1 tbsp sweetcorn
basil leaves, to serve

1. Mix together the lemon juice, zest, garlic, onion and oil with the tuna slices. Season with salt and pepper. Cover and chill for 1 hour.

2. Pour boiling water over the noodles and leave to soak for 5 minutes.

3. Whisk together the lime juice, ginger and mint.

4. Drain the noodles and toss with the dressing. Set aside for 10 minutes to allow the flavours to infuse. Add the beansprouts and sweetcorn and mix until well combined.

5. Divide between 4 serving bowls and place the marinated tuna on top. Garnish with basil.

Apple and celery salad with rice

1. Core the apples and slice thinly, tossing them immediately in the lemon juice in a large bowl. Add the celery and rice.

2. Whisk the cream until thick, then fold in the yoghurt and apple juice. Pour over the apple mixture, and toss gently to coat.

3. Divide between serving bowls and serve immediately, garnished with snipped chives.

Preparation time: 20 min
Serves 4

4 green eating apples
1 tbsp lemon juice
2 sticks celery, sliced
250g cooked rice
50ml double cream
200ml plain yoghurt
3 tbsp apple juice
snipped chives, to serve

Thai squid and pork salad

1. Heat the oil and gently cook the garlic and chillies until softened.

2. Pour in the rice wine and stock, then stir in the honey, ginger and soy sauce. Add the pork and squid to the pan, then cover and cook gently over a very low heat for 5 minutes.

3. Transfer to a bowl and mix with the shallots, vinegar and sesame oil. Season to taste with salt and pepper.

4. Divide between serving bowls and sprinkle with mint and coriander.

Preparation time: 20 min
Cooking time: 10 min
Serves 4

1 tbsp oil
2 garlic cloves, crushed
2 chillies, finely chopped
4 tbsp rice wine
200ml chicken stock
1 tsp honey
1 tsp finely grated ginger
2 tbsp light soy sauce
400g pork fillet, cut into thin
  strips
400g squid, cut into thin strips
2 shallots, sliced
2 tbsp rice vinegar
1 tbsp sesame oil
salt and pepper to taste
1 tbsp each chopped mint and
  coriander, to serve

Thai salad with chicken and mint leaves

1. Put the curry paste ingredients into a mortar and grind to a paste.

2. Mix the chicken with the curry paste and lemongrass.

3. Heat the oil in a wok or frying pan and brown the chicken on all sides then stir-fry for 2 minutes. Remove the chicken and set aside.

4. Add the onion to the wok and cook for 2 minutes, then add the tomatoes and chicken and cook gently for 5 minutes.

5. Arrange the herb and salad leaves and spring onions on serving plates and place the chicken, tomatoes and onion on top.

6. Heat the sugar, fish sauce and lime juice in the wok. Drizzle over the salad and garnish with lemongrass, coriander and mint.

Preparation time: 20 min
Cooking time: 15 min
Serves 4

For the curry paste:
2 chillies
1 shallot
½ tsp ginger, freshly grated
1 tsp shrimp paste

For the salad:
450g boneless, skinless chicken,
* cut into strips*
1 tsp lemongrass, finely grated
1 tbsp oil
1 onion, chopped
2 tomatoes, cut into wedges
1 handful mint leaves
1 handful coriander leaves
400g mixed salad leaves
1 bunch spring onions, sliced
1 tbsp brown sugar
2 tbsp fish sauce
2 tbsp lime juice

To garnish:
lemongrass, finely shredded
* lengthways*
coriander and mint leaves

Potato salad with smoked trout

Preparation time: 20 min
Cooking time: 20 min
Serves 4

800g new potatoes
4 tbsp soured cream
2 tbsp mayonnaise
2 tbsp white wine vinegar
salt and pepper to taste
1 red onion, sliced
2 spring onions, sliced
400g smoked trout, flaked
2 tbsp capers
1 punnet salad cress
2 tbsp parsley, chopped

1. Wash the potatoes and boil for about 20 minutes or until tender. Drain, let cool a little then peel and roughly chop.

2. Mix the soured cream, mayonnaise and vinegar and season with salt and pepper.

3. Mix with the dressing with the potatoes, onion and spring onions and spoon onto plates.

4. Put the trout on top of the salad, scatter with capers and herbs and serve.

Grilled pears with Stilton

1. Heat the grill.

2. Cut the pears in half and remove the cores. Brush the pear flesh with lemon juice.

3. Grill the pears for 2–3 minutes on each side until browned. Remove and set aside.

4. Place the watercress on serving plates and arrange the pears on top.

5. Crumble over the cheese and sprinkle with walnuts.

6. For the dressing: mix all the ingredients together in a bowl and season to taste with salt and pepper.

7. Drizzle the dressing over the salad and serve immediately.

Preparation time: 15 min
Cooking time: 6 min
Serves 4

4 firm pears
2–3 tbsp lemon juice
300g watercress
225g Stilton cheese
75g chopped walnuts

For the dressing:
3 tbsp walnut oil
3 tbsp olive oil
1 tsp mustard
2 tbsp white wine vinegar
1 pinch sugar
1 tsp peppercorns, lightly crushed
salt and pepper to taste

Caesar salad with chicken

1. For the croutons: rub the bread with the garlic. Heat half the oil in a frying pan and fry until crisp and golden. Drain on kitchen paper.

2. Heat the remaining oil and fry the chicken until golden and cooked through. Set aside to cool.

3. For the dressing: whisk all the ingredients together until thick. Season to taste with salt and pepper.

4. For the salad: arrange the lettuce leaves in serving bowls. Scatter over the croutons and chicken.

5. Drizzle over the dressing and garnish with grated Parmesan cheese.

Preparation time: 20 min
Cooking time: 15 min
Serves 4

For the croutons:
3 thick bread slices
2 garlic cloves, crushed
4 tbsp oil

For the dressing:
1 garlic clove, crushed
1 tsp lemon juice
½ tsp English mustard
1 tsp Worcestershire sauce
2 egg yolks
100ml olive oil
pinch sugar
2 tbsp grated Parmesan cheese
*   plus 3 tbsp to serve*
1–2 anchovy fillets
salt and pepper to taste

For the salad:
4 boneless chicken breasts,
*   thickly sliced*
1 cos lettuce

Segmenting an orange

Some recipes will call for oranges to be cut into segements and the chewy, less digestible membrane to be removed. This takes a little practice, but is worth the effort.

STEP 1 With a sharp knife, remove a slice from the top and bottom of the orange so you can sit it on a chopping board.

STEP 2 Hold the orange firmly with one hand and with the other work round it, slicing away the peel and pith.

STEP 3 Trim away any remaining pith then cut into the orange, slicing between the segments.

STEP 4 Cut along the edge of the segment, then cut along the other membrane edge to free the chunk.

STEP 5 Repeat with all the segments, then squeeze the leftover membrane into a bowl to catch any juices.

Beef noodle salad

1. Put the noodles in a large bowl and pour boiling water over. Leave until soft, then drain and rinse well with cold water.

2. Heat a frying pan until very hot. Brush the steak with oil and season with salt and pepper. Cook for 1–2 minutes. Remove from the pan and set aside.

3. Heat the butter in the pan. Drain the mushrooms and add to the pan. Cook for a few minutes until golden. Drain on kitchen paper and set aside.

4. For the dressing: whisk together all the ingredients.

5. Toss the drained noodles, steak and vegetables with the dressing. Place on serving plates and scatter with peanuts.

Preparation time: 15 min
Cooking time: 10 min
Serves 4

250g medium rice noodles
600g sirloin steak, thinly sliced
1 tbsp oil
salt and pepper to taste
1 tbsp butter
40g dried Chinese mushrooms,
  soaked in warm water for
  30 minutes
½ Chinese cabbage, shredded
3 carrots, cut into thin strips
100g chopped unsalted peanuts

For the dressing:
6 tbsp Thai sweet chilli sauce
juice of 2 limes
2 tbsp fish sauce

Mexican bean salad

1. Heat the oil in a frying pan and cook the onions and garlic until softened. Add the chilli and tomatoes and cook for 2 minutes.

2. Tip into a bowl and stir in the sweetcorn, beans, parsley, vinegar and oil. Season to taste with salt and pepper.

3. Divide between serving plates and garnish with cherry tomatoes.

Preparation time: 10 min
Cooking time: 10 min
Serves 4

1 tbsp oil
2 onions, diced
1 garlic clove, crushed
1 chilli, finely chopped
6 tomatoes, diced
450g tinned sweetcorn, drained
450g tinned kidney beans, drained
1 tbsp chopped parsley
2 tbsp sherry vinegar
3 tbsp olive oil
salt and pepper to taste
cherry tomatoes, to garnish

Aubergine salad with mushrooms, pine nuts and mascarpone

1. Heat the oven to 220°C (425°F).

2. Put the aubergines into a baking dish and drizzle with 3 tablespoons oil. Cook for 25 minutes, then add the mushrooms, remaining oil, a sprinkling of salt and pepper and the garlic. Cook for a further 20–25 minutes until softened and browned.

3. Place the aubergines and mushrooms on serving plates. Scatter with the pine nuts.

4. Place a spoonful of mascarpone on top and garnish with pea shoots.

Preparation time: 15 min
Cooking time: 50 min
Serves 4

2 large aubergines, quartered
5 tbsp olive oil
110g button mushrooms
2 garlic cloves, crushed
salt and pepper to taste
100g pine nuts
225g mascarpone
pea shoots, to serve

Jersey potato salad with radishes, feta cheese and mint

Preparation time: 15 min
Cooking time: 20 min
Serves 4

350g Jersey Royal potatoes,
  halved
1 red onion, sliced
75g feta cheese, crumbled
5–6 radishes, sliced
1 tbsp chopped oregano
1 tbsp peppercorns, crushed
mint leaves, to serve

For the dressing:
4 tbsp olive oil
1 tbsp red wine vinegar
1 tbsp capers, chopped
1 garlic clove, crushed

1. Cook the potatoes in salted boiling water for 15–20 minutes until tender. Drain well and leave to cool.

2. Gently mix the potatoes with the salad ingredients in a large bowl.

3. For the dressing: whisk all the ingredients until well blended. Pour over the salad and toss thoroughly.

4. Put the salad on a serving plate and garnish with mint.

Tomato and mozzarella tower

1. Heat the oil in frying pan and add the tomatoes and cook for 1 minute on each side. Remove and set aside.

2. Cook the mozzarella slices for 1 minute on each side.

3. Layer the tomato and mozzarella slices to form 4 'towers'.

4. Place on serving plates.

5. Whisk the basil, vinegar, peppercorns and oil and drizzle over the 'towers'. Garnish with rocket.

Preparation time: 10 min
Cooking time: 5 min
Serves 4

1 tbsp olive oil
4 large firm tomatoes, cut into 20 slices
450g mozzarella cheese, cut into 20 slices
6 large basil leaves, torn
1 tbsp balsamic vinegar
2 tsp black peppercorns, crushed
1 tbsp extra virgin olive oil
rocket leaves, to serve

Cobb salad

1. Mix together the salad leaves and place in a salad bowl.

2. Arrange the bacon, avocados, chicken, tomatoes, egg yolks, and whites and cheese over the leaves. Sprinkle with the chives.

3. For the dressing: whisk together the ingredients and serve with the salad.

Preparation time: 15 min
Serves 4

1 head Romaine lettuce, shredded
1 head frisée, shredded
½ bunch of watercress, torn
6 slices cooked bacon, diced
2 ripe avocados, pitted, peeled and
    chopped
350g cooked chicken breast, diced
2 tomatoes, chopped
2 hard-boiled eggs, separated, the
    yolk finely chopped and the white
    finely chopped
50g grated cheese
2 tbsp snipped chives

For the dressing:
70ml red wine vinegar
1 tbsp Dijon mustard
1 tsp sugar
130ml extra virgin olive oil

Orzo with vegetables and feta

1. Cook the pasta in plenty of salted water according to the pack instructions.

2. Cook the shallots in the oil, add the peppers and asparagus and continue frying for a few minutes.

3. Stir in the tomato paste and vegetable stock and simmer for about 4 minutes until the vegetables are cooked but still firm and the liquid has almost completely evaporated.

4. Stir in the lemon zest, basil and drained pasta and toss well. Season to taste with lemon juice, salt and pepper.

5. To serve, crumble the feta over the pasta, scatter with pine nuts, arrange on plates and garnish with salad leaves.

Preparation time: 20 min
Cooking time: 20 min
Serves 4

400 orzo
2 shallots, peeled and finely chopped
3 tbsp olive oil
2 red peppers, roughly chopped
2 yellow peppers, roughly chopped
500g Thai asparagus, chopped
  diagonally into 3cm pieces
1 tsp tomato paste
100ml vegetable stock
zest and juice of ½ lemon
1 tbsp freshly chopped basil
salt and pepper to taste
100g feta cheese
2 tbsp chopped pine nuts, toasted in
  a skillet without oil
lettuce leaves, to serve

Grilled fruit salad

Preparation time: 10 min
Cooking time: 10 min
Serves 4

1kg mixed fruits, e.g. apples,
  grapes, pineapple, plums
3 tbsp lemon juice
2 tbsp light brown sugar

To decorate:
2 tbsp icing sugar
mint leaves
raspberries

1. Heat the grill. Grease the grill pan.

2. Halve and stone fruits such as plums and apricots; cut large fruit such as pineapple, into wedges.

3. Toss in the lemon juice and brown sugar.

4. Grill the fruit for about 3 minutes on each side, until lightly browned. Allow to cool.

5. Arrange the fruit on serving plates and sift over the icing sugar. Decorate with mint leaves and raspberries.

Ewe's cheese and pomegranate salad

1. Put the cheese in a serving bowl, pour over the lemon juice and oil and scatter over the garlic. Leave to marinate for 3 hours.

2. Place the beetroot leaves on top of the cheese.

3. Scatter over some pomegranate seeds and place the parsley and mint on top. Sprinkle with the remaining pomegranate seeds.

Preparation time: 10 min
  plus 3 h marinating
Serves 4

350g feta cheese, cubed
juice of 1 lemon
2 tbsp extra-virgin olive oil
2 garlic cloves, crushed
1 handful beetroot leaves, cut
  into strips
1 pomegranate, seeds removed
1 handful parlsey leaves
1 handful mint leaves

Greek tortellini salad

1. Heat 2 tablespoons olive oil in a frying pan and cook the peppers and courgettes for about 4 minutes until tender. Remove from the pan and drain on kitchen paper.

2. Mix the remaining oil with the lemon juice and zest, herbs and salt and pepper to taste. Mix with the peppers and courgettes.

3. Cook the tortellini according to the pack instructions and drain well.

4. Mix together the tortellini, vegetables, cheese and olives. Season to taste and divide between serving bowls.

Preparation time: 15 min
Cooking time: 25 min
Serves 4

6 tbsp olive oil
2 small red peppers, diced
2 courgettes, chopped
juice and finely grated zest of
*   1 lemon*
1 tsp thyme leaves
1 tsp chopped rosemary leaves
1 tbsp chopped parsley
salt and pepper to taste
200g tortellini
200g feta cheese, crumbled
125ml black olives, pitted and sliced

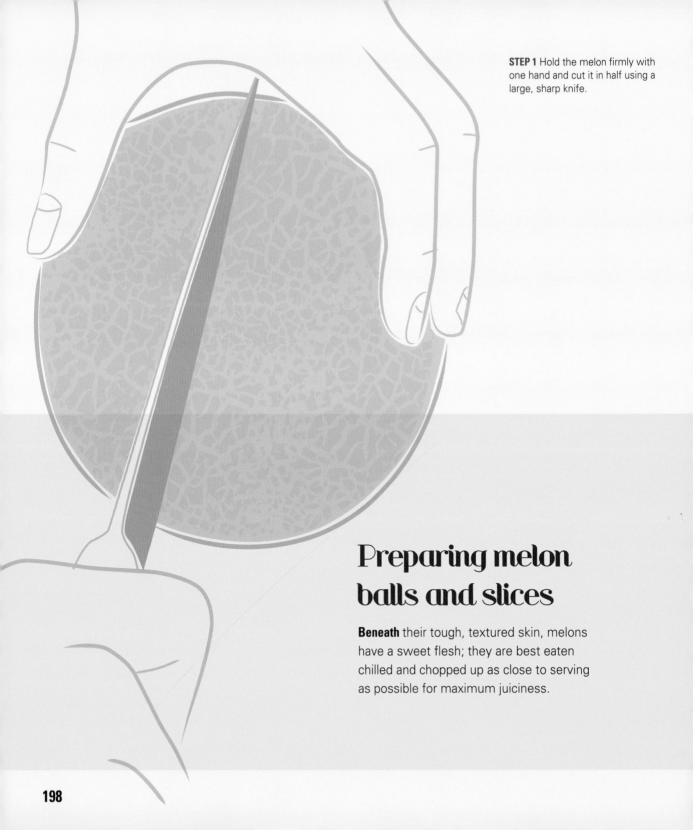

STEP 1 Hold the melon firmly with one hand and cut it in half using a large, sharp knife.

Preparing melon balls and slices

Beneath their tough, textured skin, melons have a sweet flesh; they are best eaten chilled and chopped up as close to serving as possible for maximum juiciness.

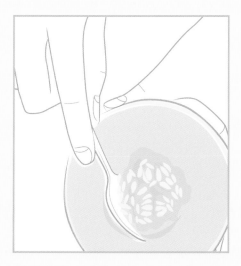

STEP 2 Hold each half with one hand and scoop out the seeds in the middle using a spoon. Discard these.

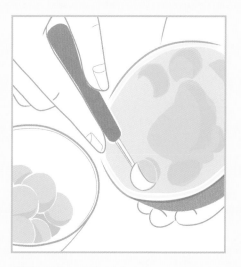

STEP 3 Using a melon baller, scoop out balls of flesh all around the melon half, avoiding the edges of the skin.

STEP 4 If you prefer to serve slices, hold the melon half in one hand and cut into slices.

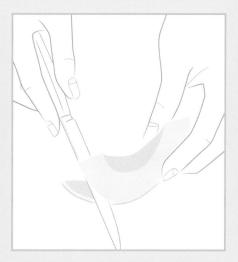

STEP 5 Once sliced into small pieces, take a sharp knife with a flexible blade and cut the melon flesh from the skin.

Insalata del contadino

1. Heat the oven to 200°C (400°F). Grease a baking tray.

2. Place the sliced vegetables on the baking tray and sprinkle with salt and pepper and 1 tablespoon oil. Cook for 20 minutes. Remove from the oven and drizzle with 2 tablespoons oil and the lemon juice and leave to stand for at least 1 hour.

3. Sprinkle half the balsamic vinegar over the vegetables. Layer the courgettes, squash and peppers, toasted bread and cheese. Top with a basil leaf and an aubergine slice.

4. Drizzle the remaining balsamic vinegar over the top.

Preparation time: 20 min
 plus 1 h standing
Cooking time: 20 min
Serves 4

1 courgette, sliced
salt and pepper to taste
1 small yellow squash, sliced
2 red peppers, sliced
1 aubergine, sliced
3 tbsp olive oil
2 tbsp lemon juice
4 tbsp balsamic vinegar
8 rounds toasted bread
4 slices Scamorza cheese
4 large basil leaves

Fish and mango salad

1. Season the fish with salt and pepper and lightly dust with flour.

2. Melt the butter in a frying pan. Place the fillets in the pan, floured side down. Fry gently for 4–5 minutes, then turn the fish in the pan and remove from the heat. Leave to stand for a further 2–3 minutes, then remove from the pan and set aside to cool.

3. Place the remaining ingredients in a bowl and toss together, seasoning to taste with salt and black pepper.

4. Put the salad into serving bowls. Cut or flake the fish into pieces and arrange on top of the salad. Garnish with lime slices.

Preparation time: 20 min
Cooking time: 5 min
Serves 4

4 × 175g firm white fish fillets,
  skinned
salt and pepper to taste
flour
1 tbsp butter
1 red pepper, diced
juice of 2 limes
2 small mangoes, peeled and sliced
2 spring onions, finely chopped
8–10 lettuce leaves, torn
1 tbsp chopped coriander leaves
4 tbsp olive oil
black pepper
lime slices, to garnish

Tuna and pasta salad

1. Heat the oil in a frying pan and cook the mushrooms until tender and golden. Stir in the peas and cook for 2 minutes.

2. Cook the pasta according to the packet instructions and drain.

3. Toss the warm pasta with all the other ingredients and divide between 4 serving bowls.

Preparation time: 10 min
Cooking time: 20 min
Serves 4

2 tbsp olive oil
150g mushrooms, sliced
150g peas
150g pasta tubes
150g tinned tuna, drained
150g tinned sweetcorn, drained

Bean salad with red mullet

Preparation time: 15 min
Cooking time: 20 min
Serves 4

1 tbsp butter
8 small red mullet fillets
400g broad beans
2–3 red peppers, skinned and cut
   into wedges
1 handful Brussel sprout leaves
4 tbsp olive oil
1 small onion, diced
1 garlic clove, finely chopped
1 tomato, diced
1 tbsp chopped thyme
4 tbsp vegetable stock
4 tbsp white wine vinegar
2 tsp pink peppercorns, crushed
sea salt

1. Heat the butter and gently fry the red mullet fillets over a low heat for 3 minutes.

2. Cook the beans in a pan of boiling, salted water for 5–8 minutes.

3. Blanch the peppers in boiling, salted water for 2 minutes. Add the Brussel sprout leaves for the last minute. Drain the Brussel sprout leaves, peppers and beans, rinse in cold water and drain well.

4. Heat 1 tablespoon oil and cook the onion, garlic and tomato gently until soft. Add the thyme, stock, remaining oil and the vinegar.

5. Remove from the heat and add the peppercorns.

6. Reserve half of the dressing and carefully mix the rest with the fish and vegetables.

7. Arrange on serving plates and garnish with the remaining dressing. Sprinkle with sea salt and serve.

Carrot and tuna salad

1. Mix together the carrots and tuna.

2. Whisk together the oil, vinegar, lemon juice, mustard and peppercorns, until thickened.

3. Divide the carrot and tuna salad between 4 serving plates and drizzle with the dressing.

4. Garnish with lemon wedges and coriander.

Preparation time: 15 min
Serves 4

8 carrots, coarsely grated
150g tinned tuna, drained and flaked
6–8 tbsp olive oil
4 tbsp wine vinegar
3 tbsp lemon juice
2 tbsp Dijon mustard
2 tsp green peppercorns
lemon wedges and coriander,
  to serve

Green lentil and Sunblush tomato salad with spicy lamb skewers

1. Mix the honey, olive oil, ras el hanout and thyme together and smear over the lamb. Place the lamb in the fridge and allow to marinade for 1 hour.

2. Cook the red rice according to the pack instructions. Drain the rice and mix with the lentils, SunBlush tomatoes and chopped parsley.

3. Thread the lamb cubes onto the skewers and grill for 15 minutes under a hot grill, turning the skewers halfway through cooking.

4. Whisk together the dressing ingredients and stir into the lentil mixture. Add in the rocket and combine. Top the salad with the lamb skewers and serve.

Preparation time: 1 h
Cooking time: 25 min
Serves 4

3 tbsp honey
2 tbsp olive oil
8 tsp Ras el hanout
1 tsp chopped fresh thyme
400g lamb leg steak, cut into
  small cubes
200g tin Puy lentils
200g red rice
100g SunBlush tomatoes
3 tbsp chopped flatleaf parsley
40g rocket leaves
4 bamboo or metal meat skewers

For the dressing:
juice of 1 lemon
60ml walnut oil

Pumpkin and orecchiette pasta salad with sage pesto

1. Cook the pasta in a large pan of salted boiling water according to the pack instructions. Steam the pumpkin cubes for 15 minutes or until easily pierced with the tip of a knife.

2. Using a mini food processor, blend the pesto ingredients until smooth.

3. Mix the pasta with the pumpkin and pesto. Toss in the rocket and serve.

Preparation time: 10 min
Cooking time: 20 min
Serves 4

200g orecchiette pasta
220g pumpkin, cut into cubes
25g rocket leaves

For the pesto dressing:
100ml extra virgin olive oil
25g sage leaves
30g walnuts
30g grated Parmesan

Piccalilli salad with English mustard dressing

Preparation time: 10 min
Cooking time: 5 min
Serves 4

250g fine green beans
3 carrots, peeled
3 asparagus spears
3 baby cauliflower heads
2 small red onions, cut into rings
15 radishes, finely sliced
20 chives, cut in half
40g mixed leaves

For the dressing:
60ml rapeseed oil
30ml cider vinegar
2 tsp English mustard
1 tbsp Greek yoghurt
1 finely chopped cornichons
1 tbsp finely chopped tarragon

1. Blanch the beans for 3–4 mins before plunging them into cold water and draining. Shave the peeled carrots and asparagus spears into a large salad bowl. Break the cauliflower in to small florets and add to the bowl along with the remaining salad ingredients.

2. To make the dressing, whisk together the oil and vinegar before adding in the mustard, yoghurt, cornichons and tarragon. Season to taste.

3. Pour the dressing over the salad ingredients and toss. Serve with leftover cold meats such as beef or lamb.

Pancetta and spinach salad with toasted macadamia nuts

1. Under a hot grill, cook the pancetta until crispy and cut each slice into 3 horizontally.

2. To make the dressing, cut the tomato into quarters, remove the seeds and grate the fleshy part, leaving the skin behind into a small bowl. Whisk in the rest of the dressing ingredients.

3. Place the spinach in a salad bowl and crumble in the blue cheese. Add in the macadamias and crispy pancetta.

4. Dress the salad by pouring over the dressing and tossing the leaves to coat them.

Preparation time: 5 min
Cooking time: 10 min
Serves 4

10 slices of pancetta
120g baby spinach leaves
100g Gorgonzola cheese
80g toasted macadamia nuts

For the dressing:
1 tomato
60ml extra virgin olive oil
30ml cider vinegar
1 tsp Dijon mustard
1 tbsp crème fraiche
1 tbsp chopped parsley

Quinoa super food salad

1. Put the pumpkin cubes into a baking tray and toss in a little olive oil, the cinnamon and sugar. Place in a heated oven and roast for 20–25 minutes or until soft and browning round the edges.

2. Cook the quinoa and giant couscous separately according to the packet instructions. Blanch the asparagus in hot water for 2–3 minutes. When the pumpkin, asparagus and grains are cooked, combine with the sprouted lentils, seeds, avocado, pomegranate and chopped herbs.

3. Squeeze the remaining pomegranate seeds over a large bowl, removing the juice and discarding the leftover seed. Whisk together with the remaining dressing ingredients with the pomegranate juice. Pour over the salad, toss and serve.

Preparation time: 10 min
Cooking time: 25 min
Serves 4

120g pumpkin, cut into cubes
olive oil
¼ tsp cinnamon
1 tsp sugar
150g quinoa
50g giant couscous
12 fine asparagus spears,
  blanched
30g sprouted lentils
1 tbsp pumpkin seeds
1 tbsp sunflower seeds
1 ripe avocado, peeled and
  roughly diced
½ pomegranate, deseeded
1 small bunch of mint, finely
  chopped
1 small bunch of flatleaf parsley,
  finely chopped

For the dressing:
juice of 1 lemon
50ml extra virgin olive oil
10ml pumpkin seed oil
seeds from ¼ of a pomegranate
1 tsp pomegranate molasses

Index

221

The Incredible Ball 1

A Comprehensive History & Price Guide

Henry Gostony and Stuart Schneider

Schiffer Publishing Ltd

4880 Lower Valley Rd. Atglen, PA 19310 USA

To Marisa and Jimmy Gostony

Library of Congress Cataloging-in-Publication

Gostony, Henry.
The incredible ball point pen : a comprehensive history and price guide / Henry
Gostony and Stuart Schneider.
p. cm.
Includes bibliographical references and index.
ISBN 0-7643-0437-2
1. Ball-point pens. I. Schneider, Sturart L. II. Title.
TS1267.G67   1998
681'.6--dc21   97-31330
CIP

Designed by Bonnie M. Hensley

ISBN: 0-7643-0437-2
Printed in China
1 2 3 4

Published by Schiffer Publishing Ltd.
4880 Lower Valley Road
Atglen, PA 19310
Phone: (610) 593-1777; Fax: (610) 593-2002
e-mail: schifferbk@aol.com
Please write for a free catalog.
This book may be purchased from the publisher.
Please include $3.95 for shipping.

Please try your bookstore first.
We are interested in hearing from authors
with book ideas on related subjects.

Contents

Foreword

The ball point pen is with us every day. It is hard to think of a day going by without using one. Here is the story behind the writing instrument that everyone takes for granted.

The authors bring the fascinating history and progress of the ball point pen to life. Henry Gostony and Stuart Schneider are experts in the field of writing instruments. Henry Gostony is the former president of the United States Ball Point Collectors Club and writes for *Pen World Magazine*. Stuart Schneider is author of four books on writing instruments and also writes a column—Ask Miss Inkly—for *Pen World Magazine*. They bring years of experience to this never before studied field.

Acknowledgments

The authors are grateful to the corporations and individuals who helped make this book possible. We especially wish to thank the Parker Pen Company for providing extensive information from their archives on Parker and Eversharp, the Paper Mate Company (Santa Monica), the Gillette Company (which owns Parker, Paper Mate, and Waterman), and the W.A. Sheaffer Company.

Susan Braden, archivist, and Vicki Hearing of Parker (Janesville) provided hundreds of pages of original press releases, memos, ads, and copies of news articles, all wonderfully arranged. Dennis Harvat of Paper Mate assisted with valuable background information and an introduction to Patrick Joseph Frawley, Jr. Paul I. Douglas of Gillette provided very useful patent information. Linda Blakesley of the Sheaffer legal/patent department was especially generous and helpful. She located rare original ad copy, patents, articles, and other valuable documents. Walter Waltz and Thomas Frantz of Sheaffer also provided assistance. Other firms such as Cross and Mont Blanc contributed material.

The authors wish to thank the following people who also graciously agreed to let the authors photograph parts of their collections or contributed information and without whose help this book would not have been possible. Fred Krinke, owner of The Fountain Pen Shop (Los Angeles), Jack Price, Leadus Armes, Dick Johnson, Gary & Myrna Lehrer, Dan Reppert, Paul Fisher (Fisher Space Pen Company), Barry Frank, Benjamin Schneider, Rebecca Schneider, Maybelle Schneider, George Fischler, Hans-Georg Schriever-Abeln, Dr. Robert Erickson, Douglas Flax, Antonio Gagean, Ken Beigel, and Fred Plewa.

These people's hospitality, desire to make this a great book, and depths of collection added significantly to the quality of this book.

Introduction

The ball point pen is one of the most amazing inventions and collectible objects ever created. People have been mesmerized with the ball point pen since its raucous introduction in New York City on October 29, 1945, and even before. Today, ball point pens are everywhere and can be purchased for next to nothing. People born in the 1960s and afterwards take them for granted. They are abundant and cheaply available even in the poorest of third-world countries. (Today, the Paper Mate plant in Santa Monica, California, alone annually makes one billion writing instruments, the majority of them ball point pens.) But this ready availability belies this product's torrid and turbulent history.

In 1946, *Nation's Business* described the first year of the introduction of the ball point pen as "America's biggest sales battle, a window-shattering, hell-raising, no holds-barred fracas…Fountain pens never sold like that before…The (ball point) pen business has become a fabulously profitable giant."

This story of the ball point pen covers its early development, its cacophonous launching, and its outrageous and scandalous promotion, making the reader feel and appreciate the public hysteria which accompanied its debut. It tells of the fabulous riches which followed, the public's rapid and total disillusionment with the product, the collapse of the market, scientific breakthroughs in 1950, the resurrection of the industry, the improvements which occurred between 1950 to 1959, and the modern period from 1960 to the present.

Not only does this book explain the human and emotional side of the birth of the ball point pen, it delves into the four basic scientific and technical areas which had to be mastered to make the pen work. These were, roughly, development of a suitable ink; reliable storage of the ink and faultless delivery to the point; a point which spread the ink properly; and the ability to reliably and profitably manufacture these components.

This book also tells the story of the first pioneers and their companies, from Milton Reynolds, visionary, snake-oil salesman, quick-buck artist, and promoter, to Patrick C. Frawley, who found a suitable ball point ink, started Paper Mate, and helped save the industry.

Finally, this is the most exhaustive work available on early ball point brands, manufacturers, and models. It includes copies of original ads, patents, and documentation and it features a comprehensive photo and price guide.

This book is written for those who appreciate the ball point pen as a collectible and an investment and wish to further their pleasure and knowledge about this fascinating object.

The Ball Point Pen History

A Circuitous Path

For an object so taken for granted today, the ball point pen has had a sometimes controversial, often turbulent, many times profitable, but always interesting past. The basic ball point pen concept has been around for over a century. Many inventors have taken a stab at creating a writing device which would hold ink in a tube and apply it to a ball and onto a writing surface. Why did it take so long to develop? There was sufficient demand in earlier days for such a device. And when the time was right for public acceptance after World War II, why did this invention, so enthusiastically received just a few years before, fall into total public disfavor? And how did the discredited ball point pen rise to the level of respect, reliability, and favor it enjoys today?

This is the story of that journey. It includes four periods: the Visionaries (pre-1945), the Pioneers (1945 to 1949), Era of Breakthrough and Acceptance (1950 to 1959), and the Modern period (1960 on). In the first period, inventors struggled to develop an idea; in the second, they made, marketed, and promoted without always knowing what they were doing; in the third, the pieces finally began to fall in place; and in the latter, the fruits of the labor of all the other periods were realized.

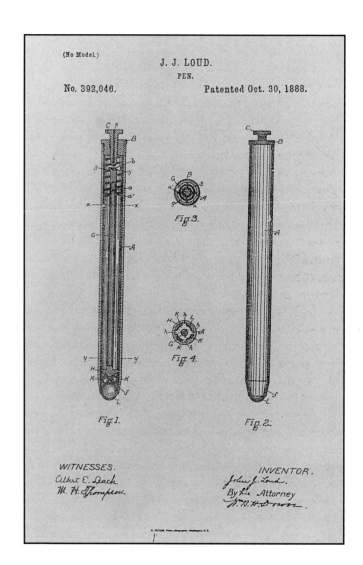

1888 patent by John J. Loud for an early ball point pen. Loud refers to his pen as "An improved fountain pen...especially useful for marking on rough surfaces."

A Simple Concept

The concept of a ball point pen dates to the early 1800s, but you won't see many ball point pens that were made before the 1940s. This is due to the complexities involved in making them. The problem areas were the ink, the size of the ball, and a way to hold the ball in place. The idea of a ball point pen is that ink in a tube is metered out to a ball at its end which spreads the ink evenly onto a writing surface. A simple concept on the surface, except that it took over 60 years to get it right.

Before the early 1940s, it was nearly impossible to make tiny metal balls that were consistent in size. Where it was possible, the cost was prohibitive. Weapons of World War II demanded ball bearings that were small and consistent in size. Since there was a demand for these small ball bearings, machinery was created to make them. As with the transistor, the initial cost of the manufacturing machinery was incredibly high, but once the machinery was paid for and in place, the product could be made by the millions. With the tremendous supply available, the price became low enough for manufacturers to begin designing ball point pens.

In the design phase, the idea was to hold the ball in place, allow it to freely rotate, and enable ink to touch the rolling ball. All of these demands were hard to meet. If the ball was not held with enough metal, the ball would soon fall out or loosen enough to allow ink to ooze out around it. If the socket holding the ball was made with too much metal, the writer would need to hold the pen almost perpendicular to the paper to write, since the edge of the socket would touch the paper and stop writing. There also had to be channels in the socket to allow the ink to reach the ball. Once all of these problems were worked out to the designer's satisfaction, they had to contend with the ink.

John J. Loud of Massachusetts is generally regarded as the father of the ball point pen. He received United States patent 392,046 on October 30, 1888. Loud thought of his ball point pen as a heavy duty fountain pen. He states in his patent that "My invention consists of an improved reservoir or fountain pen, especially useful among other purposes, for marking on rough surfaces—such as wood, coarse wrapping-paper, and other articles—where an ordinary pen could not be used."

The Loud patent was actually fairly complex. It consisted of a tube with a large ball at one end which rolled against three other "anti-friction" balls. A center rod was attached to a screw at the other end of the tube. A spring held the rod against the balls as did the threaded screw. When the screw was backed off, the rod was held in place against the ball only by the pressure of the spring. When the ball was pressed against a writing surface, it was able to retract, enabling ink to flow out of the tube onto the ball and onto the writing surface. When the user was finished writing, the screw was turned in forcing the rod to push the ball firmly against its seat and seal off the ink. The Loud concept was based strictly on the principle of gravity. His pen had to be held in an almost perfectly upright position. Loud made a few pens for himself which he used for marking boxes. However, no real commercial application was ever made of Loud's work.

After Loud, others applied for patents relating to ball point pens in the United States, England, France, Germany, and elsewhere. G.A. Werner and A.W. Askew patented a ball point pen in 1895, and for a while actually produced and sold it commercially using an ink made from lampblack and castor oil. Oscar Killebrew of Richmond, Virginia, received U. S. patent 1,028,029 (May 28, 1912) for a stylus which contained a rotating ball, the purpose of which was "...to make a large number of copies of writing by the aid of the usual carbon papers." Killebrew realized that the ball needed "...to be composed of relatively hard material such, for example, as steel, to avoid wear thereof, and the seat composed of relatively soft material..." (Later, when the ball point pen was being manufactured and promoted on a large scale in the mid-1940s, one of the selling points was that it could make seven or eight carbon copies.)

A ball point writing device was patented by Van Vecten Riesberg in 1916. In the 1930s, two Czechoslovakians, Paul B. Eisner and Wenzel Klimes patented the idea of regulating the pressure of ink with a screw at the top of the pen. Eisner and Klimes even marketed a ball point pen in Europe without much success. They were met with indifference when they approached American manufacturers. Death by neglect awaited other foreign and American ball point pens during the late nineteenth and early twentieth centuries. These pens simply weren't practical and there was little demand for this type of writing tool. Ultimately, ball point patents were allowed to die without exploitation with one notable exception.

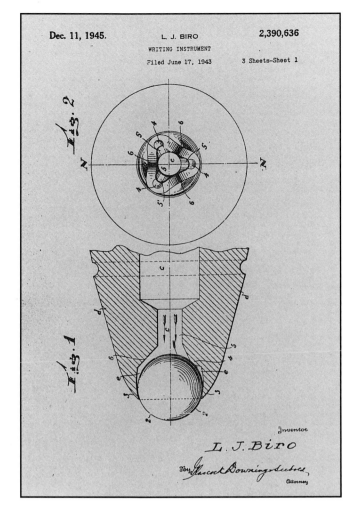

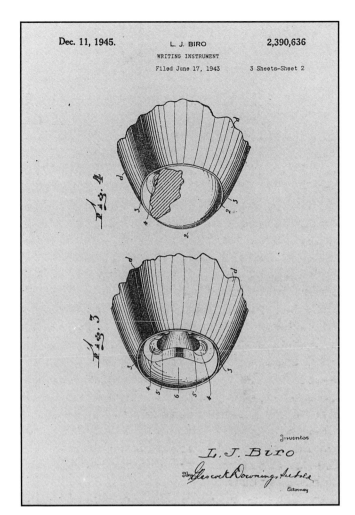

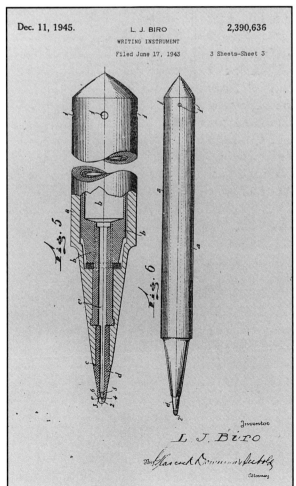

Laszlo Jozsef Biro ball point pen patent (filed June 17, 1943) using principles of capillary attraction and gravity and use of channels and grooves to flood the ball with ink.

Enter The Biros

Laszlo Jozsef Biro was a Hungarian "renaissance man." Born around the turn of the twentieth century, he had been a medical student, hypnotist, and sculptor. He was also a writer, painter, and inventor. In his various professions he had grown to dislike fountain pens. He and his brother George, a chemist, created a different kind of pen, one which employed a ball at the end of a tube to spread the ink contained therein. Like Loud one-half century before him, Biro had used three small bearing balls on which the main ball of his pen rotated. But his design was different in that he created a special ink feeding conduit by which ink could make its way to the ball once it had left the main reservoir. The pen used both the principles of simple gravity and capillary action. Biro also dealt with the problems of evaporation by using a very thick ink. Although his idea incorporated some of the concepts previously espoused, he was the first to put it all together into a coherent and workable package.

Living in Budapest and vacationing at nearby Lake Balaton, Laszlo met a fellow vacationer who showed interest in his new kind of pen. As luck would have it, the vacationer turned out to be Augistine Justo, President of Argentina. Justo invited Laszlo and George to Argentina to set up a factory to make ball point pens. At first, the Biros were not interested, but as it became more evident that the continent would soon be in the throes of another major war, Laszlo made his way across Europe to Paris (where he patented his pen) and arrived in Buenos Aires in 1940. For the first few years, Laszlo sought financial backing and set up facilities to make the pen. But his first model, based on gravity feed, was a flop. By 1943, a new pen called the *Eterpen*, using both principles of gravity and capillary action, was ready. This pen worked much better. Biro filed his design with the U.S. Patent Office on June 17, 1943, and was granted patent 2,390,636 on December 11, 1945.

The new pen worked so much better than past models, that Henry Martin, Biro's key financial backer, bought the rights and began supplying the Royal Air Force with thousands. The *Eterpen* worked at high altitude, was unaffected by climatic conditions, and held considerable ink. As more and more bombers winged their way across the skies of Europe, the advantages of new this type of pen became more apparent. The U.S. War Department expressed interest in this strategic tool and obtained a few of them. It sent samples to Eversharp, Parker, and Sheaffer and offered to buy this sort of pen if it could be made to work better. In August 1944, the War Department contacted the Sheaffer Pen Company about making ball point pens. (Laszlo Biro died at age 86 in Buenos Aires in 1985).

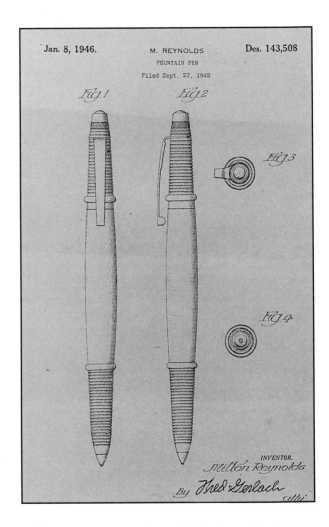

Milton Reynolds design patent filed in September 1945, barely a month prior to the public introduction of his ball point pen.

Reynolds Catches On

It was about six months later that Milton Reynolds, a Chicago businessman and promoter, got wind of the "magic" pen and flew to Buenos Aires to investigate. Informed that the American rights to Biro's patents had already been leased to Eberhard Faber and The Eversharp Company, he went on a mad scramble to produce something similar. The end result, nevertheless, was that on October 29, 1945, in New York City, Reynolds and Gimbels introduced his new pen to the world. Reynolds convinced the public that the fountain pen was a magical tool. In fact it was a miracle! The fact that it did not yet really work did not stop him from promoting his pen as though it had been perfected. The pen sold for the lofty price of $12.50.

Reynolds caught the public's attention with outrageous claims, inspired advertising, and flamboyant promotional stunts. In only a few months, he sold millions of pens and made millions of dollars. For almost six months he had the entire American market completely to himself. When Eversharp finally jumped in with its "CA" ball point pen (based on the Biro patent) in mid-1946, it had still not been perfected. And within another six months there were 150 major, and thousands of minor, companies spewing out ball point pens—none of them any good. By 1947, competition was so stiff and the product so utterly atrocious, that prices began a steep decline until most ball points sold for less than a dollar. The public had soured on ball point pens that did not work.

Improvements Remain Elusive

While the "ball point pen wars" raged from 1946 through 1949, the major manufacturers and others searched furiously for ways to make the pen work.

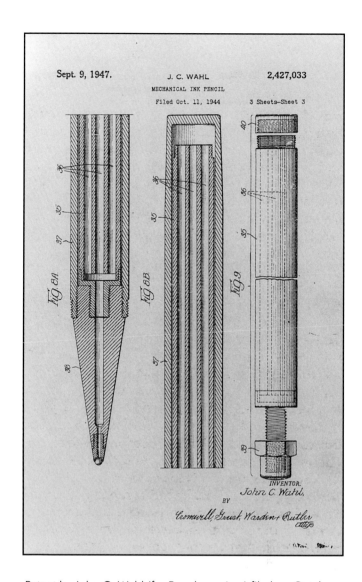

Patent by John C. Wahl (for Eversharp, Inc.) filed on October 11, 1884, for a ball point pen containing seven open-ended passages leading to a single passage culminating in a ball at the tip. This pen used the principles of a capillary attraction. The ball unit screwed into the barrel.

John C. Wahl, assignor to Eversharp, Inc., filed for a patent October 11, 1944, for a "...mechanical ink pencil." Wahl's design (patent 2,427,033, received September 9, 1947) contained seven passages which provided ink "...of a paste-like semi-fluid consistency..." to a central passage which fed the ink to a ball at its tip. Wahl applied for a patent in August 1945 (received in September 1949) for a writing instrument with a retractable point. The application was also "...for an improved refill ink cartridge for use in a retractable tip pen...using a novel push button mechanism located at the rear of the pen." The refill cartridge looked remarkably similar to the Sheaffer Stratowriter refill which debuted in 1946.

Many other patents were issued in this period for a myriad of ball point pen improvements and inven-tions. Among these, Francis E. Gruber submitted a wonderful design (patent 2,460,345) for a ball point pen in December of 1945. It contained many advanced features. The pen was streamlined, had a strong, permanently affixed clip, and had a replaceable ink cartridge. It also used a twist mechanism for propelling or retracting the point. The ink cartridge consisted of "helical coils of hollowed tubing" of a type later used in some early Eversharp *Skyline* ball point pens. The Hamilton Ross *Jet Flow*, which appeared in 1946, looked very much like the Gruber pen and had many of the same features, especially the twist mechanism.

Other inventors attempted to overcome problems concerning ink delivery by means of special air cham-

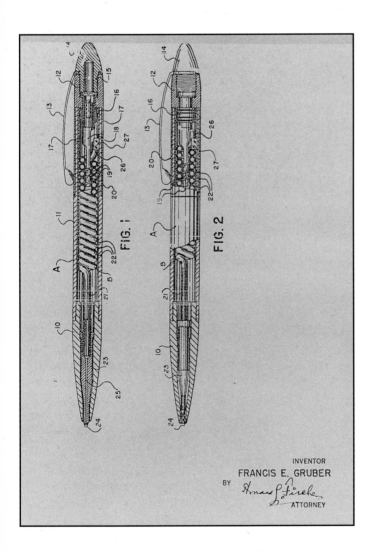

A very advanced pen for 1945, it used capillary attraction and contained a twist propel/repel mechanism, a replaceable ink cartridge, and had a streamline design. By Francis Gruber.

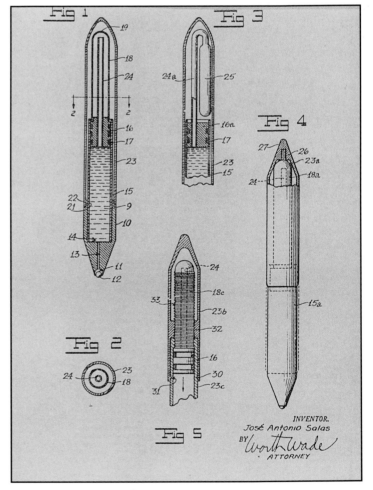

A patent by José Salas (Of Caragas, Venezuela) to regulate ink flow in a ball point pen by use of a piston and an internal air chamber. By 1950, suitable ink formulations were available which made inventions such as this unnecessary.

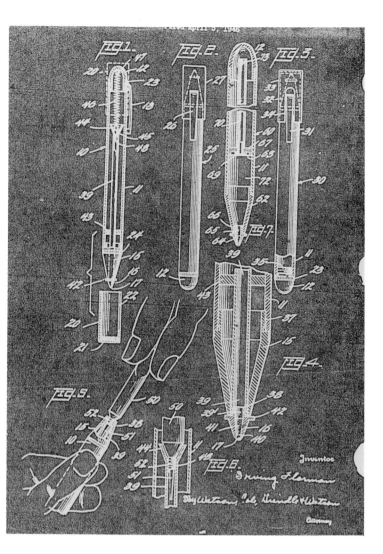

A patent by Irving Florman (filed April 5, 1946) for refilling a ball point pen by unscrewing the tip and squeezing ink into the empty chamber from a toothpaste-like tube. Easily exchangeable refills made this invention superfluous.

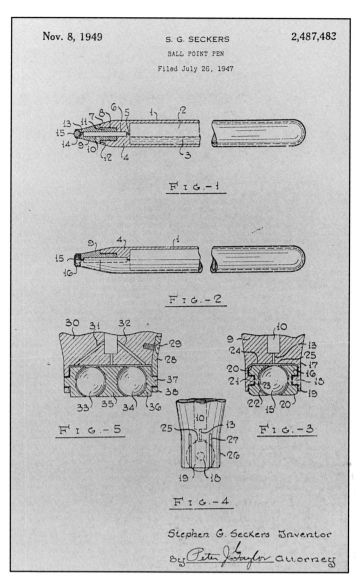

An intriguing patent by Stephen Seckers to create a ball point pen which could make lines of varying widths (shading) by using two balls at the tip.

bers and pumps. A Venezuelan inventor, Jose Salas, took the later approach and was awarded patent 2,474,865. His design seems too complicated to ever have been commercially successful. Another inventor, Irving Florman of New York City, was awarded patent 2,408,256 for an ink cartridge which was refillable from the tip. Florman's application (April 1946) explained that the writing fluid "...is supplied in flexible-walled collapsible tubes of the general type commonly employed for dispensing tooth paste, adhesives, or the like...the closure tip is unscrewed and the nozzle of the dispensing tube inserted within the opening...The body of the collapsible tube is squeezed until a charge of writing fluid is forced into the barrel of the pen...and the threaded tip replaced, all without leakage of writing fluid." The disposable refill cartridge which appeared in Eversharp's *CA Retractable* and the Sheaffer *Stratowriter* in late 1946, and in most

other pens shortly thereafter, killed outright whatever slim chance this idea may have had.

One of the ball point pen's disadvantages was its inability to vary the width of a line or "shade" like a fountain pen. Stephen Seckers devised a ball point pen which used two balls at its tip. He contends (patent 2,487,483, filed July, 1947) that his ball point pen would provide a wide range of shading depending on whether the two balls were in line with each other. When the balls were both applied to the paper horizontally (one trailing the other), there would be no shading. In any other position, shading would occur.

By late 1949, ball point sales had fallen to practically zero. Prices dropped to fifty cents or less as millions of pens piled up on counters and shelves and makers closed their doors. It looked like ball point pens, and the industry which produced them, was dead. Then, good things started to happen.

The New Ink And Other Breakthroughs

Just when it appeared no further improvements could be made, breakthroughs occurred in several areas. These included new formulations of inks, configuration of the cartridge, the "ink follower," and improvements in mass production techniques of the ball, the seat, and other components.

The main advantage of the ball point pen is that the ink is very viscous (i.e., thick), and therefore not only does not evaporate as fast as less viscous ink (used for example in fountain pens and roller balls), but also writes for a much longer time. There are many scientific concepts and terms related to the process of how a ball point pen works. Nevertheless, like the making of the atomic bomb, perfecting the process was the difficult part. (As proof, it took over a decade of active research—until the early 1950s—before the industry was able to get it right.)

The principles involving the flow of ink in a ball point pen have been known for a very long time. These include viscosity, capillary attraction, gravity, surface tension, shear, air lock, porosity, shelf life, and others. A knowledge of the chemical and hygroscopic (water absorption) properties of inks, resins, drying characteristics, solvents, and other additives is also helpful. Then there are the properties of dyes to consider, the dilution depending on the viscosity of the ink in combination with its "lay down rate," (how much goes on the paper) susceptibility to fade, and many other factors.

In general, new inks, a larger cartridge, improved manufacturing techniques, and innovations such as the sintered, textured ball, were the main developments by which the ball point pen was finally made to work right. All of these improvements together were necessary, as the success in one area without the others would have been insufficient to resurrect the ball point pen's sullied reputation.

Almost all the inks used in ball point pens up to the 1950s were derived from common printing inks. These dried very slowly resulting in smearing, blobbing, smudging, leaking, and the ability to be transferred to other documents. A company called Formulab finally developed an ink made specifically for ball point pens early in 1950. The new ink was quick-drying, non-smearing, and fade proof. Along with the new ink, the idea of a grease plug (and later, silicone) at the end of the ink cartridge was patented by an inventor named Hendrickson. This one feature allowed the diameter of the ink cartridge to be increased so that new jumbo-sized cartridges would write five or six times as long as the older style of cartridges.

The reason that wider ink cartridges were not used before the Hendrickson patent, is that when the cartridge is made wider beyond a certain point, the ink clings to the walls of the cartridge as it is used up. The grease plug, also called an ink follower, rides atop the column of ink pulling it down the cartridge to the point. The plug also has the added benefits of preventing evaporation and leaking from the back of the cartridge when the pen is put down. To compete, some manufacturers increased the quantity of ink held in their cartridges by making them longer. So called "stik pens" used this method. They were around seven inches in length. Manufacturers such as Venus began making lower cost transparent stik pens designed to be discarded after they ran out of ink. Interestingly, some disreputable manufacturers made "dummy" jumbo cartridges by making the outside of the cartridge fatter while keeping the inside diameter exactly the same size.

The quality of ball point pens increased as manufacturing techniques improved. Originally, the early manufacturers used parts made by machines which were unable to achieve the tolerances needed. As a result, often the balls would fall out of the early pens, and the only angle at which the pen would write was vertically—straight up and down. By 1950, high-precision automatic machines became available which could turn out ball point pen parts by the millions with manufacturing tolerances of almost unbelievable accuracy, sometimes running to 10 millionths of an inch. The clearance of the ball in its socket could easily be held to five ten thousandths of an inch. Rounded balls could be made to 6 millionths of an inch. Eventually, manufacturers were able to consistently produce millions of ball pen writing tips with so little variation that it was literally impossible to see variations in writing characteristics.

Paper Mate Takes the Lead

Patrick J. Frawley, Jr., was 26 years old when he got into the ball point business. With an initial investment of $40,000, he bought the Todd Pen Company, which became the Paper Mate Company. Frawley's friends thought he was crazy for going into ball point pen business, which had the reputation of being sleazy. (Frawley told the author that when he started out, the public compared people in the ball point pen business to those whose mug shots hung on the walls of post offices.)

The first Paper Mate pen looked very much like the 1946 Blythe, except that it wasn't as long and not as substantial. It had a simple retractable mechanism which consisted of a hole in the top with a button which pushed the point out of the barrel. The button had to be locked in place by tilting to the side and into a grove. (Frawley conceded in 1997, that it was a bad design.)

The next Paper Mates were modern and in tune with the times. They were "Tu-Tone" like the new cars, used new "Widco" ink, and because they were made to closer tolerances, worked relatively well. They were colorful, used one-click, positive-retraction, came in fine and medium points, and in four colors of ink. They were heavily and skillfully promoted. Soon Frawley's upbeat advertising, *Piggy Back* refill, and the double heart logo captured the public's interest. Ball point pens started selling again. Paper Mate sales skyrocketed from only $530,000 in 1950 to $20 million in just three years. So successful was the company that Gillette bought Paper Mate for $15.5 million in October 1955.

Parker Jumps In

By mid-1953, the value of ball point pen sales had overtaken that of fountain pens. Firms, such as Scripto, had emulated Paper Mate's pen sales success. Therefore, after staying out of the field for almost nine years (with two exceptions), in the fall of 1953, Parker launched "Operation Scramble," to make and put a ball point on the market in 90 days. In January 1954, Parker introduced the *Jotter*. This now legendary pen, which is still being sold, had a jumbo cartridge, a stainless steel point, a nylon barrel, and was made to very close tolerances. They were still "gun shy" of ball points, so they did not put a Parker arrow clip on the pen until a few years later. It was an immediate success and outstripped all sales projections. So successful was the *Jotter* at $2.95, that Parker added a series of more costly variations.

In June 1957, Parker launched the "T-Ball" *Jotter*, based on the original pen. Although the new pen had a revolutionary textured and porous point made by "sintering," and other new features, Parker actually lowered the price to $1.95

Not resting on its laurels, Parker bought the Eversharp Writings Instruments Division in December 1957, and gave the reconstituted Eversharp's new Fountain Ball the sintered, textured point used in the T-Ball. It sold for only 98 cents. Parker continues to offer innovations over the years and is still today a leader in the ball point pen field. In May 1993, it was bought by the Gillette Company.

Maturity and the Future

Once the technical kinks had been ironed out in the early 1950s, ball point production continued to skyrocket. From practically zero in 1949, industry-wide sales have risen steadily. In 1951, 50 million were made, 300 million by 1957, 475 million by 1958, 650 million by 1959, 900 million by 1961, and a billion the year after. Paper Mate sold over 100 million of their *98 Malibu* by 1970. The *Jotter* reached 100 million by June 1975, and topped 400 million by 1984. It continues to be made today.

But now that the ball point pen has been virtually perfected, what does the future hold? This is a difficult question, for surely the ball point will always have a place. It is sturdy, can take unbelievable abuse, and doesn't dry out for decades. Recently, however, as writing tastes have gone upscale and consumers are again becoming more sophisticated about writing instruments, attempts have been made to make the ball point write more like a roller ball, where less pressure is required and inks are more vibrant. But that means that the ink must be thinner. However, when this is done, unless the ball and seat tolerances are tightened, the pen will tend to leak at the point. So it seems that development of the ball point pen has gone just about as far as it can.

Will the roller ball displace the ball point pen? Within the limits of physics, if manufacturers could devise a way to keep the roller ball with its more fluid ink from drying out so fast, it is possible that roller ball sales or other such instruments could displace the ball point, which is over one-century old already. Certain ceramic tipped roller balls seem extremely smooth and some can hold a large quantity of fluid and write a very long time without drying out.

The ball point pen will probably be around for a very, very long time. Like the fountain pen before it, it will undoubtedly always have a future. Certainly, it has already had a most interesting past.

Reynolds

Something New

The Reynolds story begins on May 8, 1945, during the waning days of World War II. The biggest coup in ball point pen history (and some say in the annals of business) was about to begin. Milton Reynolds was lunching with Joel Goldblatt at Goldblatt's Department Store in Chicago, when Goldblatt pulled an odd writing instrument from his pocket and showed it to Reynolds. It was a ball point pen, made by Miles-Martin Pen Company, Ltd. in England for the Royal Air Force. (The need for a pen which wouldn't leak, but would write at high altitudes, had become necessary during bombing runs over Europe.) The pen had been invented by two Hungarian brothers living in Argentina—Laszlo Biro and his brother George. Goldblatt had pried the pen loose from a Pentagon official. Reynolds was intrigued and fascinated. Instinct told him that this new product could be "the big one" that promoters dream about.

Reynolds wasted no time. He hopped the next flight to Argentina hoping to secure the rights to sell the pen in the United States. Once in Buenos Aires, he found that he was too late: Biro had already agreed to let Eberhard Faber and Eversharp make and sell his pen in the United States. Unable to strike a deal with Biro, Reynolds, flew back to Chicago determined to make a pen of his own.

Making A Copy

Reynolds moved with incredible speed. He knew that Eversharp was developing a ball point pen. Reynolds realized, too, that the public had become accustomed to scientific miracles, such as rockets, jet planes, radios, and television. The ball point pen would be another such miracle—a pen that could write indefinitely for years on end, unlike old-fashioned fountain pens.

A born salesman, Reynolds, felt that the public was primed and ready for the "miracle" ball point pen. He knew that after years of war, Americans wanted to indulge themselves. During the war, workers earned lots of money, but had very little to buy. When millions of servicemen returned home, confidence and euphoria would prevail. People would be in a spending mood.

Reynolds was also excited because he knew that Eversharp had blundered by launching a publicity campaign for its ball point pen before it was ready. Due to technical difficulties, the company had held off putting the pen on the market. Reynolds rightly calculated that his pen could piggy-back on this advance publicity.

As one of the few firms permitted by the government to make nearly unlimited quantities of fountain pens during the war, Eversharp may have grown complacent. It probably didn't realize how enthusiastically the public would accept the ball point pen or the pent-up demand for a scientific "wonder" product like the ball point pen.

Reynolds worked furiously with local Chicago manufacturers to develop an alternative to the Biro capillary-attraction pen. Biro realized that ink in a narrow tube would adhere to itself based on the principle of capillary attraction or surface tension. Reynolds, unable to get around Biro's patented capillary principle, settled on using simple gravity to deliver ink to the point.

A gravity-feed system requires less viscous, thinner ink. Because thinner ink runs out faster, the pen needed a wider barrel to hold more of it. A vent hole was also needed, since in a gravity-feed pen "air locks" would develop. Air lock occurs when bubbles form in the ink tube as the ink travels down to the point or when the pen is laid on its side. Without a vent hole, the bubbles would block the flow of ink. Another problem was that unless the pen was held in an upright position, ink would leak out of the hole. To solve this problem, Reynolds placed a drop of oil and a plastic plug, called a "follower," atop the supply of ink. This didn't fix the leaking problem. A suitable ink (neither too thick nor thin, quick drying, non-smearing, transferable, and non-fading) couldn't be found, and

Reynold's *Satinflow* ink proved a deplorable failure. Moreover, the design and manufacture of a satisfactory ball and socket continued to proved illusive. The steel balls routinely fell out of their sockets and developed "flat spots" resulting in seizing. None of this deterred Reynolds.

In the summer of 1945, Reynolds informed his partners that the pen was now "commercially practical." On July 26, 1945, with an initial investment of $1,000, Reynolds and four associates formed the Reynolds International Pen Company. They later added additional capital. In late September, Reynolds persuaded the United States Office of Price Administration (OPA) to set a retail ceiling of $12.50 on the pen. The pen itself cost only eighty cents to make.

Since Reynolds had been in business selling his *"Printasign"* machine to department stores, he knew many of the owners and top buyers. He convinced Fred Gimbel to place an order for 50,000 pens. With orders in hand, Reynolds hired Chicago manufacturer Titus Haffa to make the pens. With the war now over, aluminum, manufacturing facilities, and skilled labor were readily available. The pen's barrel, cap, clip, and most other parts were made of war-surplus aluminum. The tip was brass, and the ball stainless steel. Reynolds got the balls from SKF which had a million 1 millimeter balls (in little bottles of five hundred each) left over from the war.

Production began on October 6, 1945, when Titus Haffa's machine shop turned out its first seventy-five pens. The model was the Reynolds *"International."* Everything was falling into place. On October 29, only 23 days after production began, the first Reynolds pens were offered at Gimbels' New York City store, barely a month-and-one-half after victory over Japan and the end of the War.

Hysteria Ensues

Gimbels ran a huge ad for the Reynolds pen in the October 28, 1945, Sunday edition of the New York Times. It announced that, "The fantastic, atomic era, miraculous fountain pen that you've read about, wondered about, waited for..." would be available for $12.50 on Monday morning.

In typical Reynold's fashion, the ad made vastly exaggerated claims. It called the pen "...Buck Rogers' baby" and said it could "write in the stratosphere at 20,000 feet or higher," and even on cloth. It could write in the "remotest ice floe in the Aleutians," under water, and for two years without refilling. In short, it was "the perfect Christmas gift for anyone from eight to 80!"

In line with its outlandish claims, the pen's packaging was as flamboyant as the rhetoric describing it. Long and thin, the pen was positioned vertically atop a stepped, aluminum base, set within a clear plastic tube, and enclosed inside a spherical cardboard tube with "Reynolds Pen International" elegantly lettered in gold on its exterior. The pen gave the appearance of a rocket ready to be launched.

As Reynolds had guessed, the timing was right. That Monday, a crowd of 5,000 thronged in front of Gimbels, blocking the entrances, waiting anxiously to be let in. Hastily, fifty extra policeman were dispatched to control the crowd. An eyewitness, recalls, "Everyone was excited. People were pushing and shoving to get inside. There was a near panic. No one wanted to be left out or even minded paying the $12.50 for the pen, a huge amount in those days." Gimbels sold $100,000 worth of Reynolds *International* pens that day.

The following day, ball point pen hysteria swept the nation based on news reports and word of mouth. People everywhere began to clamor for the pen. Within a few days, Reynolds received more orders than he could possibly fill.

A 1946 Reynolds ad extolling the virtues of the pen. An unsuspecting public would soon learn just how exaggerated the claims were.

In the month following the introduction of the pen, sales climbed to 100,000 pens per day. By the beginning of December, there was a backlog of over a million orders. Reynolds started selling certificates promising the owner a pen as soon as it was available. By February 1946, Reynolds had made a profit of $1.5 million.

The introduction of the Reynolds pen caught Eversharp by surprise. An article which appeared in Fortune months later (July 1946) stated that the introduction of the Reynolds pen was "...a rude shock to Eversharp, Inc. which thought it had the ball pen sewed up by joint control with Eberhard Faber, of the Biro Argentine patents."

The Fever Breaks

In April 1946, Eversharp brought out its long delayed version of the Biro pen. (Reynolds simultaneously brought out his 400 model that had a retractable protector which slid over the point, instead of a cap.) Called the Eversharp CA (for "capillary attraction") and able to be refilled in a few seconds (although priced at $15), it began cutting into Reynolds' sales.

Reynolds tried to expand the market for the pen by taking it abroad, and by late summer of 1946, it was being sold in 37 countries. However, criticism of the pen began to take a toll. Banks and government agencies warned that signatures written with Reynolds pens could be easily transferred by pressure onto other documents and that the ink faded. In late 1946, as reliability and performance problems became widely known and competition increased, Reynolds sales and prices began to drop dramatically. Profits slid to $350,000 per month by October 1946, and continued on a downward slide. By the Christmas season of 1946, there were at least 150 other manufacturers churning out ball points.

To stimulate sales, Reynolds came out with a succession of new models. The *Rocket*, launched in October 1946 for $3.85, cost only thirty cents to make. It was guaranteed to write for fifteen years or 32 miles, non-stop (whichever came first!). Macys touched off a price-war in February, 1947, when it offered the Reynolds *Rocket* Threesome at just $2.79 for all three. (The Threesome, consisting of a Rocket and two new models, the *Rockette* and the *Stubby Rocket*, had been introduced in time for the 1946 Christmas season at $9.95.) Macys, which had obtained the pens from a Chicago jobber, sold 60,000 the first day alone. After that, Gimbels retaliated by lowering the price still further. Later in February, it offered the Rolls ball point (by Continental) for ninety-eight cents.

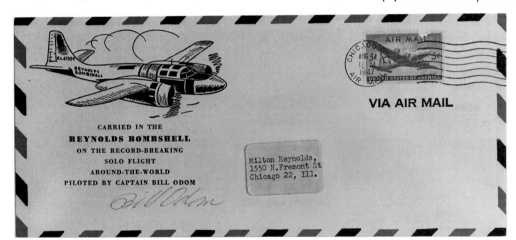

Envelopes carried aboard Milton Reynold's round the World flight, autographed by Reynolds and the pilot.

Reynolds decided to garner publicity, and, hopefully, increase sales by breaking the around-the-world speed record set in 1938 by Howard Hughes. He bought an A-26, two-engine, WW II bomber (named the Bombshell), converted it for the flight, and enlisted the help of William P. Odom, a famous flyer. Departing on April 12, 1947, the crew of three did set a new speed record (62 hours, 46 1/2 minutes) and later met with President Truman. (A year later, Reynolds flew to China in a converted C-87, named the Explorer, in search of the world's tallest mountain. He was arrested by the Communist government, and barely made it out in a daring escape.)

The Milton Reynolds China Expedition

Here, for the first time, is the story behind the Reynolds expedition to China.

Reynolds hurled the bag of pens at the Chinese.

BY W. T. BRANNON

Take the Money and Run

Although the flights generated extensive publicity, sales and profits continued to slide. The flying adventures had been expensive, costing a quarter-of-a-million dollars each. As the number of defective and returned pens mounted, Reynolds brought out the *Flyer* priced at only thirty-nine cents. It cost eight cents to make, but by now competition was intense. Reynolds pens began to be disparaged too. A common joke was that the Reynolds pen could make up to 8 carbon copies, but no original.

In 1948, following the China expedition, Reynolds called his remaining staff together. In light of declining sales (1947 was the last year in which the Reynolds pen business posted a profit), and inasmuch as the firm had no tradition of making pens, it decided to go out of business. Reynolds walked away with $5 million.

Reynolds left quite a legacy. He was the first to bring out a ball point pen which captured the public's attention. But he remains an enigma. Perhaps, he was just a relatively unscrupulous, promotional genius, in the right place, at the right time. He single-handedly forced the premature birth of the ball point pen industry, was largely responsible for the weakening and demise of several established pen companies (notably Eversharp), helped sour and disillusion the public on the ball point pen, and nearly destroyed its future. On the other hand, although Reynold's pens were barely functional, they did lead the way. As for Milton Reynolds, personally, he made history and was a most fascinating character. He knew an opportunity when he saw one, gave no quarter to competitors, made a fortune, and totally enjoyed his moment in the sun.

The 1948 story of Milton Reynolds expedition to China. Here he is shown throwing pens to the hoards of Chinese surrounding his plane.

Eversharp

A Long History

In April 1946, Eversharp was the first traditional fountain pen manufacturer to put a ball point pen on the market. The firm had started in the writing instruments field 31 years earlier when in 1915, the Wahl Adding Machine Company purchased the Eversharp Pencil Company. In 1917, Wahl bought the Boston Fountain Pen Company and moved the business to Chicago.

By the late 1930s, after a history of making fountain pens and mechanical pencils, Wahl-Eversharp was on the ropes financially. The Great Depression had taken its toll. In May 1940, Martin L. Strauss and others bought the company for $200,000 and changed the name to Eversharp Inc., with Strauss at the helm. Strauss commissioned famous industrial designer, Henry Dreyfuss, to fashion a brand new pen. In May 1941, the deco-styled, teardrop-shaped *Skyline* fountain pen was offered to the public and was a "hit." As luck would have it, the War Production Board awarded Eversharp a generous production quota while limiting other manufacturers. During World War II, Eversharp prospered.

Eversharp Gets A Leg Up

By the time Eversharp learned about Laszlo Biro's ball point pen in 1943, Eberhard Faber had already struck a deal with Biro. Eversharp vied with other manufacturers to join with Faber to make and sell the pen. Eventually, Eversharp paid Faber $300,000, and five and one-half percent on each ball point pen produced. They believed that they had the inside track. Therefore, when the Reynolds ball point was introduced in New York City on October 29, 1945, Eversharp was stunned and unprepared.

April 1946 advertisement for Eversharp's CA pen.

Eversharp had been working on a ball point pen based on the Biro patent, but development had been slow. For over a year, it had been preparing the public for its arrival. When the Eversharp CA was finally rushed to dealers in April 1946, it still hadn't been perfected. But the CA was well received. Sales of the pen were spectacular. Eversharp revenues jumped, up over $4 million in the first three months after the CA was introduced. A thousand new employees were hired to make the pen. But by the end of the year, it became apparent that the bugs hadn't been worked out. Warranty claims, quality control problems, litigation, and legal expenses mounted. Price wars with Reynolds and others broke out. And then sales began to fall.

Ball Point Pen Problems

Eversharp brought out a series of other ball point pens. In 1947, Eversharp signed an agreement with the Kimberly Corporation of Los Angeles, another ball point maker, to supply Eversharp with ball point pens and refills. None of this stemmed the tide of red ink. By May 1948, Eversharp had to borrow $3 million just to stay in business. It ended the year with a $3.4 million loss. Strauss admitted that the firm had "...expended so great a portion of its time and attention in solving the problems of the ball point pen that certain developments in its conventional business (i.e., fountain pens; mechanical pencils, etc.) were, perhaps, under-emphasized." In 1949, the Eversharp Board of Directors forced Strauss out.

Parker Takes Over

Eversharp ball point pen history can be divided into two periods: April 1946 to December 1957, and January 1958 through January 1973. In the first period, Eversharp helped pioneer the development of the ball point pen. It had a full line of ball points, from top-of-the-line models to lower-priced variations. These included the CA, the CA Retractable, the Wahl Ball, and the Slim Jim. There was the diminutive Pockette and several other variations made by Kimberly, including the Eversharp KIM. Pens with removable caps include the Reporter and Star Reporter. There

were several variations of Eversharp and Kimberly retractable pens such as the Small Ball. After 1947, Eversharp pens all used refills made by Kimberly. In 1953, Eversharp advertised that its new pens used Inca Ink which cost "hundreds of thousands" to develop. Inca Ink, which captured "the secret of the centuries," came in Fire Red, Leaf Green, Temple Blue, and Jungle Black. In 1954, Kimberly built a modern 22,555 square manufacturing plant. In 1955, Eversharp acquired controlling interest in Kimberly.

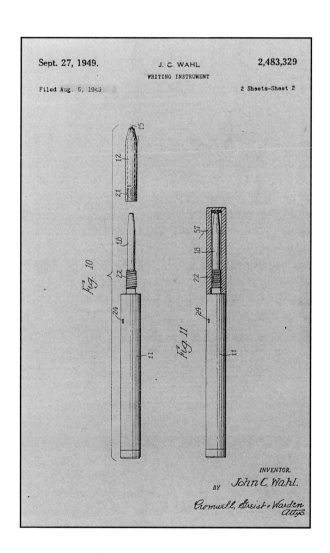

September 1949. The patent for a ball writing instrument with a retractable tip by John C. Wahl of Chicago assigned to Eversharp, Inc.

Eversharp continued to introduce new ball point models with a variety of inks in the 1950s, while the quality of its other products, notably fountain pens, continued to deteriorate. In January 1954, Parker put the *Jotter* on the market. It was the first ball point pen to bear the Parker name and offered many new features. These included a huge refill cartridge and a retractable mechanism which turned the point each time it was actuated. The pen was priced at $2.95. In June 1957, Parker brought out the T-Ball *Jotter* and reduced the price from $2.95 to $1.95. This was probably the last straw for Eversharp. The firm entered into negotiations and in December 1957 was acquired by Parker. In January, the Eversharp Pen Company became a Parker subsidiary as did the Kimberly Corporation. Parker relegated Eversharp to the lower end of the ball point pen market, reserving the upper tier for itself.

In September 1958, the new Eversharp Pen Company (a subsidiary of Parker), introduced the *Fountain Ball* priced at 98 cents. This entirely new model constituted Eversharp's entire product line. The *Fountain Ball* was a well designed, handsome pen, and featured a textured point like that on Parker's T-Ball *Jotter*. Eversharp claimed the pen individualized writing style and "added character to handwriting," similar to a fountain pen. The pen was available with either a triangular, or round barrel.

From 1958 to the early 1960s, Eversharp introduced a variety of new pens. Meanwhile the company offered to buy back any Eversharp pens made before 1958 still in dealer stocks. From 1958 on, Eversharp models incorporated modern ball point pen technology and improved inks. In 1958, the *Tu-Tone Slim Deluxe* was introduced. In 1959, a whole series of pens "designed with a gal in mind" debuted. These included the *Teena* at $1.29, *Gamin* at $1.95, and *Tiara* at $2.95. In 1960, the *Lightening*, a thin, see-through pen with a six-inch long refill, was introduced to compete with similar models offered by Venus, Eagle, and others. The *Lightening* cost 49 cents with a clip, or 39 cents without one.

In 1961, Eversharp introduced two ball point pens as a tie-in to the Civil War centennial. These were the *Johnny Reb* and the *Billy Yank*, each priced at 98 cents. The *Johnny Reb* was colored in "Confederate" gray, and included a lithographed replica of the Confederate flag. It used gray refills. The *Billy Yank* model was blue, and included a lithographed replica of the United States shield. It had a blue refill. Both models had a saber-shaped, gold electroplated clip. On the back of the cards holding the pens was a listing of significant Civil War dates.

Demise

On December 19, 1967, Parker announced that Eversharp would relocate from Culver City, California, to Parker's plant in Janesville, Wisconsin. The reason was to "gain efficiencies from integrated manufacturing, administrative and computer facilities." On January 10, 1968, Parker's Alfred P. Diotte announced that "Eversharp will cease to exist as a separate operating entity." On March 1, 1968, the Culver City operation was shut down and the building sold. The transfer of Eversharp to Janesville was completed on April 25, 1968. Eversharp limped on for a few years more, but finally, on January 15, 1973, after 58 years of operation, the Eversharp Pen Company ceased to exist. Thus, the book was closed on one of the early ball point pen pioneers and a great pen company.

The W. A. Sheaffer Pen Company

As one of the major old-line makers of fountain pens and mechanical pencils, Sheaffer had no choice but to enter the ball point pen field once this new type of writing instrument had been introduced by Milton Reynolds in October 1945. Actually, Sheaffer had been aware of the ball point pen since August 1944, and probably even before.

On August 11, 1944, a small rectangular-shaped package was sent by Air Mail Special Delivery to The Sheaffer Pen Company, Fort Madison, Iowa. It was sent by the United States War Department, Office of the Quartermaster General, Washington, D.C. (Sheaffer had been misspelled "Shaeffer.")

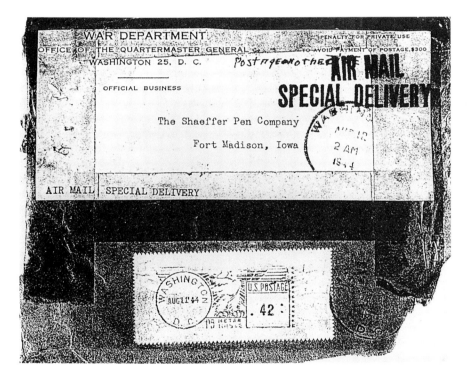

The wrapper of the package of pen samples that the War Department sent to Sheaffer in August 1944 to determine if Sheaffer could make a satisfactory ball point pen for military use.

Inside was a writing instrument which looked like an ordinary fountain pen of the day. It had no lever or any other visible means of filling. Simultaneously, a letter was posted which explained that in accordance with previous telephone conversations between Sheaffer's George Holt and Mr. Ronald Senseman, War Department Special Assistant, the special pen was being forwarded under separate cover. The pen was an *Eterpen* ball point pen, invented by Biro and manufactured in South America. Would Sheaffer be interested in making an improved model for the Army? The letter went on to say that if "...after inspection of

the pen you feel that you would be interested in making some for the Army, please have a representative of your company come into this office and discuss the matter at the earliest possible date." It requested return of the *Eterpen* sample. The letter concluded, "Your cooperation in this development work will be very much appreciated."

On October 25, 1944, a year and a few days before the Reynolds pen went on sale to the public, Sheaffer sent samples of its version of the *Eterpen* to the War Department. Barely a week later, on November 3, 1944, the Quartermaster General wrote back thanking Sheaffer for the prototypes, but noting that these pens had the same drawbacks as the *Eterpen*, a failure to feed ink to the point and a ball recessed to such a degree that the pen had to be held vertically to work. Of the eleven Sheaffer samples sent, one had been filled with the ink from the original *Eterpen* and the others with "Michigan" ink.

The Quartermaster General informed Sheaffer that "The writing ability of these (pens) has been recorded and they are of no further use to this office unless the tip is corrected and a tube of ink is supplied." However, it invited Sheaffer to continue development. "When these pens are corrected or others produced which you feel are satisfactory, this office would appreciate twenty samples at the earliest possible date so as to initiate testing now being held up. Your cooperation in this development work is greatly appreciated." Sheaffer had been given plenty of early warning about the ball point pen. It apparently did not realize it, but another war—the ball point pen war—was about to erupt.

The Stratowriter Debuts

Milton Reynolds had one great advantage on his side when Gimbels introduced his version of a ball point pen in New York City. Unlike the Sheaffer Pen Company, Reynolds had never been in the pen business; he cared little about his reputation or longevity in the writing instruments business. He only wanted to make a quick profit. Although Sheaffer had been working on a ball point pen for several years, it had mostly been preoccupied with production of war-related products and instruments. Sheaffer wouldn't offer a ball point pen until it worked right.

There is no doubt that Sheaffer had been working on a ball-point pen in advance of Reynolds. By September 1946, just ten months after the debut of the Reynolds *International* pen, Sheaffer introduced its sleek *Stratowriter* ball point pen. It was designated by the company as the RA1. Its retail price was a lofty $15. It was a streamlined, gold-filled, push-button model measuring just over five and one-quarter inches in length. It had a spring-hinged clip. Unlike the crude Reynolds, it had a replaceable ink cartridge. The patent number on its *"Micro-Crafted"* ink cartridge was 2,444,003. This patent had been filed on January

19, 1945, by Isidor Chesler and was assigned to the Eagle Pencil Company.

In his patent application for the ink cartridge, Chesler states that it "...relates generally to dispensers for applying minute quantities of liquid or paste...with writing implements, more particularly with what may be correctly designated ink pencils or ball point writing pens. The object is to create a cartridge which requires substantially no service or replacement, but inherently includes a sufficient supply of ink to last for years, even to outlast the implement itself and which makes a line that is substantially smudge-proof and requires no blotting."

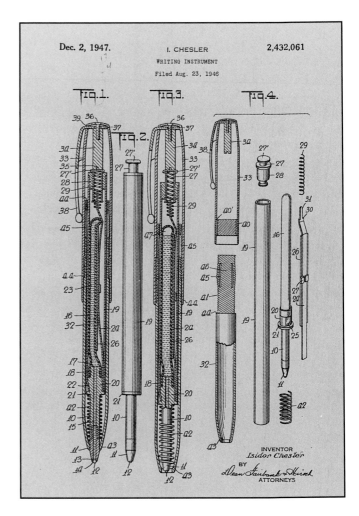

1947. The Isidor Chesler patent for a method, when using a less than spherical ball, to apply the ink and avoid the problem of ink forming at the tip of the point when the pen is not in use ("weepage"). The patent was assigned to Eagle and shared with Sheaffer.

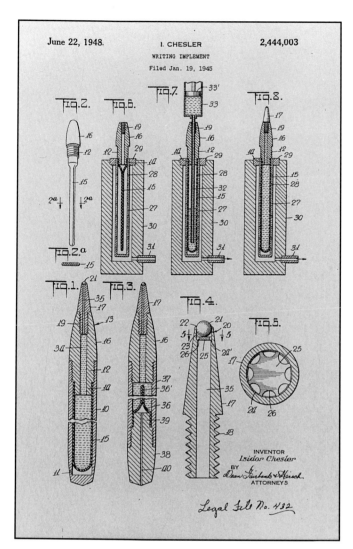

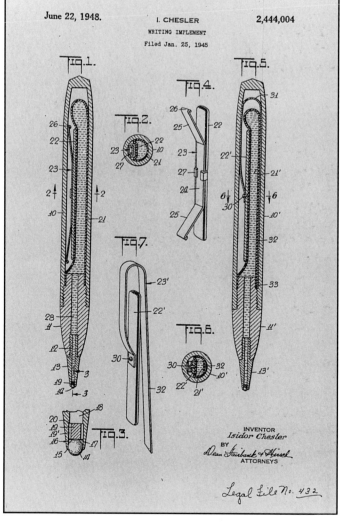

1948. The Isidor Chesler patent for an improved method of applying minute quantities of liquid or paste designed not to flood under extreme temperature, humidity, or atmospheric pressure. The patent was assigned to Eagle and shared with Sheaffer.

1948. The Isidor Chesler patent for an improved method of applying minute quantities of liquid or paste with a pressure bar. The idea was that the flexible SAC would always be in contact with the ink supply under all temperatures and atmospheric conditions. The invention of the "ink follower" atop the column of ink made this mechanism superfluous. Patent assigned to Eagle and shared with Sheaffer.

Chesler filed at least three ball point pen-related patents in 1945, and one in 1946. Interestingly, the patents were all assigned to the Eagle Pencil Company. The Eagle ORBIC ball point pen, like the *Stratowriter*, was introduced in late 1946. Its ink cartridge was shaped like that of the *Stratowriter*, but was about one-half inch longer. Both cartridges, however, were threaded near the tip, although the thread sizes were different. The ORBIC refill screwed into the barrel (it was not retractable), whereas the *Stratowriter* dropped in and was button actuated. Obviously, Sheaffer and Eagle shared patent rights to some degree.

In 1947, within a few months of the *Stratowriter* introduction, Sheaffer added what it called a "White Shirt Guard." This was a removable hood, made of the same gold-filled metal as the pen. Its purpose was to cover the pen's point to prevent leakage. The guard was slotted so that it could be slipped on the back end of the pen when in use.

Sheaffer added other *Stratowriter* models to its line in 1947. In all, there were fourteen variations. The *Stratowriter Tuckaway* was a diminutive, all gold-filled clipless model priced at $15. Most of the others had black plastic barrels. These included the *Valiant Stratowriter* ($12.50), the *Valiant Tuckaway Stratowriter* ($12.50), *Crest DeLuxe Stratowriter* with gold-filled cap ($17.50), *Crest DeLuxe Tuckaway Stratowriter* with gold-filled cap ($17.50), and the *Sentinel DeLuxe* and *Sentinel DeLuxe Tuckaway Stratowriters* with steel and gold-filled trim caps ($12.50). The caps of the full-sized *Stratowriters* screwed on while the *Tuckaway* models simply pushed on. Two additional versions of the *Stratowriter*—both of solid gold—were available in 1947. One was plain and the other machine chased. These were priced at $75 and $81, respectively.

Stratowriter models were also packaged with mechanical pencils and fountain pens. The two basic Threesome sets included a *Fineline* pencil, *Triumph* fountain pen, and *Stratowriter* ball point pen in the larger *Crest* or smaller *Tuckaway* series. Eventually, *Stratowriters* were offered in colors other than black including blue, brown, green, and burgundy. Caps were available in gold and gold-filled metal, brushed and bright chrome, and plastic with bands of varying length.

The public's huge appetite for ball point pens soured in less than two years of the ball point pen's introduction. Their performance had not lived up to the hype. By 1948, Sheaffer lowered prices on its *Stratowriters*, but not as dramatically as most others. The gold-filled *Stratowriter* went from $15 to $12.50; and the solid-gold model from $75 to $62.50.

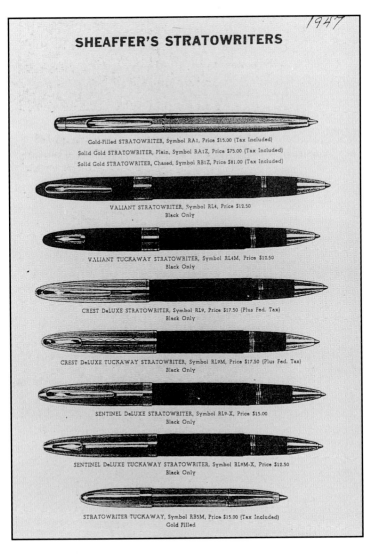

The Sheaffer *Stratowriter* family of ball point pens.

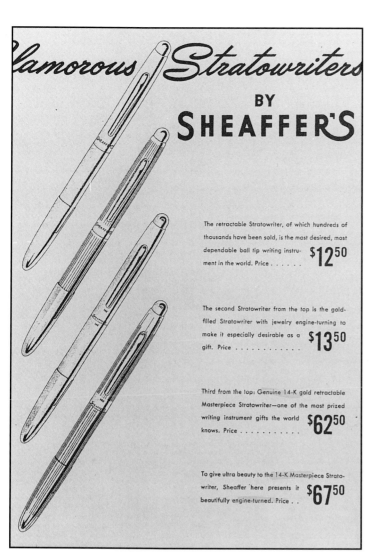

The Sheaffer gold and gold filled *Stratowriter* ball point pens.

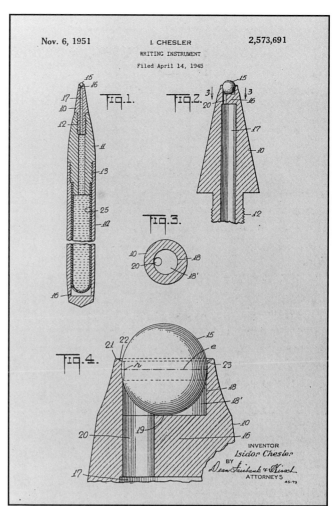

1951. The Isidor Chesler patent for an improved method of applying minute quantities of liquid or paste with constant flow through an offset flow channel. Patent assigned to Eagle and shared with Sheaffer.

Although *Stratowriters* were still being sold after 1950, it was around this time that great improvements in ink technology resulted in better pens and renewed public faith in the ball point pen. *Stratowriter* production was phased out in favor of newer models, to take advantage of this resurgence. Sheaffer's models in the 1950s quickly emulated those of other manufacturers, particularly Paper Mate's newest one-click, positive-retractor action model.

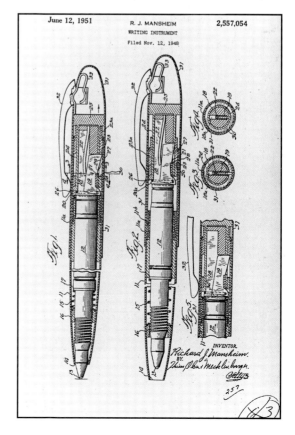

1951. The Richard J. Mansheim patent for an improved mechanism to extend and retract the point. Patent assigned to Sheaffer.

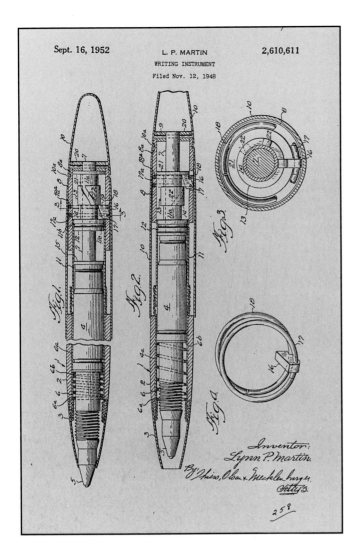

Sept. 16, 1952   L. P. MARTIN   2,610,611

WRITING INSTRUMENT

Filed Nov. 12, 1948

1951. The Lynn P. Martin patent for an improved mechanism to extend and retract the point (push/twist control). Patent assigned to Sheaffer.

The Sheaffer *Clicker* model had been under development for years. Assigned patent #2,709,989 in June 1955, it used a "slide-collar" type click mechanism consisting of six clutch-like "fingers" located in the cap just below the button. When the button was pushed, a shaft extended allowing the "fingers" to rest in a preset groove, locking the refill in the extended position. Another push of the button released the fingers and allowed the spring to propel the cartridge upwards into the barrel and up into the cap. The *Skripriter* cartridge used in the *Clicker* was the large diameter type as was the original Sheaffer cartridge, but much sleeker, made of plastic, and with a visible ink supply. It received patent 2,678,634 and had been under development since sometime in the late 1940s. Later cartridges were given a sterling silver tip and heavily advertised as corrosion proof.

The Next Generation

Sheaffer offered an increasing range of models from the middle 1950s onward. One of the most attractive was the all-metal *Skripriter* made of iridescent, anodized aluminum. It boasted the full-sized *Skripriter* cartridge and used the clicker push-button mechanism. It came in six "high-fashion" colors and was priced at $2.95. The cartridge cost 89 cents. Sheaffer also made ball point pens under the "Fineline" name. Fineline had traditionally been Sheaffer's lower-end brand, but the *Fineline "500"* was priced at a relatively expensive $2.10 in 1953. This was at a time when the Paper Mate DeLuxe was selling for $1.69. The "500" looked almost exactly like the Paper Mate, and came in metal or plastic caps and colored barrels. The "500" was guaranteed to write "five times longer" and had the "...biggest capacity of any pen!"

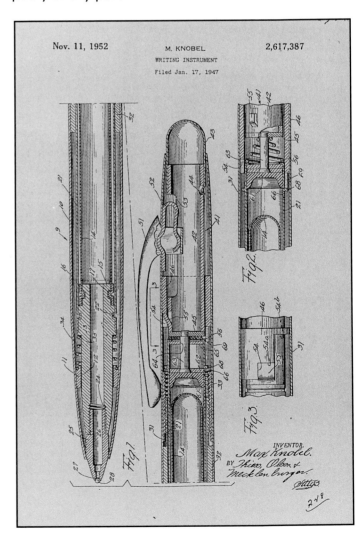

Nov. 11, 1952   M. KNOBEL   2,617,387

WRITING INSTRUMENT

Filed Jan. 17, 1947

1952. The Max Knobel patent for manually applying pressure to the ink while writing and releasing the pressure when not writing. Patent assigned to Sheaffer.

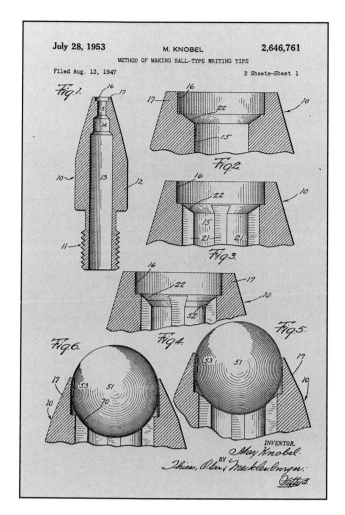

1953. The Max Knobel patent for making ball type writing tips. Patent assigned to Sheaffer.

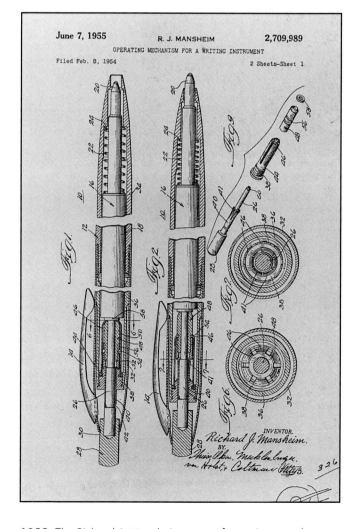

1955. The Richard J. Mansheim patent for an improved operating mechanism to extend and retract the point. Patent assigned to Sheaffer.

Sheaffer introduced a new push-button mechanism in 1957 (patent 2,685,532) with a sliding "N" shaped spring. The next major change occurred in 1961, when Sheaffer introduced a clip operated mechanism (patent 3,130,710) which it originally named the *Reminder* clip but later called the *Safeguard* clip.

In 1965, Sheaffer returned to the use of a smooth-polished stainless steel ball and socket. A new ink called *Dokumental Skrip* was introduced ostensibly to match the characteristics of the new ball and socket.

The *Dokumental Skrip* refill cost 98 cents. In 1976, a totally new mechanism to extend and retract the writing unit was developed for the new Targa line. This mechanism (patent 4,025,204) is still in use in the *Targa* and other Sheaffer luxury ball point pens. In the years which have ensued since then, Sheaffer has introduced many varieties of ball point pens. The firm has changed ownership a number of times. It continues to make ball point pens and other writing instruments, and is still based in Fort Madison, Iowa, where operations began in 1911.

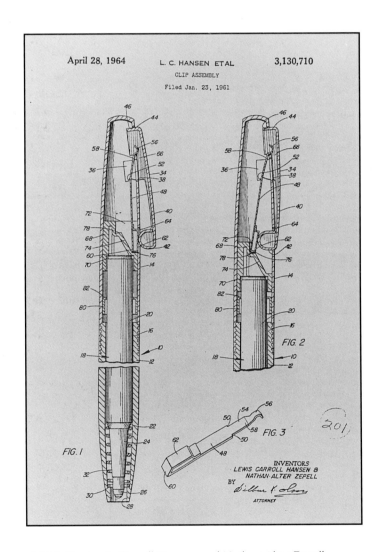

1964. The Lewis Carroll Hansen and Nathan Alter Zepell patent for an improved clip that will also extend and retract the point. Patent assigned to Sheaffer.

The Paper Mate Company

Saving the Ball Point Pen

Many say that the Paper Mate Company saved the ball point pen. By the end of the 1940s, people had stopped buying ball points. After four years, the public lost faith in them because of exaggerated, unrealized claims combined with poor performance. The pens leaked, globbed, smeared, and were largely unreliable and unpleasant to use. For the first year or so after their introduction in October 1945, an eager public paid dearly to acquire them. Many models fetched $12.50 and up. Within a year, prices fell, although firms like Sheaffer tried to hold the line on certain models like their *Stratowriter*. However, like a roaring forest fire, the craze eventually burned itself out.

By 1949, the ball point pen industry was barely smoldering. Very few of the hundreds of firms making pens from late 1945 through 1949 survived. Even the Reynolds *International* Pen Company, which had started the inferno in 1945, quit the business in 1948. Other firms like Eversharp and Waterman's had been weakened substantially due to the fierce and debilitating competition.

Patrick Frawley

When Patrick Frawley decided became interested in ball point pens in 1949, the business resembled a battlefield, except that instead of being littered with bodies, it was littered with the carcasses of defunct ball point pen companies. Many ball point pen makers were also in other businesses such as tool making and the like; they were able to change course when the tide turned. Frawley had no prior experience making writing instruments. His expertise was in importing and exporting, and he had served with the Royal Canadian Air Force in World War II. He became interested in making ball points just when about everyone else was bailing out.

Patrick Joseph Frawley, Jr., was born in Nicaragua on May 26, 1923. His family moved to San Francisco in 1928. Mr. Frawley, in a 1997 interview, shed some light on aspects of his early ball point pen days.

Frawley became involved with the Todd Pen Company of Burbank, California, in the late 1940s. He developed a genuine interest in why no one had been able to make a ball point pen that worked properly. He went to the library and read everything available on inks, dyes, and the physics involved in the ball point pen. He discovered that the German firm of A.G. Farben had developed excellent inks. However, after the war, German patents were unenforceable. To protect itself, the firm spread out production among forty smaller companies making their formulas inaccessible to all, including Frawley.

Laying The Groundwork

When he started making ball point pens, Frawley says, those in the business were considered "swindlers." Bankers and businessmen viewed them as disreputable. At social gatherings, friends would joke about mug shots on Post Office walls with the caption "last known making ball point pens" underneath. The public viewed the ball point pen with scorn and contempt.

Frawley and a chemist, Fran Seech, worked to find a suitable ball point ink formula. Early Paper Mate documents state that the firm made its own *Widco* ink. (Later, in 1957, *Widco* was replaced with an improved *Flogen* ink which made it possible for the ball of the pen to turn "up to 5,000 r.p.m.") In early 1950, a firm called Formulab introduced a ball point pen ink which worked very well and which was rapidly adopted by the industry, but it is unclear whether it made ink for Frawley.

Frawley raised $40,000, took over the Todd Pen Company, and changed its name to the Frawley Corporation. He later renamed it the Paper Mate Company. Paper Mate Company, Inc. was located at 8790 Hays Street, Culver City, California. Paper Mate Eastern, Inc. was located at 752 Broadway, New York City. The first Paper Mate model, (which Frawley called "a bad design") was similar to the early Blythe retractable. It featured a button in its cap which locked the point in place when pushed down and over. Frawley admitted that this pen, "didn't work too well".

The Right Product

The next Paper Mate pens were different. They were modern looking and colorful. Instead of aluminum, they were made of plastic, or plastic with metal caps. The flagship of the early Paper Mate line was the *Retractable*, priced at $1.69. The *Retractable* had a modern, clean, streamlined look. It was lightweight, well balanced, had a strong clip, and was easy and convenient to use. The Frawley Corporation applied for a patent for the pen on August 4, 1950, and received one (2,624,314) on January 6, 1953. The essence of the patent was that alternate depressions of the button extended and retracted the point, the point would automatically retract when the pen was dropped, and that the pen was simple and inexpensive to make and assemble.

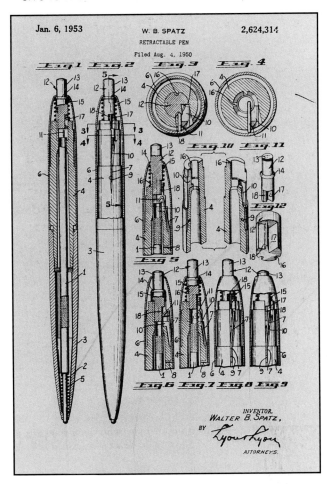

Patent for the "Retractable" assigned to Frawley Corporation of Los Angeles (Paper Mate), filed August 4, 1950.

The *Retractable* was available in at least a dozen *Tu-Tone* color combinations, from red and black, yellow and green, blue and white, to pink and gray. Paper Mate ads invited readers to match the colors of their Paper Mate to those of their two-tone cars. Paper Mate "piggy-backed" on the automotive motif naming its pens, among others, the *Capri* and *Malibu*. In advertisements, "*Capri*" appeared within what looked like an automotive badge. There was even a *Capri* series—the *Mark III*, *Mark IV*, and *Mark V*—just like the cars.

Inspired Promotion

Frawley remembered his first early attempts at promotion. He didn't advertise at first. Instead, he traveled around the country for six months setting up a sales network. One early customer was Macys Department Store. He had convinced Macys to buy his pen, and Macys insisted on running a large ad in the San Francisco Examiner. Frawley remembers, "The ad cost $5,000, a huge amount in those days." The ad said, "Now Macys Brings You Paper Mate." Macys even guaranteed the pen's performance. Frawley questioned the wisdom of the campaign, but Macys was adamant. On the day of the sale, pens were piled high on tables and half a dozen Macy clerks waited to take orders. The pens were priced at one dollar. Twelve hours later, only eighteen had been sold. For Frawley this was just a beginning.

Paper Mate began to advertise heavily around 1953. The ads were upbeat and light-hearted. They appeared in major magazines like the Saturday Evening Post and showed people smiling as they admired a colorful group of pens. Above the faces it said, "Paper Mate pleases everyone." Celebrities such as George Burns and Gracie Allen appeared in testimonial ads. "I simply adore Paper Mate's style and smart new colors!" Gracie exclaims in one. Other celebrities included Groucho Marx, Arthur Godfrey, Art Linkletter, Bert Lahr, Gary Moore, and Imogene Coca. In 1954, and for years afterwards, Paper Mate sponsored TV shows such as *People Are Funny*, *Cavalcade of Sports*, *The World Series*, and many others.

1953. Advertisment Famous Mates (Gracie Allen and George Burns) Pick Paper Mate.

Paper Mate's effective advertising is undoubtedly what made the brand such a well known household word. Paper Mate claimed that its pens were "…guaranteed not to leak or smear, always a clean point." Their "bankers approved" ink "…dries permanently on paper in 1/89th of a second." In 1956, Paper Mate introduced the piggy-back refill. Instead of a standard length refill, the piggy-back consisted of two smaller refills back-to-back, each with its own point assembly. The idea was that when one refill ran out, the user had a spare. The standard refill cost 49 cents, the piggy-back version 69 cents. In fact, the standard refill probably held more ink than the two piggy-back refills due to the space taken up by the extra point.

1955. Advertisment for Paper Mate's Tu-Tone pens to match the colors of the new Tu-Tone cars.

But what really caught on and endeared Paper Mate to the country was the Paper Mate symbol—two hearts adjacent to each other. The logo appeared on the clips of the pens. It became so widely recognizable, that it became interchangeable with the name Paper Mate itself.

An Icon Emerges

Paper Mate sales soon took off, from $530,000 in 1950 to $2 million in 1951, $20 million in 1953, and upwards every year thereafter. In 1955, Paper Mate pens were being made in Salinas and Culver City, California, and in Puerto Rico. The Puerto Rico plant employed 800 workers and turned out 125,000 pens a day. Such success did not go unnoticed by others. In January 1954, after waiting almost nine years after the introduction of the ball point, Parker brought out its first ball point, the Jotter.

Frawley reportedly tried to interest the Waterman Pen Company in buying Paper Mate, but Waterman, in financial trouble, turned him down. However, The Gillette Company, a leading worldwide consumer products firm, became a suitor. In October 1955, at the age of only 32, Frawley sold Paper Mate to Gillette for $15.5 million. In a letter dated December 28, 1955, Frawley advised clients that the new Paper Mate Company—now a wholly owned Gillette subsidiary— would take over on January 1, 1956. Frawley stayed on with Paper Mate for a few months thereafter, and later worked for Eversharp and Schick, among others.

Sales of Paper Mate ball point pens continued to grow. When in 1956, Paper Mate introduced the *Capri* with the piggy-back refill, it was priced at $1.95. By 1957, 40 million of their 98 pens had been sold. In 1958, Paper Mate introduced a number of models, including the *Capri Mark III* ($2.49) and gold electro-plated *Mark IV* ($3.50), the diminutive *Lady Capri* ($2.95), and the erasable *School Mate* (39 cents). In 1959, the *Holiday* and its jumbo refill debuted at $1.79. In the 1960s, the *Profile, Trio,* and *Lady Petite* appeared. By 1970, 100 million 98s had been sold. Paper Mate now offered eight basic ball point pens and four pen and pencil sets.

In January 1956, Paper Mate executive offices moved to 444 Merchandise Mart, Chicago and in 1957, a new 100,000 square-foot plant costing $1.5 million was opened in Santa Monica. The Puerto Rico plant was closed in 1960. Paper Mate became an operating division of the Gillette Company in 1967, and in 1968, the Santa Monica Manufacturing Center was expanded to 240,000 square feet.

Today, Paper Mate is a part of the Gillette Stationary Products Division. It continues to make and introduce new ball point pens. Its Santa Monica Manufacturing Center alone produces more than 1 billion writing instruments a year, the majority are ball point pens.

Parker Pen Co.

Parker Introduces a Ball Point Pen

The Parker Pen Company was a latecomer to the ball point pen market. In an internal 1953 position paper, Parker said that it had been researching ball point pens since the 1940s. On January 5, 1954, the Parker Information Service announced "Among the country's major writing equipment makers, only the Parker Pen Company has never marketed a ball-point pen. Today the firm announced that it is ready to invade the field." Bruce Jeffris, Parker president, explained "We've been waiting until such time as we could offer a ball pen worthy of inclusion in our price and quality bracket. We now have such a pen, and this new product does justice to both our customers and our reputation." Jeffris was talking about the brand new *Jotter*, a ball point pen truly worth the wait, one of the best selling ever, and still in production nearly a half century later. Today, most people believe that the *Jotter* was indeed Parker's first ball point pen. But what the company said was not entirely accurate.

Four years earlier, in 1950, Parker prepared a memo for internal use at a meeting of distributors soon to receive a new product. It was titled, "*Hopalong Cassidy Ball Point Pens*." Its purpose was both to introduce the new 98 cent novelty pen bearing the likeness of "Hoppy" and to make it clearly understood that Parker was not in the ball point pen business. Its content was contradictory. "Although you will be selling ball point pens next week...and a lot of them...Parker is not in the ball point pen business. One of these days, if a few of our plans work out, we might be in that business but the ball point pen you will be selling next week is the *Hopalong Cassidy Ball Point Pen*...made and distributed by the Parker Pen Company...but not a Parker ball point pen." Parker went on to state that undoubtedly, many of its retailers will "view with alarm" the ball pen's introduction and will say, "I'm sorry to see Parker getting into this business." The memo also stated that, "Mechanically, the *Hopalong Pen* is a good ball point pen. It is a

good writing instrument. It does not have the features we would want in a Parker ball point pen but 'performance wise' it will more than hold its own in competition with any of the ball points on the market today, regardless of price." How could Parker not be in the ball point pen business but be making, distributing, and selling a ball point pen? Was this a trial balloon, of sorts?

Two years later, in 1952, a Parkette version of the *Hopalong Cassidy* ball point pen was offered by Parker solely at U.S. military post exchanges. The only real change to the pen was that Hoppy's head and name had been removed and replaced with a tassle.

"Operation Scramble"

After waiting almost nine years to officially enter the ball point pen business, Parker put the *Jotter* into production in just 90 days. The effort, officially called "Operation Scramble," began in the fall of 1953. On Tuesday, December 22, 1953, a Parker Pen Bulletin proclaimed, "Operation Scramble is Paying Off!!! The first 100 Parker *Jotter* ball pens will be completed late tonight. We are sure you will be interested in seeing them, writing with them, and asking questions about them." The Parker employee magazine "Shoptalker" of January-February 1954, called Operation Scramble "90 days of hectic rush to production." It described the tremendous effort involved: "To move the *Jotter* from the drawing boards of Research to the production lines of Arrow Park took a near miracle of sweat and skill...It meant long hours—ten to twelve a day for some folks—and it took courage. The engineering department was given the greatest freedom in its work on the *Jotter*. They were told to make whatever changes in design would move the *Jotter* faster. But, any change had to work! If not, time, the all-important factor, would be lost."

What prompted Parker to launch "Operation Scramble" when it did? Since the introduction of the Reynolds *International* ball point pen in 1945, Parker steadfastly claimed that it was not interested in ball point pens. On May 13, 1946, and again on June 10, *Time* magazine wrote about the surprising sales of ball points in the United States and the mad scramble and confusion of manufacturers to get on the ball pen band-wagon. Kenneth Parker's response was that Parker, "…didn't have a ball point in its stable of products because it didn't want one." He stated that two years earlier Parker had decided that it could make a "fast bulge in sales and profits" but that ball point pens of the day were not good writing instruments. Said Parker, "If and when we bring out a ball pen it won't resemble anything now on the market."

Parker was correct in his assessment of the quality of early ball points. In addition, the *Jotter*, when it finally emerged on January 5, 1954, soon became the standard by which others were judged. By why did Parker wait so long and then move so quickly with "Operation Scramble"? Had Parker been hoping to have the pen in place by the 1953 holiday season? Perhaps the changing economics of the writing instruments field had something to do with it.

In 1946, eight million ball point pens were sold, but by 1950, total ball point pen sales were down dramatically. Starting in 1951, the ball point pen began a miraculous recovery. This resurgence was led largely by Paper Mate, due in large part to the development of new and better ball point pen inks and manufacturing techniques. In 1953, the value of ball point sales overtook fountain pens and by mid-1953, aggregate U.S. ball point pen sales had risen from almost nothing in 1950 to about $40 million. During this same period, fountain pen sales declined from $45 million to about $40 million. By the beginning of 1954, ball point sales continued to rise to about $48 million while fountain pen sales continued a gradual, but steady, decline. Ball point pen unit sales showed an even more dramatic recovery, from 50 million in 1951 to about 150 million by 1954. Fountain pen sales stayed relatively flat at about 44 million a year throughout the 1950s. The *Jotter* was Parker's answer.

1954. A store window showing the first year Jotter.

The Miraculous Jotter

The Parker *Jotter* was, and possibly is, one of the best designed ball points ever made. The design was so good that it is still made today. The exterior remains basically unchanged from the early models. It was introduced in 1954 with a plain, smooth ball-bearing tip and cost $2.75. The pen's ink was non-smearing, dried faster, darkened under exposure to light, and was acid neutral so that the tip did not deteriorate. The first 100 pens were completed on December 22, 1953, and made available for the employees to try out. Thirty-two thousand demonstrator models were reportedly made and sold for 75 cents to pen stores. In January 1954, all 1,600 Parker employees were given one of the new pens. Parker planned to produce 4,500,000 *Jotters* in the first year.

Judging by the sophistication of the *Jotter*, the pen was probably on the drawing board for several years, although it only took three months from design to engineering and into production. No doubt, Parker could have produced the pen earlier. Once out, it was a clear winner. Its cap was stainless steel. Its nylon, plastic barrel was available in black, blue, rust, and gray. Ink came in blue, green, and red, and fine, medium, and broad point sizes were offered. Within a few months, black ink and an extra-fine point were added.

The *Jotter* was Dan Parker's project; Parker's designer, Don Doman was instrumental in the design. The company was not comfortable with the Jotter when it was first introduced. It was one of the most expensive ball points at the time. Parker was well aware of the problem with Eversharp's first pen in 1946, and the resulting company image problem in the late 1940s. Parker was reluctant to commit their name and reputation to the new technology and corresponding product. This shows in the lack of a Parker "arrow" clip on the pen during the first few years of production. The arrow clip was Parker's trademark and sign of Parker quality. Kenneth Parker felt that if the product was a dud, no one would be able to tell that it was a Parker by just looking at it and it would not reflect badly on the company. This seems naive in light of the heavy advertising that said the pen was a Parker.

The *Jotter* had only 3 moving parts, the extender/retractor button, the refill and the spring in which the refill sits. The original barrel was grooved nylon. The cap was stainless steel with a brass screw thread liner. When the button is pushed, the refill travels down and rotates. When the button is released, the rotating action of the notched top of the refill against the button moves it to a short groove (extended) or a longer groove (retracted). The original models had no metal tip on the barrel. Listed originally at $2.75, public acceptance and demand was so great that by March 1954, Parker raised the price to $2.95. Clearly it had a winner on its hands.

Part of the reason for the *Jotter's* immediate acceptance was that Parker's staff of sixty-six researchers had done its work well. The pen simply had a myriad of wonderful features which made it stand out. These included a brass refill cartridge which held 1.6 grams of ink and offered six times as much writing. (Most refills of the day held one-half gram of ink. The *Jotter* cartridge could write from 60 to 80 hours, depending on the size of the ball, compared to 10 to 14 for others). Parker said this translated into 393,000 words. The cartridge also contained a newly developed fiber seal to prevent leakage and ensure continuous write-out. The pen's propel-repel mechanism had a rotating ball-seat which turned the cartridge 90 degrees every time the button was depressed, thus ensuring even wear of the ball and socket. The ball itself was made of stainless or chrome steel, and was rounded to within six millionths of an inch. The ball seat was made of "work hardened brass." On top of all this, the pen was well-balanced, attractively designed, and felt solid.

Once launched, Parker scrambled to meet demand. On April 4, 1954, Parker announced that it was sending 100,000 *Jotters* to the New York area, "…the largest single shipment of pens the company has ever made." This was the first full-scale introduction of the pen to that area although it had been available three months earlier in Janesville. Through the rest of 1954 the company scrambled to offer higher-priced variations of the *Jotter*. These included the all-metal *Jotter Custom* in *Lustraloy* at $3.95, and the Parker *51 Ball Point* with stainless steel cap at $5. In July 1954, claiming sales "exceeding forecasts," Parker introduced its gold-filled cap *51 Jotter* at $8.75. All these pens used the same Jotter cartridge. Parker estimated it would sell 4.5 million *Jotters* in 1954 alone.

Parker had delayed almost nine years in entering the ball point pen field, but once it did, it met with much greater success than ever anticipated. In June 1954, Parker began to sell the *Jotter* in Europe. On June 6, Ivan Tefft, Parker's legal counsel, expressed concern upon returning from Europe aboard the S.S. United States that "Germany's existing low wage scale" posed the danger of the production of cheap imitations. Therefore, the firm continued to aggressively follow up with a series of Jotter improvements, changes, and new designs. By June 1956, Parker introduced the *Pardners* set. This set included its *Liquid Lead* ball-point pencil with the *Jotter*.

During the first three years of production the *Jotter* remained basically the same, except for the addition of a few new colors. After that, the barrel was changed from nylon to plastic. In June 1957, three and one-half years after the Jotter made its debut, Parker pulled another rabbit out of its hat—a new and better pen at an even lower price—the *T-Ball Jotter*.

Enter the "T-Ball"

In January 1954, simultaneously with the launching of the *Jotter*, the director of Parker research began talking about something called a "sintered" pen point. "In fact," he said, "there are years of work involved in perfecting the idea of such a sintered pen point. Right now we're devoting our efforts to Jotter ball-pen improvements." In June 1957, the new *T-Ball Jotter* had a sintered ball.

The sintered ball was achieved by heating and compressing five million powdered metal particles into a one millimeter ball. The result was a porous tungsten carbide ball of uniform texture which contained 35 feet of microscopic, connecting channels, none over 39/1000ths of an inch long. The channels permitted ink to pass through the ball as well as around it, while 50,000 microscopic paper "grippers" on the surface kept the ball rolling.

The new *T-Ball* was indeed revolutionary. (The "T" refers to the textured ball, but *T-Ball* was also the trade mark name for the new *Jotter* cartridge and *Jotter* pen.) The ball itself held 167 times as much ink as a smooth stainless steel ball in 25,000 microscopic veins. The T-ball was harder than stainless steel. It was able to cut glass or steel and had a compressive strength of about one-half million pounds per square inch.

From a design standpoint, the *T-Ball Jotter* looked much like the original *Jotter*. A metal nose ring had been added at the point end of the barrel to prevent breakage at this point of stress. What also changed was the price. Parker introduced the new and improved T-Ball at only $1.95, one third lower than the original *Jotter*!

T-Ball sales took off immediately. Although the first deliveries were not available until around early August 1957, by February 28, 1958, Parker had produced its five millionth T-Ball. Eventually, the design of the pen's clip was changed to emulate Parker's distinctive arrow. An entire range of T-Ball variants and offshoots emerged. These included the "window" *Jotter* in March 1958, where advertising and alternating messages could be placed and which rotated as the pen's cartridge revolved. This same pen was later made into a four nation currency converter. There was even a *Jotter* from which paper could be pulled from an opening in the barrel. By September 1959, 15 million T-Balls had been made. By June 1961, this number had climbed to 30 million made at "Arrow Park." By July 22, 1963, the 50 millionth *Jotter* had been made; in June 1975, the number reached 100 million. Parker even issued a 100 Millionth limited edition *Jotter* to commemorate this milestone. By January 1984, total *Jotter* production reached an incredible 400 million. And the story continues today. *Jotters* are still being made and are in strong demand worldwide. It seems it will be a long time before the final tally is in.

Beyond the "T-Ball"

In the midst of the rush to introduce its new T-Ball in mid-1957, Parker commenced negotiations for the purchase of the Eversharp Writing Instruments Division of Eversharp, Inc. The purchase was concluded in December 1957. In January 1958, the newly constituted Eversharp Pen Company introduced its first model, the *Fountain Ball*. This pen had the same sintered ball as the *Jotter*. The *Fountain Ball* sold for 98 cents. It seems that Parker bought Eversharp for a variety of reasons. One may have been so that it could sell lower-priced writing instruments under the Eversharp name. Although Eversharp made pens until 1973, it was always relegated to the lower segment of the market, a tier below Parker. Parker has always been conscious of its name and reputation.

In 1957, Parker introduced a series of ball point pens based on the *Jotter*. The Parker *Jotter* gift line included three new, uniquely designed female models called the *Debutante*, which quickly became the *Princess* line. In addition, there was a small, clipless model called the *Minim*, and the *V.I.P.* (basically a "51") *Jotter* with a chrome cap. The *Princess* models ranged in price from $5 to $10. Two of the models had a lattice of filigree engraved on pink, beige, turquoise, blue, or black enamel caps. The third model, the most expensive, had a hand-engraved floral pattern over a white or black cap. (Later as many as eight models were added to the *Princess* line.) The *Minim* was advertised as "Just a filter tip taller than a king-size cigarette," and as "a pen for the boss." It was "The ideal size for pocket or purse. Made like fine jewelry…packaged like fine jewelry, too." The 12-karat gold-filled cap and plastic barrel Minim retailed at $5, the all gold-filled at $8.75, and the 14-karat solid gold cap and barrel model at $25. Since then, Parker has introduced hundreds of attractive and innovate ball point pens. Some, such as the *Spanish Treasure* and *"T-1"* ball point pens, are highly collectible; many newer pens are also becoming collectible.

In 1986, the Parker Pen Company was bought by its English management. The firm became Parker Pen Holdings Ltd. In May 1993, the Gillette Company acquired Parker for $450 million. The changes in management have been relatively smooth with some shifting of production to England, but with little noticeable effects otherwise. Under Gillette, Parker has continued the tradition of quality products and is adding strong and distinctive designs with a flavor both forward looking and yet hearkening back to the company's roots.

Parker Ball Point Pen Models

Since 1950, Parker has introduced over 400 different variations of ball point pens. The following listing gives many models through 1980.

PARKER BALL POINT PENS (1951-1980)

YEAR	MODEL
1950	*Hopalong Cassidy Ballpen* at 98 cents
1951	*Hopalong Cassidy Ballpen*, price raised to $1.49
1952	*Parkette Ballpen*
1954	*Jotter* ball point (nylon barrel), intro price $2.75, raised in March to $2.95
	Colors available: black, gray, blue, and burgundy
	32,000 clear grooved barrel demonstrators sold to dealers for 75 cents
July	*51 Ball Point* (stainless steel cap w/arrow clip) at $5.00
	51 Jotter (gold filled cap w/arrow clip) at $8.75
	Custom Jotter (burnished stainless steel cap & barrel) at $3.95
Nov.	*51 Jotter Deluxe* (*Lustaloy* cap w/arrow clip) at $5.00
	51 Jotter Custom (gold filled cap w/arrow clip) at $8.75
	51 Smart Set (fountain pen & *Jotter* w/arrow clip)
1955	Ball point *Jotter* Desk pen
	21 Jotter (with Parker 21 clip & button action)
	21 Jotter (with Parker 21 clip & cap actuated action)
1956	Ball point *Pardner Set*—*Jotter* pen & *Liquid Lead* pencil
1957	*51 Jotter* commemorating Mayflower II crossing in June 1957
June	*T-Ball Jotter* (textured Ball) at $1.95, (believed to have a 21 style clip)
	Barrel colors: black, blue, turquoise, coral, and charcoal
	Deluxe ("51" style) *T-Ball Jotter* (satin finish cap) at $2.95
	Insignia Jotter—Gold filled

	Laboratory Jotter—a stainless steel *Jotter* for laboratory work w/21 clip
Nov.	*Debutante* models—decorated cap w/plain colored barrel and decorated cap and decorated barrel
	Colors available: charcol, turquoise, blue, and coral
1958	Arrow clip now used on *Jotters* made after about mid year
	Super 21 cap actuated *Jotter* w/arrow clip
	Window Jotter w/imprinted cartridges introduced (21 style clip)
	Minim—available in colors, gold filled, and 14kt gold
	Custom T-Ball Jotter (all metal lustraloy—grooved barrel)
	Princess (formerly *Debutante*) models—added floral engraved pattern on cap,
	Colors available: pink, beige, turquoise, blue, and black and white
	V.I.P. Jotter (51 style), more feathers in arrow & longer clip, 3 styles of finish
1959	Silver overlaid *Jotter* (overlay form slips over $1.95 *Jotter* barrel)
	T-Ball Desk Jotter
	International Flighter set—*Lustraloy*
April	*Executive* ball point (possibly sold in Europe) renamed *VIP* ball point
1960	*Insignia Jotter* (all gold) and *International Insignia Set*
	Plastic *Minim Deluxe*
	14kt gold *Jotter*
	Imperial Pardner Set
	Step Cap *Jotter* (Deluxe) (plastic and gold)
	Step Cap *Jotter* (Custom) (plastic and chrome)
1961	*45* cap actuated *Jotter* (*Lustraloy* cap, plastic barrel)
	45 Ball Point Desk Pen
	61 Ball Point Desk Pen
1962	*45 Classic Jotter* (steel cap, plastic barrel)
	45 Jotter (gold filled cap, plastic barrel)
	45 Flighter Jotter (steel cap & barrel)
	45 Insignia Jotter (gold filled cap & barrel)
	61 Classic Jotter—cap actuated, *Lustraloy* cap, plastic barrel
	Sterling silver *Jotter*
	Black *Jotter* Desk Pen with chrome finish (matches the 51 desk pen)
	V.I.P. Custom Jotter—black
	Custom Jotter with Hallmark—matches the fountain pen and pencil
	Doric line introduced (looks like standard Cross ball point)
1963	*Laboratory Jotter*—a stainless steel *Jotter* for laboratory work w/arrow clip, less detailed feathers in arrow clip, $2.49 list price
	45 Insignia Ball Point pen
	61 Jotters—gold-filled cap, plastic barrel and gold-filled cap and barrel
	Sterling silver *75 Jotter* with flat crown
	Arrow Ballpen Jotter—cap actuated w/plastic cap and barrel and chrome trim
1964	Cap actuated *Jotter*—plastic cap and barrel, chrome trim
	Jotter point inside diameter reduced and spring revised.
1965	*Compact* or *Girl's Jotter* (smaller size)

Jotter with cross symbol—*Lustraloy* cap
Arrow Window Jotter with window and snap in magnifying lens. Message printed on shell that fits over refill (Can be removed when refill is empty) cap actuated—plastic cap and barrel with chrome trim
Sterling silver *75 Jotter*—cap actuated—antiqued grid engraved cap and barrel
75 Insignia Ballpen—gold-filled—grid engraved

1966 *75 Vermeil Ballpen*—14K gold-filled on Sterling silver—cut grid pattern
International Classic Sterling Silver *Jotter*—Antiqued grid pattern
Classic 75 Sterling Silver *Jotter*—button actuated, grid pattern
75 Insignia Jotter 14K gold-filled grid pattern
75 Tiffany Sterling Silver pattern *Jotter* (made for Tiffany & Co. N.Y.C.)
Calendar *Jotter* (regular T-Ball Jotter with 1 year calendar attachment)
75 Sterling Silver *Jotter*, chrome trim, grid pattern (made for Cartier)

1967 *Tiara*—lady's model with a star burst design on the cap
Treasure Pen (Parker 75) made from silver salvaged from 1600s Spanish wreck
75 Keepsake with a smooth finish for engraving dates and events
International Classic Desk pen
International Classic Jotter, chrome plated or stainless finish
International Classic—gold plated silver, grid pattern
Calendar Jotter (perpetual version) good for 12 months

1968 *Presidential Jotter*—cap actuated—14K gold cap and barrel—bright finish
Window *Jotter* with currency converter

1969 Jotter with arrow clip having less feathers
Stainless steel redesigned *Custom Jotter*
Vase top *Jotter*
International Classic 14K gold *Presidential Ballpen*

1970 *45* Ball point desk pen—plastic barrel and shell, Sel-Rex trim
45 Ball point desk pen—chrome trim, plastic barrel and shell
T-1 ball point introduced, sold for about two years
Stainless steel Desk pen with black tip taper
Perpetual calendar desk pen

1972 *Big Red* men's pen: plastic barrel and cap
Big Red women's pen: plastic barrel and cap with

neck ribbon
75 Classic sterling silver pen has new indented crown
75 Classic brushed stainless steel ballpen
75 Flighter pen: stainless steel cap and barrel, gold electroplated trim

1973 Company symbol stamped on button of Jotter and button top flattened
Big Red pen in colors—black, yellow, green, blue, white
Parker *Filigree* Pen, Silver filigree wrapped around a black *Big Red*

1974 *Jotter Ballpen*: stainless steel cap and clip, plastic barrel, chrome trim
100 Millionth Jotter Ballpen: 1954-1974 (engraved on barrel of *Jotter*): stainless steel cap and clip, plastic barrel (*Pompei* red), chrome trim

1975 *Bicentennial* red, white and blue pen: blue cap w/ white stars, white barrel w/red stripes, chrome trim
Jotter Desk Ballpen: brown plastic barrel and taper, gold trim (used with the laser engraved walnut cube desk sets)
Big Red (white) pen: soft-tip pen with Bicentennial emblem

1976 The *Swinger Ballpen*—plastic cap and barrel w/shoe-lace neck rope
180 silver pen
180 gold pen
75 Place Vendome pen

1977 *Jotter* Desk Pen with new *Jotter* taper design—thinner
Queen Elizabeth's 25th Anniversary pens

1978 *Laque Ballpen*: brass cap and barrel with colored lacquering
Big Red: stamping on clip changed from Parker U.S.A. to Big Red U.S.A.

1979 *Aarrow* ballpen, matte black plastic cap and barrel, chrome trim (large arrow clip is part of cap assembly)

1980 Bushing in cap is now plastic rather than brass
Flighter Jotter of brushed stainless steel
Classic Keepsake pen: polished sterling silver cap and barrel
Classic Laque pen: lacquered brass cap and barrel, gold electroplated trim
Classic Ambassador pen: silver electroplated brass cap and barrel, blackened longitudinal grooves, chrome electroplated trim
Window Jotter: button actuated, lustraloy cap, plastic barrel (imprinted) with new "flush type" window and lens design

Early Manufacturers

Many firms made ball pens. Most in existence during the period 1945 through 1949 were out of the business by 1950. Therefore, many no longer exist. In some instances, we know very little about the maker other than the pens it produced. In many instances, however, the location of the firm, the models made, advertising claims, information about its principals, production figures, and other particulars are available and are provided here. We have included most quality ball point pen brands and manufacturers known to us at the time of printing. Undoubtedly, there are some that have not been mentioned, especially those of foreign manufacturers. However, this listing is the most comprehensive available.

Acme Pen. Extremely early, all aluminum ball point pen, with permanently affixed refill. Features a gold-tone clip. Has a ribbed section with a ring around its barrel for securing the push-on cap. Early model measures only 4 1/2 inches in length. Little else is available about this firm or its products.

Arkon. Arkon Pen Company, Chicago. In 1946, Akron offered a large, colorful, aluminum pen for $6.95. It had a unique, threaded rod located under its removable end cap. To force ink to point, the user had to screw in the thin, threaded rod as needed. The pen was listed as not acceptable by Consumer Reports as it failed to write after a short period of use.

All-Rite Pen Company, Inc. All-Rite was located in Hackensack, New Jersey. Made slim, contemporary, quality, push-button retractable ball point pens starting in the late 1950s. Used oversized refill cartridge made of brass. One model had a chrome-plated cap and plastic barrel. Later versions were all plastic.

American Pencil Company. Hoboken, New Jersey. Like Eagle, Faber, Unipenco, Venus, and other pencil manufacturers, this company was an early entrant into the ball point pen market. It produced a model very similar in appearance to the bullet shaped Kimberly. This model had a permanently affixed refill. *See Venus.*

Autopoint. Chicago, Illinois. This venerable mechanical pencil maker also briefly produced a ball point pen. It was purchased by The Gillette Company in 1970, but was resold in 1979. Autopoint ball point pens were relatively dependable, but lacked flair and failed to distinguish themselves in the marketplace.

BB Pen Company, Inc. One of the original ball point pen manufacturers in the United States. 6245 Santa Monica Blvd., Hollywood, California. In its advertisements of the early 1950s it claimed to be the largest selling ball point pen maker in the United States. BB produced a variety of models between approximately 1946 and 1953. By 1948, BB claimed that "In just three years, performance and styling have made BB the world's largest selling pen." In 1949, the company claimed over 26 million pens sold. By 1952, its ads trumpeted "World's Largest Selling Pen—Over 50 Million Sold."

BB offered a variety of different sized models, some of higher quality than others. In 1947, the full-sized "Executive" sold for 98 cents. The "VP" was a smaller, purse-sized pen (similar in shape to the Kim by Kimberly). These were offered in three colors, all with silver colored caps: dove gray, maroon, and black. By 1948, the cap had been streamlined and a stylized clip and logo added. Caps and clips were offered in gold or chrome color. The models for this year included the "VP" and the "Retractable" which featured a twist mechanism. BB pens were also available in Canada. By 1948, the "VP" model had been streamlined. Refills cost 49 cents at that time. Later models were more contemporary and similar in style to the 1954 Paper Mate retractable, but with a red crown on the button.

Unlike the extravagant and often outrageous claims of other makers (for example, Reynolds),

BB conservatively claimed that their refill was "good for six months average use." The company also claimed that "One million people each month buy a BB pen." According to BB, their pens "...won't clog, blot, skip, scratch...(and)...contains exclusive perma-dry ink, rolls on dry." In 1952, their pens were still priced at only 98 cents. The firm seemed to fade from sight after this year.

Bendell. Bendell Pen Company of Stamford, Connecticut, made a pen in 1946, similar in appearance to a mechanical pencil. It was constructed with an aluminum top and plastic barrel. It wrote relatively smoothly, although its dark blue ink faded considerably. The point retracted using a twist mechanism. Refills cost 35 cents.

BIC. BIC Corporation (USA), Milford, Connecticut. Founded by Marcel Bich and Edouard Buffard in Clichy, France. Bich made plastic ball point pen parts in France in 1948. In 1949, Bich introduced its first ball point pen in France under the BIC name. The Societe Bic was formed in 1953. Bich purchased the Waterman Pen Company (USA) in 1958 as a way of introducing Americans to his product. The firm was named the Waterman-BIC Corporation. The first BIC pen in the U.S. was the see-through, disposable "Crystal" stick-pen. Originally sold in the Northeast United States at 29 cents, the price was soon reduced to 19 cents nationwide. By the early 1960s, the manufacture of Waterman fountain pens was discontinued. BIC ball point pens use tungsten carbide balls obtained from General Electric. BIC relocated from Seymour, to Milford, Connecticut, to larger and more modern facilities. In 1967, BIC and Biro Pens Ltd. (England) merged and became Biro BIC Ltd. BIC is still head quartered in the United States in Milford, Connecticut.

Birome. Manufactured in Argentina and distributed by R.H. Macy & Company, New York City, and also by Biro, Meyne & Biro Inc., 46 East 57th Street, New York. United States manufacturing rights based on the Biro ball point patents were licensed to Eberhard Faber and shared with Eversharp in 1944. However, In 1946, Birome introduced a "Ball-point Perfume Flacon" in the United States. This device was a gold-colored, bullet-shaped cylinder with a removable cap. A full page ad in *Time*, December 16, 1946, stated that, "Biro, creator of the ball-point pen applies its leak proof principle to a jewel-like Ball-point flacon containing concentrated, long-lasting perfumes of enchanting fragrance..." Biro reportedly sold his ball point pen patents to Parker in 1954.

Blythe. The Blythe Ball Pen Company of Hollywood, California, was one of the earliest American ball point makers and a significant pioneer in the ball point pen design. Blythe appears to have started in the ball point business in May 1946 with a push-button retractable. One 1946 model was priced at $9.95 and included a spare refill. It was a well-designed pen with an aluminum case. The barrel was enameled in black. There was no time-limit on its ink supply, but the amount of ink held was small and the refill was difficult to install. The original Paper Mate model of 1949 appears to be a copy of this early Blythe, although instead of having a machined aluminum barrel, the Paper Mate was made of plastic and was smaller in scale. Both the Blythe and Paper Mate had a post which protruded from the center of the cap of the pen. When this button was pressed down and pushed to the side, it caused the pen's point to protrude and locked it in place. Another model was made entirely of aluminum. The barrel was anodized and the refill permanently affixed. The streamlined cap even had a spring-loaded clip similar to many quality Sheaffer fountain pens. In February 1947, Gimbels Department Store of New York offered the Blythe "B2 Ballero" as an alternative to the Reynolds "Rocket." Gimbels sold both brands, but preferred Blythe stating "We recommend the B2 Ballero, which we consider a far superior pen in the lower-priced pen field."

Carter's. John W. Carter founded a firm in Boston, Massachusetts, in 1857 that would later become the Carter Ink Company. Carter was best known for its ink products but made very nice fountain pens during the 1920s and 1930s. Fountain pen manufacture began about 1926. Carter abandoned the fountain pen business about 1931 and returned to just selling ink products. The Carter's Ink Company made a ball pen in the late 1940s that was designed to mark clothing. They may have felt that as they were "burned" by their fountain pen business, they did not want to jump into the ball point business. Their marker was called the Carter's Retractable Ball Point Cloth-Marking Pen. The firm claimed that "Carter's Quickset indelible ink withstands weather, repeated washings and dry cleanings and writes on almost any surface."

Conklin Pen Company. Conklin was located in Chicago, Illinois. They were the successor to the Conklin Pen Company of Toledo, Ohio, in name only. The original Conklin was one of the pioneers in fountain pen manufacturing and sales. The original Conklin Pen Company was founded by

Roy Conklin in 1898 and was best known for their "Crescent Filler" pens (1901-1928). Conklin ran into financial difficulties during the Depression and sales lagged. In 1938, the company was sold to a syndicate in Chicago. This syndicate also made other fountain pen brands such as the Park-O-Type, the Waltham, the Winchester, and the Starr Pen.

This company made an early foray into ball point pen field. The Conklin model had a permanently affixed ink cartridge with point and barrel similar to Scripto's tilt-tip point. The pen consisted of a light-weight, ribbed metal cap with clip in the shape of an arrow and plastic barrel similar in design to a Parker "51."

Cross, A.T. A. T. Cross, located in Providence, Rhode Island, was founded by Alonso Townsend Cross, a jeweler by trade, who perfected a stylographic fountain pen in the late 1870s. In 1916 the company was sold to Walter Russell Boss, Sr. Ownership has stayed in the Boss family to the present. Cross first introduced a ball point pen in 1953, "The Century" a 12-karat, gold-filled model utilizing a propel-repel twist mechanism. Its design was similar to their mechanical pencil of 1946. In later years the firm claimed that their pen was the first to utilize the twist mechanism. However, this is not the case. For example, the Hamilton Ross "Jet-flow" employed a very good twist mechanism in 1946.

Eagle. Eagle Pencil Company, New York City. Made lower priced ball point pens. In 1949, Eagle offered the non-retractable Glider for $1. This pen had an excellent clip and reportedly could write for up to 65 hours. Later, Eagle merchandised reasonably priced "stick pens," offered largely through drug stores and other outlets where students could purchase these pens. Eagle relocated to Danbury, Connecticut, and became Berol USA which was owned by the Empire Pencil Company. In 1988 Empire was acquired by a New York investment group and the company moved its operations to the southeastern part of the country. Eagle apparently shared its patents with Sheaffer. *See also Orbic.*

Eberhard Faber. Eberhard Faber bought the rights to manufacture a ball point pen in the United States based on the Biro patents. Faber shared its patent rights with Eversharp in 1945. Eversharp introduced its "CA" ball pen in April 1946, and also produced a model for Faber. Faber's version had a ribbed barrel, a stylish, sloped cap and clip. The pen had a stainless steel socket and a steel

ball and utilized both capillary action and gravity feed principles. The cartridge was replaceable. Eberhard Faber moved from Brooklyn to Wilkes-Barre, Pennsylvania, in 1956. In 1988 EF was acquired by A.W. Faber-Castell Corp.

Esterbrook Pen Company. Esterbrook was located in Camden, New Jersey. Produced ball point pens to match their fountain pens and mechanical pencils, and others. In 1956 they claimed a "floating ball construction" and "new exclusive ink with controlled surface tension…no smear…no stall…no spreading." The pen sold for $2.50, $3.75 with a metal cap. Other models included the 1959 "Scribe" costing $1.69. It had a "super tex" ball, and an oversized cartridge which was claimed to "outwrites ordinary ball points 5 to 1." Its "Wordathon" refill sold for 69 cents. In 1967 Venus Pen & Pencil Corporation bought Esterbrook and became Venus-Esterbrook. Esterbrook's New Jersey facilities were moved to Mexico, England, and Tennessee. In 1973, The remainder of Venus-Esterbrook was bought by Faber-Castell.

Evant. Evant Pen Corporation, Hollywood, California. In 1949, Evant offered a non-retractable ball point pen for $1. The refill cost 50 cents with "write out" reportedly at 40 hours. This firm also made a midget-sized, clipless, non-retractable, refillable ball point called the Evantte priced at $1.95.

Everlast. Everlast Pen Corporation, New York City. Everlast made reasonably priced pens from at least 1949 on, of which some were promotional items. One model had a gold-colored metal cap and was offered by Westinghouse in 1952 for 25 cents. "Writes like a $1 pen." Everlast pens generally exhibited poor writing and fading characteristics. The firm also produced mechanical pencils.

Eversharp, Inc. 1800 Roscoe Street, Chicago. A leader in the development of the ball point pen, Eversharp shared rights to the Biro patents with Eberhard Faber. Eversharp introduced their first model, the "CA", in April 1946 and offered a wide range of ball points until December 1957, when Eversharp sold its writing instruments division to Parker Pen. Originally located at 1800 Roscoe Street, Chicago, the pen division relocated to Culver City, California, when sold to Parker. It transferred to Janesville, Wisconsin, in April 1968. Parker liquidated the Eversharp Pen Company on January 15, 1973. Parker relegated Eversharp products to the lower-priced segment of the ball point market. The Eversharp story appears in greater detail elsewhere in this book.

Faber. *See Eberhard Faber*

Ferber. Ferber Corporation, Englewood, New Jersey. Made a "stick pen," among others, called the Vu-Riter which sold for 25 cents in 1952.

Fieldson. Fieldson Ball Pen Company, Bronx, New York. Made the Re-Tract-O for $5.98 in 1946. The pen was made of aluminum with a brass clip, and similar to a mechanical pencil in appearance. Its blue ink faded appreciably. It was one of the few pens of the time which wrote smoothly and evenly with little effort. In 1949, made a midget-sized, clipless, retractable pen which retailed for 98 cents. Reported ink permanence was excellent, but writing time was only eight hours.

Fineline. (See Sheaffer) A brand of ball point pen made by a division of W.A. Sheaffer Pen Company, Fort Madison, Iowa. These pens were Sheaffer products. The "500 Retractable" sold for $2.10 in 1953. It claimed to write longer than any other pen and also to have the "biggest capacity of any pen. No other ball point can write as long because no other ball point holds as much ink!"

Fisher. The Fisher Pen Company, originally located in Van Nuys, California, was founded by Paul C. Fisher, machinist, designer, contemporary, and former associate of Milton Reynolds. Fisher is best known for their Space Pens that were used in the manned space missions. They began production in 1948 making parts for other pen companies. In 1953, Fisher invented the "Universal Refill" which fit most pens of the time. Later he developed the Fisher "AG-7 Space Pen," a nitrogen pressurized refill which was first used in the Apollo 7 space mission of October 1968 (Before this, astronauts used pencils and felt tip pens). The refill did not depend on gravity for operation and therefore could be used in the weightless environment of space. All following manned space missions, including Soviet space missions, used these pressurized cartridge pens. In 1993, the Fisher Pen Company split in two. Paul Fisher heads up the firm located in Boulder City, Nevada. The other firm is located in Chicago, Illinois.

Flo-Ball. Flo-Ball Pen Corporation. New York City and Hollywood, California. Flo-Ball advertised "Flo-Control...the new point developed by Flo-ball to control the flow of ink." Made pens from the late 1940s. Displayed the "Guaranteed by Good Housekeeping" seal in their advertisements. Models in 1949 included the "Little Jewel" for $1 which came with or without a clip and in five colors. It was shaped similar to an early Kimberly but with an elongated metal cap. It reportedly had

excellent ink permanence and wrote for 20 hours. The "Senior" was a larger pen with a removable cap which covered the point when the pen was not in use. It cost 98 cents. Another model had an oversized, screw in, replaceable cartridge, similar to that of the original Sheaffer ball point. It had a plastic barrel, aluminum gripping section, and steel cap and clip. The cap was distinctive in that it had eight three-eighths inch "cutouts" which give it an easily recognizable profile. The "48" came in four colors with chrome or gold-colored caps. The "Tri-Tone" was available in 1953. The barrel and cap of this pen were triangular shaped. The pen wrote in three colors—green, red, and blue. The user simply rotated the pen so that the point of the refill of the color desired faced the paper. The Tri-tone retailed for $2.50; refills cost 50 cents. Interestingly enough, Flo-Ball was one of the very few ball point makers who later introduced a fountain pen. The "Scribe" cost 98 cents, had a steel press-on cap, came in four point sizes, and had an aerometric fill mechanism. By 1954, Flo-Ball had become the Morse Flo-Ball Corporation of Holland, Michigan.

Hamilton Ross. Hamilton Ross Jetflow Corporation (HRJC) was located at 666 Lake Shore Drive, Chicago, Illinois. The factory was at 2824 University Avenue, S.E., Minneapolis, Minnesota. HRJC was an early (1946) maker of very high-quality ball point pens. Their pens employed a twist activated refill (propel/repel) mechanism. The pens were machined of solid aluminum with an electrically anodized finish. The firm recognized the deficiencies of ball points of the time and addressed itself to correcting the failures of the Reynolds and other poorly made pens. Like Reynolds, however, it played on the public infatuation with scientific developments to promote its product, especially aviation. Its ads claimed that "The emulsion (ink) container is perfectly sealed to prevent leakage in any atmospheric pressure." This was written in 1946 when few members of the public ever flew in an airplane. Nevertheless, the design of the pens was superb. The firm did not exaggerate when it stated its pens were "...fashioned with the artistry of fine jewelry."

Holt. The George Holt, Inc. was located in Providence, Rhode Island, and later in Crompton, Rhode Island. It was active in the ball point pen field in the early to mid 1950s.

Ingersoll. The U.S. Time Corporation of Waterbury, Connecticut, sold the Ingersol pen. Before getting into ball point pens, Ingersoll was known for its

"Dollar" fountain pens and wristwatches. It claimed to make a high value product for only one dollar. In 1949, Ingersoll offered a ball point pen featuring the likeness of Mickey Mouse on its gold-tone metal cap. The pen may have been made by BB as it looks similar to the BB "VP" model. The barrels came in green, red, and blue. Offered in the same collection were a Mickey Mouse wristwatch and clock (made by US Time) and a girl's and boy's ring, all bearing the likeness of Mickey.

Kimberly. Kimberly Corporation was located in Los Angeles, California. It was one of the early ball point pen pioneers whose product, worked fairly well. Kimberly began production in late 1946. Its early model, the "Pockette," retailed at $9.75 and was available in six colors and a metal finish. In 1947, Eversharp entered into an exclusive agreement with Kimberly, to supply Eversharp with pens and refills. They marketed their products jointly under the Kimberly and Eversharp names. The Kimberly "Pockette" was promoted in ads by Humphrey Bogart and other celebrities. The company was largely known for its small, clipless pens which were advertised as "...not much longer than your cigarette!" They came in a large variety of bright colors including yellow. They were touted as a fashion statement for men and women. One Kimberly ad suggested, "Buy one for your wife...in feminine high-style colors." Eversharp used Kimberly refills in most of its ball points up until the 1960s.

In 1955 Eversharp acquired controlling interest in Kimberly and in December 1957, Parker bought Eversharp and Kimberly became a separate Parker division. In 1964, Parker reincorporated Kimberly to protect the rights to its name. Kimberly produced a push-button retractable ball point pen. The pen was similar to the Eversharp "Small Ball" pen, except more substantial. It used the Kimberly KEC-54 or KEC-55 Small Ball refills in blue, black, red, or green permanent ink. The KEC-54 was a medium sized point, and the KEC-55 a fine point. The diminutive Kimberly Pockette and the Eversharp Jr. and Kim were essentially the same pen.

Merlin. An extremely unique, substantial, early ball point pen. It had an aluminum cap with a steel clip and anodized aluminum, machined barrel with a heavily ribbed gripping section. The ink cartridge was permanently affixed. Little else is known about this firm or its other products.

Minuet. A mid-1940s, early, though diminutive (4 3/8 inches long, closed), streamlined stainless steel barrel and cap ball point pen with spoon-feed shaped clip (similar to 1920s Wahl metal pens). Most had a plastic barrel with a brass refill. It is distinctive because of its handsome, refined design. Little else is known regarding this maker or any other possible models.

Mont Blanc. Mont Blanc, Inc., 75 North Street, Bloomsbury, New Jersey. Mont Blanc launched its first ball point pen in 1956, the PIX. The first retractable mechanism employed a lever which protruded from the side of the cap to retract the refill. It was a bit noisy and Mont Blanc switched to a twist mechanism. This system is today used exclusively in Mont Blanc ball point pens. Refills were originally provided by a firm called Ballograph. In the 1960s, the firm began making their own refills employing a ball seat made of a bronze alloy. Although Mont Blanc says that it favors the fountain pen over the ball point, it states that "...this view was not confirmed in the marketplace, where the ball point pen was received like no other writing instrument before." Even a company concerned about exclusivity like Mont Blanc could not permanently close itself to the demands of the market.

Morrison. The Morrison Fountain Pen Company was located on Fifth Avenue, New York, New York. The ball point pen probably came from the same firm which made lower-end fountain pens. Usually found as a plastic-bodied, retractable ball point pen with a sterling filigree overlay. Morrison sometimes chrome plated the silver to prevent tarnishing, giving the pen a very cheap look. These appear to be one of its few ball point models and is notable only in that it had a sterling overlay.

The Morse Flo-Ball Pen Corporation. Morse was located in Holland, Michigan, and appears to be the successor to the Flo Ball Company of New York and Hollywood, California. It offered relatively expensive pens for 1954 ranging from $3.95 to $10. It referred to its pen as "a jewel-crafted ball pen that instantly obeys every writing impulse." It advised owners to "treasure it...but don't coddle it."

National. National Pen and Pencil Company, Inc. was located in Los Angeles, California. Originally it was a pencil manufacturer (like Eagle, Venus, Faber, Unipenco, and Universal) which entered the ball point business. National made an early, machined, all-aluminum, Kimberly-shaped ("Pockette") ball point pen with a brass refill. Little else is known about this firm or its models.

Norma. Norma Pencil Corporation was located at

137 West 14th Street, New York City. They offered the "Combination," a ball point pen and mechanical lead pencil combo. The "Combination" retailed (chrome model) for $5.95. Ink refill were 49 cents. Norma had produced "Multikolor" pencils since the late 1920s and carried this idea of four colors to the production of four color pencil/ball point pen combinations.

Normandy & Norman. Norman Gerstenzang, Inc. was located at 715 Fifth Avenue, New York City. Normandy had five models available in 1948. The "Four-Riter Retractable Pen" cost $2.95. It had four colored bands on the lip of its cap in blue, green, black, and red, the colors in which it wrote. Four other models were available at one dollar. These were the "Two Riter Retractable" which wrote in red and blue; the "Long John" (capable of "...over 58 miles of writing"), the "Knight" (retractable), and the "Page," a ball point pen/pencil combination. The pens were solidly build and heavy. Normandy claimed to be the "World's Largest Manufacturer of All-Metal Pens." Normandy also made the Norman ball point pen.

Orbic. The Orbic was produced by the Eagle Pencil Company, Fountain Pen Division, New York, London, Toronto. It was introduced in the latter half of 1946, possibly to keep pace with Eberhard Faber, another long-standing pencil manufacturer with an early venture into the ball point pen field. Their early ball point pens cost ten dollars. Orbic claimed to make better pens than other makers. In October 1946, Orbic ads referred to the Eagle Orbic as "The perfected ball point pen. Really writes better." Other claims were "No skip! Continuous, clear, crisp writing. No Drip! Ink can't blot, won't leak. No stall! Just pick up and write. Orbic is unconditionally guaranteed." Early Orbics were well made with a solid stainless steel cap, clip, and band.

Packet. The Reynolds International Pen Company, 1550 N. Freemont Street, Chicago, Illinois. Canadian plant, Oshawa, Ontario. This rather stubby pen, priced at $5.85, had a huge clip disproportionate to its overall length. Reynolds may have elected to hide the parentage of this pen, as the Reynolds name had lost its luster by the time this pen appeared in mid-1946. The Reynolds name does not appear on the clip on later examples. Nevertheless, this two-piece, all aluminum pen was typical of the other poorly performing Reynolds pens, although its ink faded very little in the few instances it ever reached the paper.

Paper Mate. The Frawley Corporation, later the Paper Mate Company, was founded by Patrick Joseph Frawley Jr., in 1949. It is still in existence today. The ball point pen industry was on the verge of extinction when Frawley acquired the Todd Pen Company in Southern California. By 1949, annual ball point pens sales in the United States had plummeted to 50,000 down from millions in the preceding years. Frawley used the first new ball point ink, available in 1950, which worked properly. Coupled with Frawley's marketing acumen, Paper Mate, took the lead in reviving the ball pen industry. In a few years, sales had rebounded into the millions. Other companies followed Frawley's lead and jumped into the field. In 1955, Frawley sold Paper Mate to Gillette for $15.5 million. (Frawley later took positions at Eversharp and Schick.) Paper Mate continues to be a major ball point pen and writing instrument manufacturer. In 1996, its Santa Monica, California, plant alone produced more than one billion writing instruments. Paper Mate also produces writing instruments in sites around the world. See the Paper Mate chapter.

Parker. The Parker Pen Company is located in Janesville, Wisconsin, with production facilities throughout the world. This major manufacturer officially held off putting a ball point pen on the market until 1954, when it introduced its highly successful *Jotter*. However, in 1951, it made and sold the *Hopalong Cassidy* ball point pen although the company advised its dealers that "Parker is not in the ball point pen business...but the ball pen you will be selling...is made and distributed by the Parker Pen Company...but not a Parker Ball Point Pen." In 1952, Parker removed Hopalong's head and sold the same pen as a *Parkette* at military post exchanges. Parker Pen Holdings Ltd., was acquired by the Gillette company for $458 million in May, 1993. See the Parker chapter.

Presdon. Presdon Manufacturing Company, New York City. In 1949, Presdon made a non-retractable, non-refillable ball point pen priced at 39 cents. Writing time was reportedly 36 hours.

Presto. An early, high-quality, heavily gold-plated ball point pen. The clip is arrow shaped and the pen was button actuated. It used a large, three-staged, stepped-down cartridge. Little else is known about this firm or other models.

Redipen. A very early, machined-aluminum ball point pen with a permanently affixed ink cartridge. It was simply made with a two-tone body (matte silver color with black mid-section or another color). It used a twist mechanism to extend and retract the point. Little else is known about this firm or its models.

Reynolds. The Reynolds International Pen Company was located at 1550 N. Freemont Street, Chicago, Illinois. A Canadian plant was in Oshawa, Ontario. Milton Reynolds kicked off international panic buying when he introduced his ball point pen in October 1945. A marketing genius, he promoted his pen so skillfully that he sold $5.3 million worth within three months of introduction in October 1945 (on an initial investment of $26,000). He quickly became a multimillionaire. However, although his pens appeared futuristic, they worked poorly, if at all. They leaked, faded, blotted, and the balls dropped out, among other things. But millions kept buying them as he introduced one new model after another. Within several years sales dried up and he closed down operations in 1948. Reynolds moved to Mexico and surrendered his United States citizenship (and all I.R.S. obligations) to become a Mexican citizen. He spent the rest of his life living like royalty in Mexico City. See the Reynolds chapter.

Rich Marco. This firm produced a relatively heavy, gold-tone double ended ball point pen. It had red ink on one end and black on the other. Both sides had caps which pulled off, one side containing a clip. Little else is known about this firm or any other models.

Ritepoint. Ritepoint was located in Saint Louis, Missouri, and later moved to Fenton, Missouri. They produced ball point pens in the early 1960s. They produced a very uniquely shaped contemporary ball point pen noteworthy because of its space-age look. It had a uniquely designed clip which gave the appearance of being hinged with three slots on either side. The pen had a distinctive, over-sized, red, tear-drop shaped button and a red center band. Its "Micro Tip" refill cost 49 cents in 1963. Later models were more contemporary in appearance. One all-plastic, push-button retractable model had a button on top to expose the point, and a lever on the side to retract it.

Roger. Roger Pen Company, New York City. In 1949, produced a double-pointed (red and blue), non-retractable, 98 cents ball point pen. The pen exhibited poor writing qualities and fading of both ink colors.

Rolball. Rolla Ball Pen Corporation, New York City. This firm produced a two-piece pen with a plastic barrel and metal top. It was priced at $4.95, with refills costing $1. Its lightly colored ink faded significantly.

Rolls. The Rolls pen was made by Continental Mfg. Co. It was a thick aluminum pen, first made in 1946.

Rollit. The Rollit was made by the Diversey Machine Works, Inc., Chicago, Illinois, and in Canada, by Rollit Ltd., Brockville, Ontario. It was advertised as "The pen you're proud to own or give." In 1947, the Rollit "Convertible" model was advertised as "World's only ball pen that refills through the tip in 3 seconds." This was accomplished by pressing the pocket clip which allowed the ink cartridge to slide out of the point-end of the barrel. A new refill was pushed in without the need to disassemble the pen. The "Convertible" retailed for $1 with refills costing 35 cent. In 1948, three models were available. These were the "Petite," a pen that looked like the early diminutive Kimberly, the "Retractable," a longer pen, and the "Director," which had a removable cap. All three models sold for one dollar each. These pens had anodized gold, silver, or chrome-colored caps with plastic barrels in deep colors or pastel shades.

Rolpoint. An early maker (ca. 1946) of ball point pens. One Rolpoint model is nicely machined and made entirely of metal, largely aluminum. It had a permanently affixed ink cartridge with slip-fit cap and an arrow style clip. Some models were made with a colored barrel and white-metal cap and end piece. It was similar in design to Faber and Eversharp "CA" models. Little else is known of the firm.

Ro Mur. Robert-Murrary Company, New York City. The Tri-Color model sold for $2 in 1949. Refills cost 50 cents. It contained three colors (blue, green, and red), but exhibited fading and poor writing qualities.

Ronnie. A very early, all aluminum, bullet-shaped ball point pen. Less than four inches in length, shaped similarly to an early Kimberly. Its cap has two sets of grooves, each containing four rings. Little else is known about this firm or any other products.

Scripto. Scripto, Inc., located in Atlanta, Georgia, and Scripto of Canada, Ltd., in Toronto, Canada (as of the 1950s). The Scripto name is still in use. Scripto become a major player in the ball point market in the early 1950s. Their pens were always reasonably priced The firm advertised heavily in major national magazines. Their later models used "Rx" ink and were retractable. Scripto introduced the "Feather Tone" in 1956 in six colors: turquoise, gray, orange, black, yellow, and lime. In 1958, Scripto introduced the "Satellite," undoubtedly named due to the influence of the "space race" of the late 1950s. This pen had a massive transparent ink cartridge with ink follower. Ads showed it floating in space. It wrote in "brilliant atomic red", "stratosphere blue", "jet black" and "jade green." Scripto continued to produce a line of reasonably affordable and functional ball points which had mass market appeal.

Sheaffer. Sheaffer Pen Company is located in Fort. Madison, Iowa. It was one of the original early pioneers of very high quality ball pen pens and is still a major manufacturer of them today. Sheaffer was approached by the United States War Department in 1944 to produce a ball point pen and they made bomb sights and ball bearings during the second World War. They still produce high-quality ball point pens. See the Sheaffer chapter.

Stratford. Stratford Pen Corporation was located in the Salz Building, New York City. They produced ball point pens from approximately 1947. Stratford made fountain pens and was probably related to the Salz Company which also made fountain pens and other products. They produced the "Celebrity" model in 1947, and advertised it with testimonials from movie stars such as Hedy Lamar. The pen was relatively flat and uniquely shaped, made largely of plastic. It sold for $1.95. The Celebrity was guaranteed to write "friction free" for "up to three years without refilling." It came in "Venetian red," "cloud blue," "fawn," and "midnight black." In April 1948, Stratford introduced a long, streamlined pen which had a very small cap. The clip extended beyond the cap itself. This pen was called the "$1 Prize Pen" because Stratford offered a $2,500 prize for the best name suggested for the pen. In 1949, Stratford offered the Peter Pan ball point pen for $1. It used the same refill as the Celebrity, was clipless, and non-retractable.

Style King. The Style King Magic Flow was made by S. Buchsbaum & Company, Chicago. They made a very early (1946), heavy ball point pen, with permanently mounted ink cartridge and press fit cap. It had a ribbed gripping section. The pen had an all aluminum case. Style King guaranteed some models to write five years without refilling and had the largest reservoir of any pen of the time. Its blue-violet ink faded considerably in sunlight.

Tucker. Tuckersharpe Pen Company, Inc. was located in Richmond, Virginia. It produced the "Mustang" retractable ball point pen in the mid-1960s which sold for 39 cents and was guaranteed to write for one year.

Unipenco. The Union Pen & Pencil Company was located in Mount Vernon, New York. They made a variety of pens from around the mid-1950s. Various mechanisms were used to make the point protrude. The "Magic Clip" model had a push button mechanism and a lever in the center of its clip to retract the point. Another model used the oversized "Everglide Carbide Ball" refill which cost 59 cents. Later models were triangular shaped. One was very similar to the Paper Mate Capri Mark V. In later years, Unipenco made nondescript models such as the "Fine Riter." They are most often found with advertising on them.

Universal. Universal Ball-O-Matic Corporation, New York City. It was an early producer of ball point pens with unique models with varied features. An early model consisted of a gold, electroplated slip cap, permanently mounted ink cartridge and plastic barrel with plunger button at the end of the barrel. The ink was advanced to the point by pumping the button which served to prime the cartridge, the same principle used by the Arkon pen. Another Universal model featured refills mounted on opposite ends, one with a fine point filled with red ink and the other a medium point with blue ink. A third Universal model had a gold tone cap and barrel. The point protruded when the entire cap was depressed, similar to a Parker "51" ball point pen. The "Buck Ball" had a permanently mounted ink tube which was covered with a vented fountain pen type ink sack. The purpose of the sack may have been to prevent leaking. The Ink-N-Trol non-retractable model was priced at $1.95. Refills cost 95 cents. This pen had a weak clip and reportedly could write for up to 49 hours. In 1949, the Klip-O-Matic non-retractable model cost $1, with refills at 39 cents. It had a tendency to fade and was rated as not acceptable. Many Universals survived and they can be found quite readily.

Van Cleeve. Cleveland Corporation, New York City. This corporation offered a pen in 1946, which may have been based on the Reynolds concept. It cost $2.69 in aluminum, $12.50 in silver, and $62.50 in solid gold (all prices exclusive of a 20% Federal Excise Tax). It was an extremely bulky pen with the point covered with a pull down sheath (similar to the Reynolds 400). It had a very weak clip, and like the Reynolds, a large ink supply contained solely in the barrel. Its very dark blue ink showed no signs of fading, but the pen came with no guarantee or indication of servicing.

Venus. Venus was made by the American Pencil Company of Hoboken, New Jersey. Like Eberhard Faber and Eagle (Orbic), Venus was a pencil manufacturer that entered the ball point pen field. The firm made ball points from the mid-1950s. Many of its pens are lower priced elongated "stick" ball points. Venus offered a choice of a regular and smaller-sized ball, and later offered points in broad, medium, fine, and extra-fine sizes. The balls were made of chrome steel. They also made a retractable pen with replaceable cartridges. These "extra full-length" refill cartridges came in red, blue, green, or black ink and cost 25 cents. In 1956, Venus became Venus Pen & Pencil Corporation and moved its headquarters from Hoboken to New York. Private investors bought Venus in 1966 and Esterbrook the following year. In 1973, Venus-Esterbrook was bought by Faber-Castell.

Wahl Ball. (See Eversharp) Eversharp's low-end models under a different name.

Waterman. The manufacturing arm of the Waterman Pen Company was located in Seymour, Connecticut. The company was begun in 1884 by Lewis E. Waterman. Due to diminished sales of fountain pens, it was losing money in 1945, at the time of the introduction of ball point pens. Generally conservative and staid, Waterman's put out its first ball point pen around 1949, the "Ball Pointer." It retailed for one dollar. The firm, attempting to emphasize quality and performance and trading on their past reputation, advertised "Avoid regrets—get famous Waterman's quality for sure performance!" Several styles appeared under the Ball Pointer moniker. One of these was a model designed after the "Crusader," Waterman's low-end fountain pen. Interestingly enough, the Crusader mechanical pencil was priced at $3, triple the price of the ball pen, a sure sign of the low esteem with which the public held the ball point by this time. By 1952, the Ball Pointer was offered in two sizes and in five colors with a free 30-day trial offer. Finally, in 1953, the "Sapphire" model was introduced. This slim, metal pen had a synthesized diamond point. It was billed as "the world's largest selling jewel point pen." To boost sales, it was offered in combination with wallets and other items for $10. One of Waterman's nicest pens made about, was the "CF" or cartridge filler. The CF line was made in the USA or Canada from 1955 to 1958. In 1958, the Waterman Company (USA) was sold to the French importer of Waterman pens—BIC—and its pens were sold under the "Waterman-Bic" name. In the early 1960s, BIC discontinued production of most Waterman products, moved its offices to Milford, Connecticut, and began manufacturing the CF and its higher priced pens in France.

Wearever. David Kahn, Inc. of North Bergen, New Jersey, was the maker of Wearever pens. Wearever claimed to be the "world's largest pen maker." They were a fountain pen maker and became an early producer of ball point pens. One of the first models was all aluminum, about five inches in length (with cap screwed on) with a steel clip. This model had a slip-on cap. The back end screwed off, apparently to permit the manufacturer to inject ink directly into the barrel. Later, Wearever pens were more conventional. They were reasonably priced at around one dollar. In 1955, Wearever offered four basic models. One was the "Press Clik," a metal retractable with "giltone" trim in red, green, gray, or black barrels, priced at 98 cents (which included an extra refill). Another was the "Slim Style," also a retractable, was priced at 98 cents, made of "luxurious giltone" metal. There was a "Slim Style Jr.", purse-sized "giltone," retractable pen for 98 cents. The most interesting and innovative model, the "Flipit" was priced at only 29 cents. It was an all plastic model with a lever or "peg" on the top of the cap, similar to a toggle switch. When the lever was pushed to one side or the other the point protruded for writing. It had a replaceable cartridge and came in many colors.

Valuing Pens

Valuing ball point pens can be approached several ways. Pen collectors use a "Supply and Demand" valuation or what would a willing buyer and a willing seller agree to as a value. An examination of the components of value are helpful. A valuable pen is usually rare, but a rare pen is not always valuable. A rare pen, of which only one or two are known may not have the broad appeal of the Reynolds pen for example. There are many Reynolds in collections and yet the demand for the Reynolds continues. A Stratford pen, of which there are only a few known, may sell for less. Obviously, the rarity factor is not the main determinant of value. It depends upon who is buying, the availability and how badly the collector wants that pen.

Here is how pen collectors describe pens to each other:

Mint	No sign of use.
Near Mint	Slightest signs of use.
Exc	Imprints good, looks new, all moving parts work.
ExF	One of the following: some wear, some darkening, or some moving parts stick.
Fine	Used, parts show wear.
Good	Well used, imprints may be almost gone, plating worn.
Fair	A parts pen.

Things to consider when valuing pens:

Condition is the most important criteria. Ball point pens were made by the millions and collectors want them to be in Mint condition. A pen in Ex. Fine condition may be worth much less than that of a Mint example. Damage is a major problem. A pen with a small crack in the cap or barrel may be valued only as a parts pen unless historically important. Repairs are possible, but to repair the pen, one needs parts or another pen with that part. Is it still a bargain when you have to find, buy, and strip another pen for parts.

Regular rubbing alcohol may remove old ink leaks at the front or back of the pen.

Color: Tens of millions of pens were made in black, less were made in other colors. The quality of the color is also important. A perfect pen in a crisp, rich color may demand a premium over a standard, well colored pen. The pens illustrated generally show good examples of color.

Advertising: Some collectors are looking for pens that are imprinted with advertising. In order of desirability, from most to least: Pen company advertising, Dated advertising, Large companies no longer in business or selling products no longer made, Major company's advertising, Unusual advertising, Specific products, and Local advertising.

Working Condition: Many ball point pens do not work and are not expected to work. (Some never worked when new!) Collectors may pay a premium for pens that can be put in working condition and can take a modern refill, such as the Parker Jotter. Most collectors would rather not try to repair a broken pen or resize a modern refill to fit an older pen.

Size: At this time, size does not seem to be a factor. In fountain pen collecting, the larger pens are usually valued higher than the standard size pens.

Original Packaging: Displays, boxes, instructions all add value.

Original Parts: Not all pens need to have original internal parts, especially if you are trying to make an early pen write with a modern refill, but they are very important to some people. A writing pen that is cosmetically original is worth the same or more than the same pen that is all original.

Early Pens (1957 and before): Collectors are looking for the earliest pens made. Rarely do they expect to use them.

When deciding whether to buy a pen, remember that in a few years you will rarely regret paying too much for a pen that you own, but you will always regret having not bought a good pen when it was available.

Important Notice

1) The pens illustrated vary in condition. Most are excellent to near mint. Due to the large number of ball points made, the prices are based upon a pen in **Excellent to Near Mint condition**. Add 20-50% if the pen is Mint in its original box or packaging. Subtract 75% if the pen is missing any parts. Subtract 25% if the condition is Extra Fine, 60% if in Fine condition and 90% if in only Good condition. These are retail prices. If you are trying to sell your pen to a pen dealer, expect 50% or so of the above figured value to be a reasonable offer. Do not fool yourself into believing that a defect or flaw will not affect value. Look over the pen with a magnifying glass, most dealers will do the same.

2) The fact that a pen is not illustrated here does not mean it is rare or valuable. It may be extremely common. We purposely left out hundreds of cheap and low quality pens. European pens were mostly not included. The same is true for many novelty pens. Both may become the subject of another book. This book is a guide and at the time of preparation, these were the pens that were available to illustrate it.
(Note: If you are interested in Fountain pens and their makers' history, read *Fountain Pens and Pencils—The Golden Age Of Writing Instruments*, *The Book Of Fountain Pens*, and *The Illustrated Guide to Antique Writing Instruments*, all by Stuart Schneider and George Fischler. In total, they contain over 2,500 color photographs of fountain pens, mechanical pencils, histories and pen company advertising.)

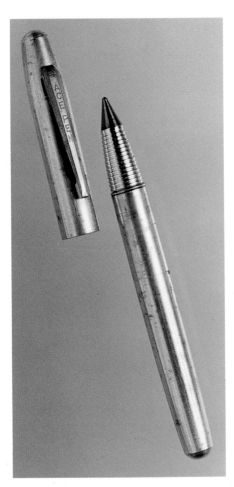

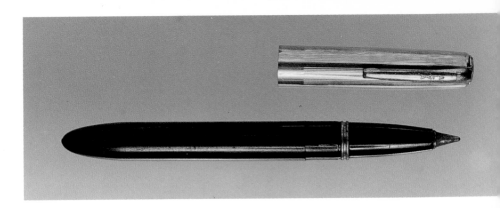

ALVA, ca. 1953. An unexceptional plastic and metal pen with an interesting name. Thomas Alva Edison may have been the inspiration for the name. There were two Edison Pen Companies from prior years that made fountain pens. Value $8-$10.

ACE PEN, ca. 1948. An aluminum pen with a gold plated brass clip. Value $20-$25.

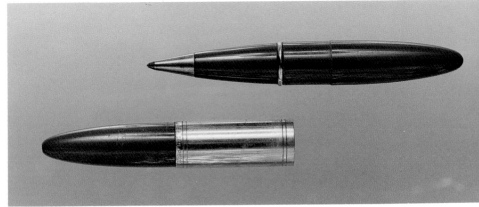

AMERICAN, ca. 1949. The well made American pen bears a strong resemblance to the Kimberly pen but is slightly longer (4 inches). Value $15-$20.

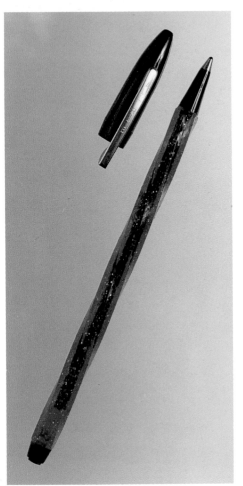

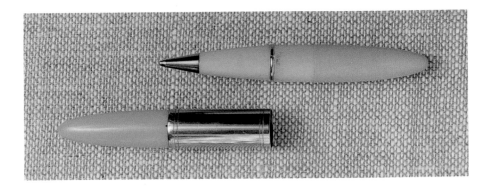

AMERICAN, ca. 1950. A small pink plastic pen, 4 inches long, made by the American Pencil Company as a copy of the Kimberly pen. Value $12-$16.

ALLRITE, ca. 1963. An Allright sparkly red plastic twisted stick style ball point. Value $6-$9.

AMERICAN, ca. 1952. The American ball pen is plastic and gold plated metal. Value $10-$12.

ANSON, ca. 1957. A well made gold plated pen that was similar in shape to the Cross Century. Value $10-$15.

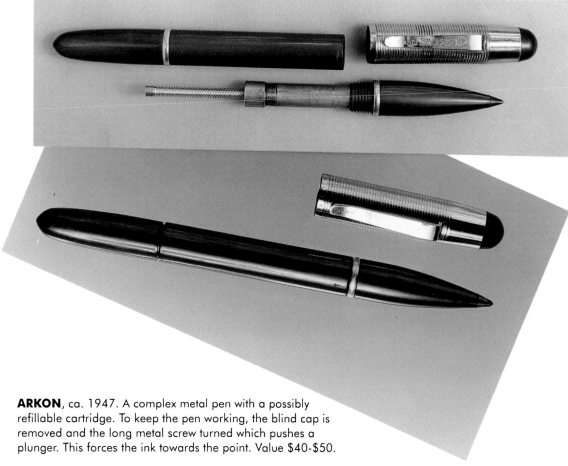

ARKON, ca. 1947. A complex metal pen with a possibly refillable cartridge. To keep the pen working, the blind cap is removed and the long metal screw turned which pushes a plunger. This forces the ink towards the point. Value $40-$50.

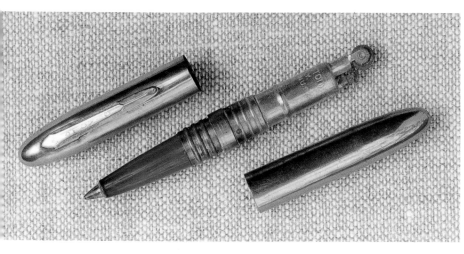

ATOMIC, ca. 1957. A gold plated pen/ cigarette lighter combination with a plastic grip. The lighter was made by the Weston Co., New York. Value $20-$30.

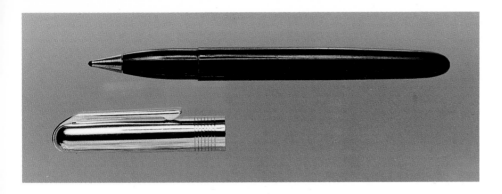

AUTOPOINT, ca. 1950. Autopoint is known for mechanical pencils. The company was in business in Chicago from 1929. They were a medium quality ball pen maker. This pen has a nice design to its clip. Gillette bought Autopoint in 1970 and sold it in 1979. Value $15-$18.

AUTOPOINT, ca. 1960. A simple gold plated pen found mostly with advertising on it. Value $5-$7.

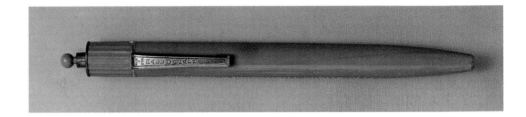

BALL-O-GRAPH, ca. 1949. A gray metal pen with a locking cam. The ball on the cam is pushed down and then pushed to the side, locking the point in the extended position. Value $20-$30.

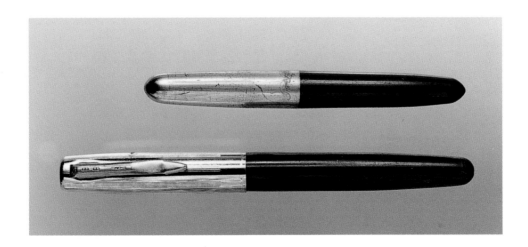

BB, ca. 1947. Two plastic pens with metal caps. The shorter model is called the "VP". Value $10-$15 each.

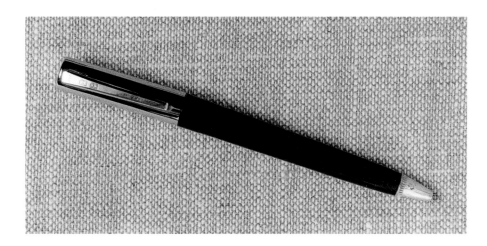

BB, 1947. Advertisement for BB pens.

BB, ca. 1948. A plastic, chrome, and aluminum point pen. Value $10-$15.

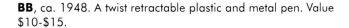

BB, ca. 1948. A twist retractable plastic and metal pen. Value $10-$15.

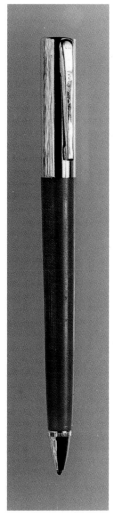

BB, ca. 1948. A good looking BB "Executive" pen in black plastic and gold plated metal. The pen originally cost ninety eight cents. Value $8-$12.

BB, 1948. Advertisement for BB's ninety eight cent pens.

BB, 1949. Advertisement for BB pens.

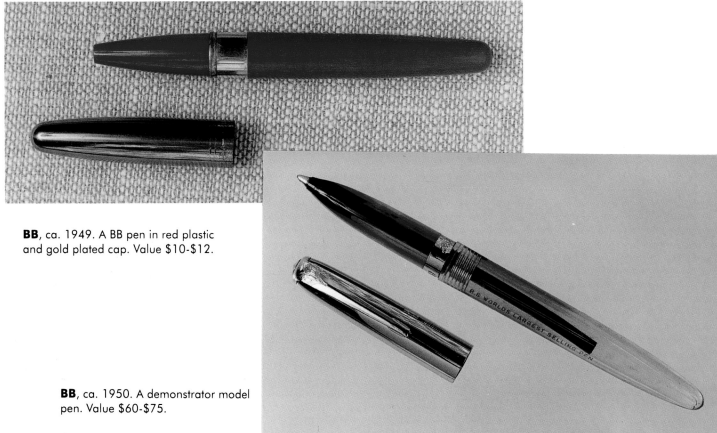

BB, ca. 1949. A BB pen in red plastic and gold plated cap. Value $10-$12.

BB, ca. 1950. A demonstrator model pen. Value $60-$75.

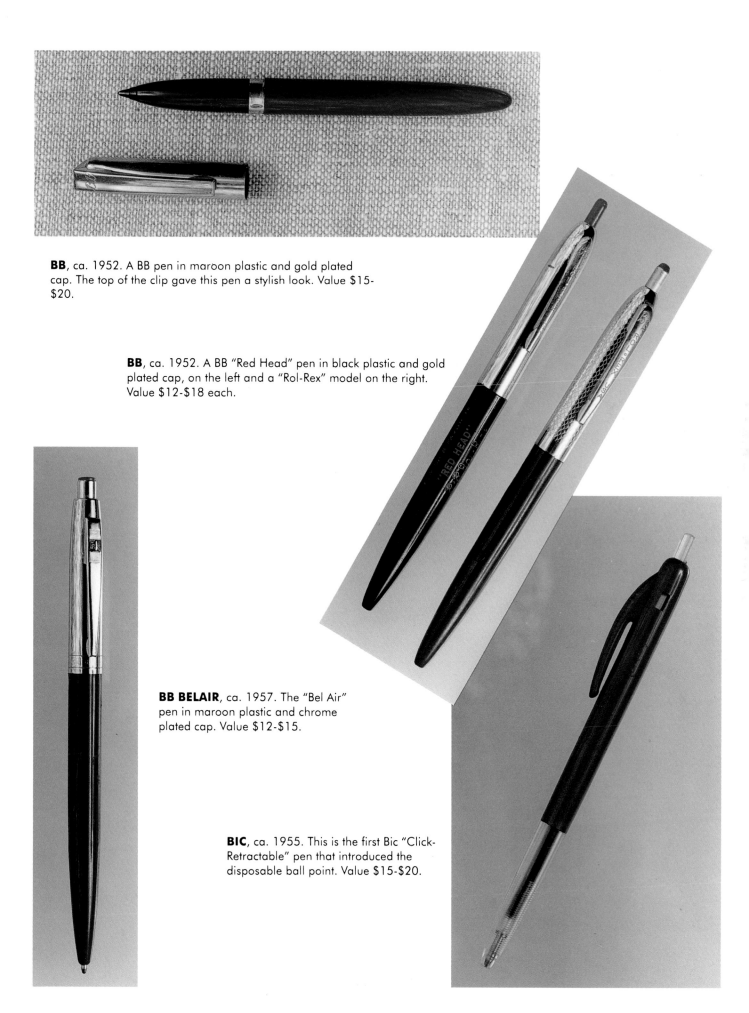

BB, ca. 1952. A BB pen in maroon plastic and gold plated cap. The top of the clip gave this pen a stylish look. Value $15-$20.

BB, ca. 1952. A BB "Red Head" pen in black plastic and gold plated cap, on the left and a "Rol-Rex" model on the right. Value $12-$18 each.

BB BELAIR, ca. 1957. The "Bel Air" pen in maroon plastic and chrome plated cap. Value $12-$15.

BIC, ca. 1955. This is the first Bic "Click-Retractable" pen that introduced the disposable ball point. Value $15-$20.

BIRO, ca. 1956. Biro may be said to be the inventor of the modern ball point pen. On this later interesting model, the clip moved down and to the side to extend the point and over and up to retract the point. Value $35-$40.

BIROME, 1947. Advertisement for Birome Parfum.

BIROME, ca. 1949. A tough to find retractable model where the clip extends and retracts the point. Value $30-$35.

BLYTHE, ca. 1947. Aluminum barrel with maroon top. Replaceable metal refill unit, long spring, push button "shoulder clicker." The top has a locking cam. The flat end is pushed down and then pushed to the side locking the point in the extended position. Clamped ring on refill to hold spring in place. Blythe was a small California firm and one of the original makers of aluminum ball point pens. Note similarity to later Paper Mate of similar design. Extremely high quality. Value $50-$55.

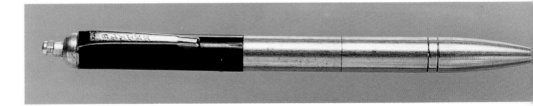

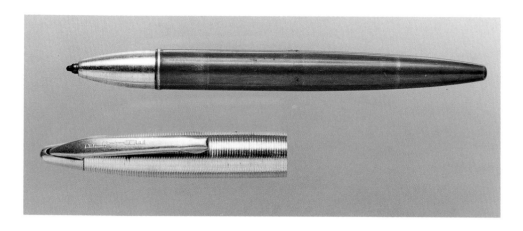

BLYTHE, ca. 1947-50. All aluminum, machined, balanced pen. Factory installed refill. Ribbed cap with spring-loaded clip. Extremely high quality. Value $50-$55.

BURGESS, ca. 1947. An early streamlined pen from this maker. It is possible that the Burgess Battery Company produced this shortly after World War II when it had employees who were no longer needed for the war effort. Companies often branched out to find business to keep the employees employed. Value $15-$20.

C & D, ca. 1962. An advertising pen filled with shredded money. Value $4-$6.

CARTERS, ca. 1954. Carters was a major pen maker in the 1920s and 30s. They stopped making fountain pens and continued to sell inks and glues. This four color pen is an attempt to get into the ball point pen market. Value $15-$20.

CHAMPION, ca. 1954. A swirled plastic barrel with a gold plated pocket clip. May be missing a cap band. Value $15-$20.

CHROMATIC, ca. 1959. A brass pen that writes in two colors. Twist it one way and the red point comes out. Twist it the other way and the blue point comes out. Value $12-$15.

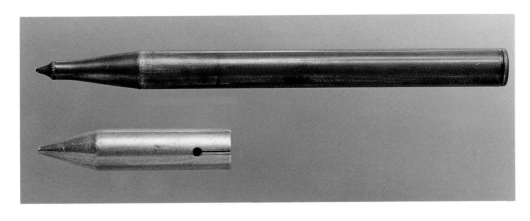

CLEEVLANDT, ca. 1946. The Cleevlandt pen is copper with an aluminum cover. It was most likely only refillable at the factory. It has a primitive style to it. Value $40-$50.

COLORKING, ca. 1954-58. A metal four color pen. This is similar to the Norma four color pen but to retract the points, you had to push the slide button back up Value $12-$15.

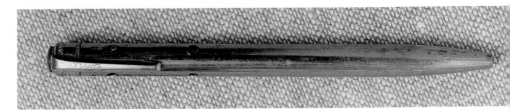

CONKLIN, ca. 1952. Black plastic and metal fixed point pen with an angled point. Note that this is a Conklin in name only. It is not associated with the earlier Conklin firm. Value $20-$25.

CONQUEROR, ca. 1950. This Conqueror closely resembles the Tower pen. Value $12-$15.

CONSTELLATION, ca. 1957. A gold plated pen/cigarette lighter combination. The lighter was made by the Negbauer Lighter Co., New York. Value $25-$35.

CROYDON, ca. 1953. An interesting design of this aluminum and plastic pen is the open slots cut in the cap. Value $10-$12.

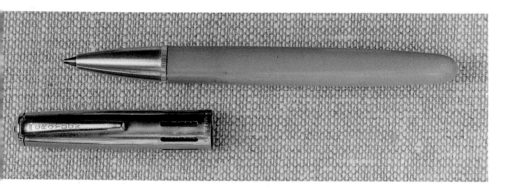

DEPENDO, ca. 1956. A combination pen and lighter. The lighter was made by Weston, New York. Value $15-$20.

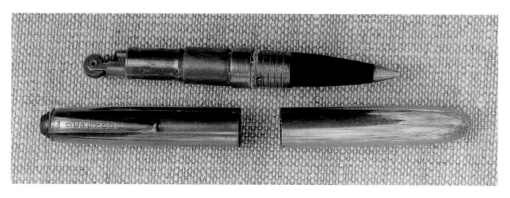

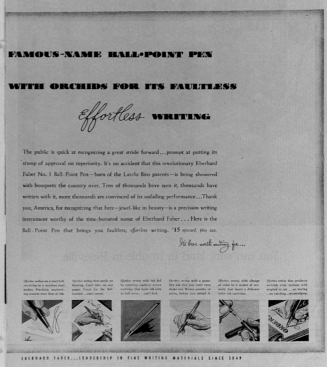

EBERHARD FABER, 1946. Advertisement for the Eberhard Faber pen.

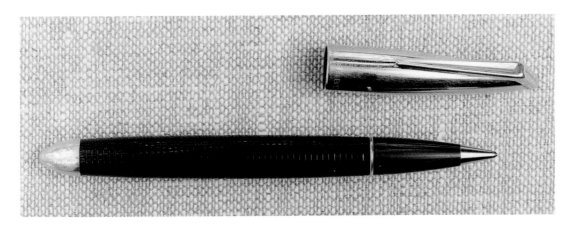

EBERHARD FABER, ca. 1946. A great early Faber pen with beautiful styling. The gold filled cap tapers upward and the clip is set at an angle to the top. The bullet end of the barrel compliments the cap. Original cost was $15.00. Value $45-$60.

EBERHARD FABER, ca. 1948. An interesting Faber pen that could be mistaken for an Eversharp CA pen with a bullet end. The cap is clearly marked "Eberhard Faber". Faber and Eversharp had a relationship whereby Eversharp produced models for Faber and royalties were paid. Value $30-$40.

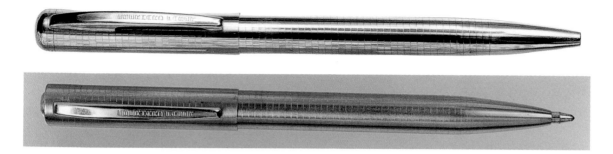

EBERHARD FABER, ca. 1948. Faber pens with a push cap retractor that looks like an Eversharp CA Retractable pen. Value $25-$30.

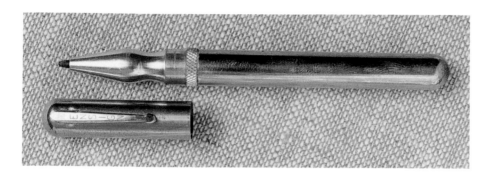

ENSIGN, ca. 1949. An aluminum pen with a molded grip. Value $20-$25.

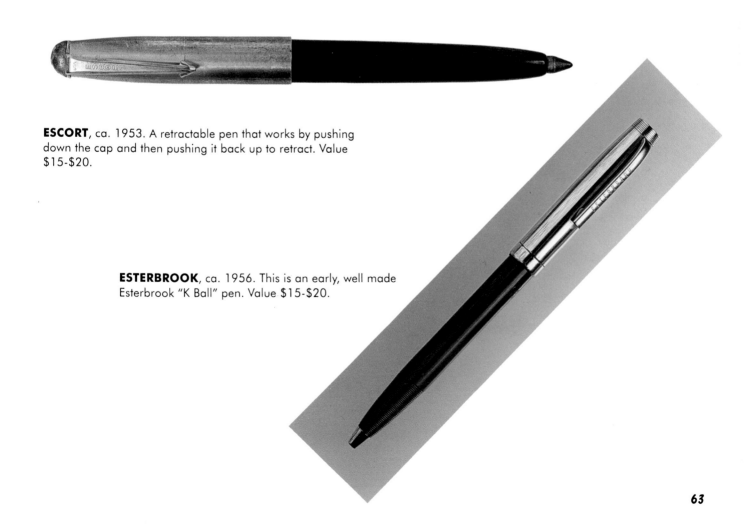

ESCORT, ca. 1953. A retractable pen that works by pushing down the cap and then pushing it back up to retract. Value $15-$20.

ESTERBROOK, ca. 1956. This is an early, well made Esterbrook "K Ball" pen. Value $15-$20.

ESTERBROOK, 1956. Advertisement for the Esterbrook pen.

ESTERBROOK, 1956. Advertisement for Esterbrook's pen.

ESTERBROOK, ca. 1960. A gold plated metal convertible pen which can use a ball point or a felt tip. Value $12-$16.

EVERLAST, 1952. Advertisement for the twenty-five cent Everlast pen as a premium for buying light bulbs.

EVERLAST, 1952. The twenty-five cent Everlast pen offered as a premium. Value $4-$6.

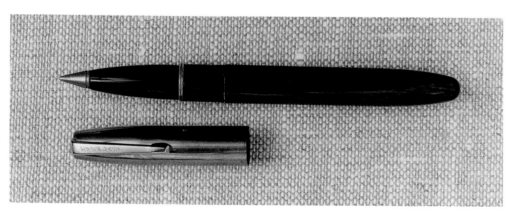

EVERLAST, ca. 1952. A rather simple pen that originally cost about twenty-five cents. It was popular as a premium; i.e., Buy so many light bulbs and get a free pen. Value $5-$9.

EVERSHARP, ca. 1946. Eversharp's CA or capillary action pen was available in a regular size and a demi size. The demi size was 4.5 inches with the cap in the closed position. The pen has been opened to show the curled ink cartridge. Value $20-$25.

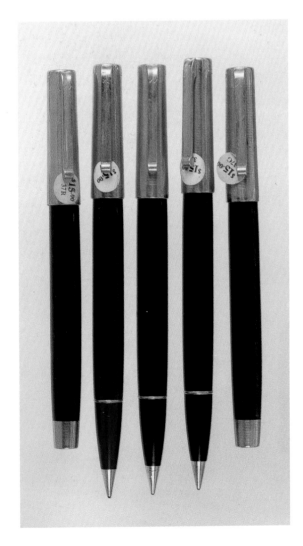

EVERSHARP, ca. 1947. Eversharp's CA with a stainless steel cap and trim in two sizes. Value $20-$25.

EVERSHARP, ca. 1946. Eversharp's CA or capillary action pen, their first ball point pen, was available in several colors—blue, maroon, brown, black, and green. Value $25-$45

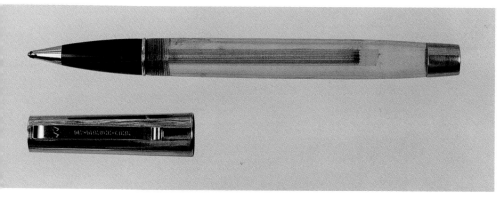

EVERSHARP, ca. 1946. A rare demonstrator version of the Eversharp's CA or capillary action pen. Value $75-$100.

EVERSHARP, ca. 1948. Eversharp's CA "Repeater" retractable pens, one in Gold Filled metal and the other with a Gold Filled cap on a brushed stainless steel barrel. Although the GF cap looks wrong on the Stainless barrel, they originally came this way. Value $25-$45.

EVERSHARP, ca. 1947. Eversharp's "Wahlball" pen, one in Chrome and another with a gold filled cap on a plastic barrel. Value $15-$20.

EVERSHARP, ca. 1948. Maroon plastic and metal "Slim Jim" pen, button press, clip release retractable. The original cost was $1.95. Value $12-$15.

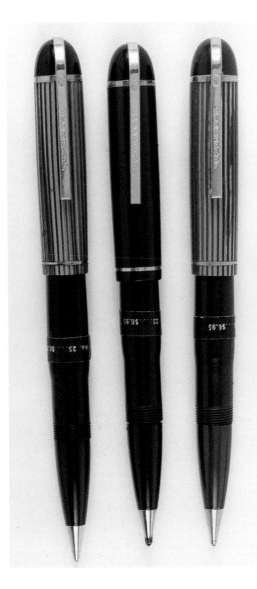

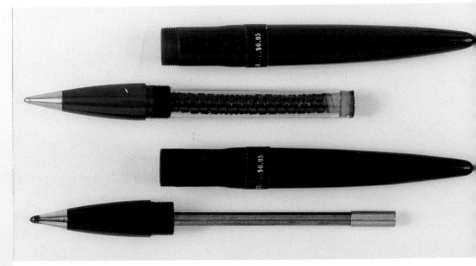

EVERSHARP SKYLINE, ca. 1948. Three skyline ball point pens. The Eversharp Skyline fountain pen was introduced in 1944. The ball point is harder to find than the fountain pen. The inner cap of the ball point pen has no blind cap and the barrel has no lever. The earlier refill had a spiral tube, the later models had a straight tube. Value $50-$55.

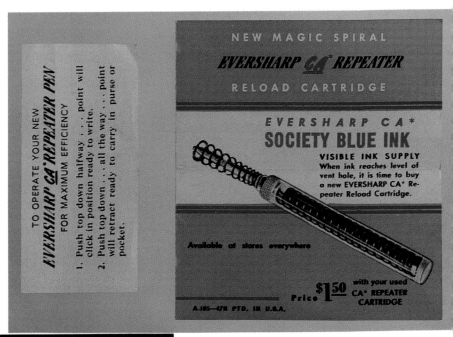

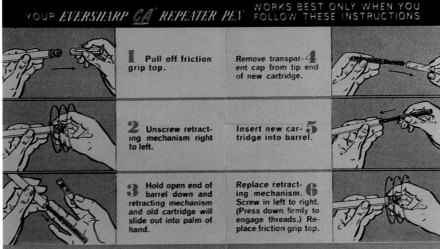

EVERSHARP, ca. 1948. Eversharp's CA Repeater refill advertising and ad insert.

EVERSHARP, ca. 1948. Black plastic and metal "Slim Jim" pen, button press, clip release retractable. The original cost was $1.95. Value $12-$15.

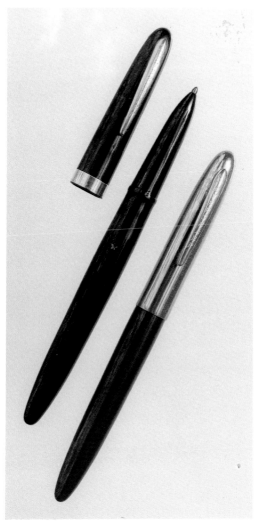

EVERSHARP, ca. 1948-54. Plastic "Star Reporter" and metal capped "Reporter" pens. Original cost was $1.00. Value $15-$20 each.

EVERSHARP, ca. 1948-54. A nice group of mint, plastic "Star Reporter" pens. Original cost was $1.00. Value $15-$20 each.

EVERSHARP, ca. 1948-54. Nice high quality "Small Ball" retractable pens with a click mechanism to extend the point and a small release at the top of the clip to retract the point. It used the long Kimberly refill. Original cost was $1.95 in plastic. Value $20-$25.

EVERSHARP, ca. 1948-54. Nice high quality "Kimberly Retractable" pens, similar but a bit larger than the "Small Ball". Value $25-$30.

EVERSHARP, ca. 1948-57. Maroon plastic "Retractable" pens and matching pencil with gold-colored electroplate trim. Refill marked "Eversharp Kimberly." Wide, clear plastic refill. Stylish, button press, clip release retractable. High-end, dependable, popular model. Original cost was $1.29. Value $20-$30 each.

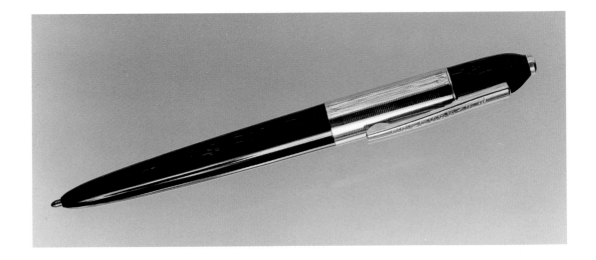

EVERSHARP, ca. 1948-57. Maroon plastic "Deluxe Retractable" pen with gold-colored electroplate trim. Refill marked "Eversharp Kimberly." Wide, clear plastic refill. Stylish, button press, clip release retractable. High-end, dependable, popular model. Value $25-$35.

EVERSHARP, 1948. Advertisement for the Eversharp "Kimberly Pockette" pen.

EVERSHARP, ca. 1948-59. A Kimberly advertising model. Value $25-$30.

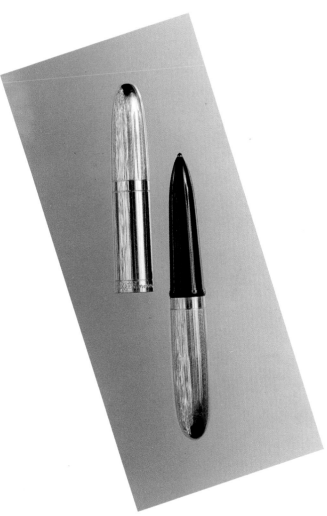

EVERSHARP, ca. 1948-59. A gold filled Kimberly "Pockette by Eversharp" pen. Value $35-$40.

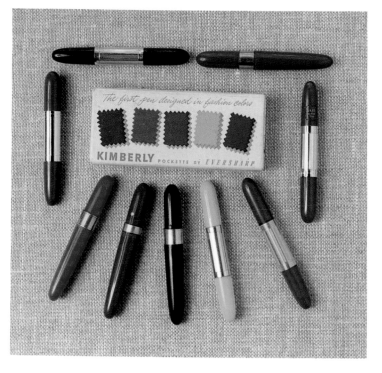

EVERSHARP, ca. 1948-59. The Kimberly claimed to be the first pen made in fashion colors. Eversharp bought the Kimberly purse size pen and continued to make it in varied colors, band styles, and advertising models. Value $20-$25 each.

EVERSHARP, ca. 1948-59. The Men's Pocket Edition "Kimberly Pockette." Black with a gold filled band. Value $20-$25.

EVERSHARP, 1953. Advertisement for the Eversharp "Reporter" pen.

EVERSHARP SKYLINE, ca. 1949. The economy model skyline ball point pens. The clip does not go over the top of the cap. Value $35-$45.

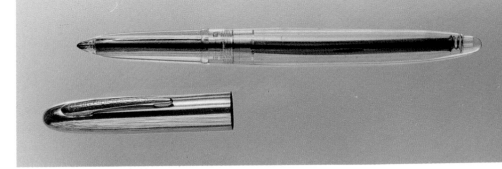

EVERSHARP, ca. 1951. Eversharp "Reporter" demonstrator model. Value $60-$75.

EVERSHARP, 1953. Advertisement for the Eversharp "Inca-Ink" pens.

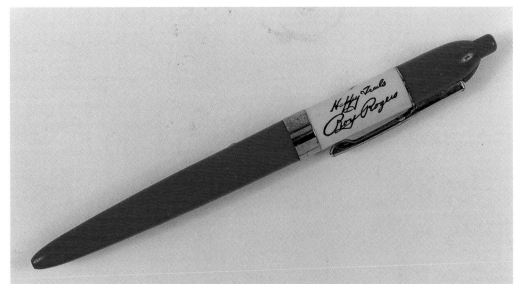

EVERSHARP, ca. 1953. The Roy Rogers "Retractable" Eversharp pen. Value $70-$85.

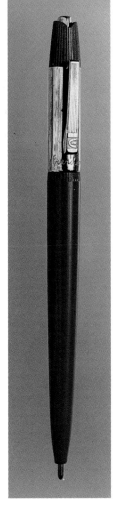

EVERSHARP, ca. 1957. "Deluxe Reporter" retractable pens with a circular cross section and no metal tip. Value $15-$18.

EVERSHARP, ca. 1957. Colorful plastic pens, stylish, button press, clip release retractable. Value $15-$18 each.

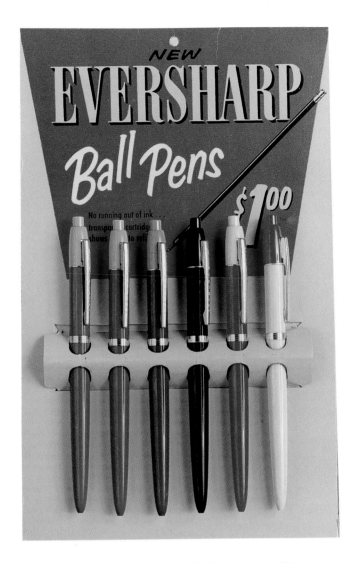

EVERSHARP, ca. 1957. Colorful plastic pens, stylish, button press, clip release retractable. Value $15-$18 each.

EVERSHARP, ca. 1958. These are the "Fountain Ball" retractable pens with a triangular cross section and metal tip. One is an advertising item given to pen shops to introduce the pen. Value $15-$18 (pen company advertising $30-$45).

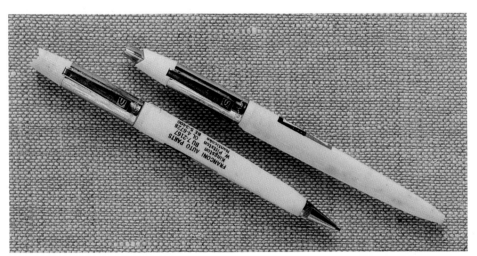

EVERSHARP. ca. 1958. White retractable "Fountain Ball" pen and matching pencil. Champion spark plug advertising pen in cardboard box. Stylized Eversharp "E" emblem. This is the first pen produced by Eversharp after Parker purchased them in December 1957. It is marked "Eversharp" with modern-day Parker oval and arrow. Available with triangular or round barrel. Value $20-25 (set).

EVERSHARP, 1958. Advertisement for the Eversharp "Small Ball" pen.

EVERSHARP, ca. 1959. A button retractable pen with a very Parker Jotter look. Value $20-$25.

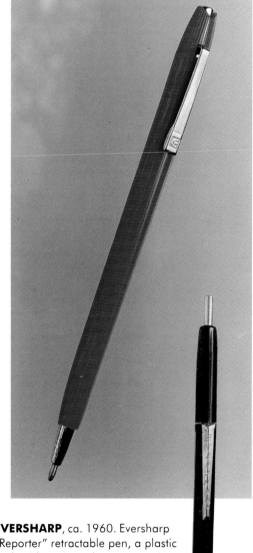

EVERSHARP, ca. 1960. "Teena" (no.814) retractable pens with a gold electroplated cap and clip with a plastic crown. 4.5 inches long. Originally cost $1.29. Value $10-$15.

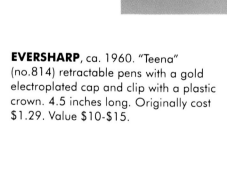

EVERSHARP, ca. 1960. Eversharp "Reporter" retractable pen, a plastic body with a triangular cross section and chrome plated tip. Offered in black, red, blue, green, gray, white, and yellow. It used Kimberly reload cartridges. Value $15-$18.

EVERSHARP, ca. 1960. Eversharp's office retractable pen, six inches long. Value $8-$10.

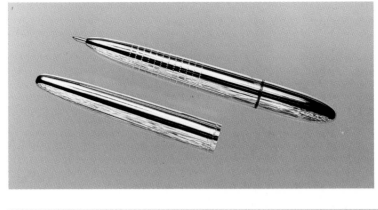

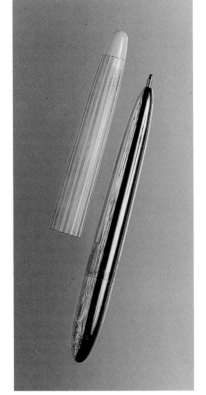

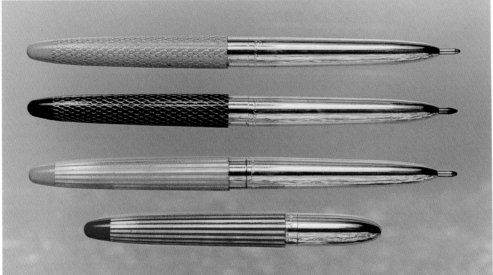

EVERSHARP, ca. 1960. Small (3.5 inch long when closed) "Tiara" pens with the Parker arrow insignia. Original cost was $2.95. Value $35-$55.

EVERSHARP, ca. 1961. Retractable "Reporter" button. Gray plastic with polished steel trim. Stylized Eversharp "E" emblem. Marked "Eversharp" with modern-day Parker oval and bisecting arrow. Plastic refill also similarly signed. Average quality for era. Value $15-$20.

FERBER VU-RITER, 1956. Advertisement for Ferber's "Vu-Riter" pen.

FERBER VU-RITER, ca. 1956-60. Disposable see through stick pen made for office use. Value $3-$5.

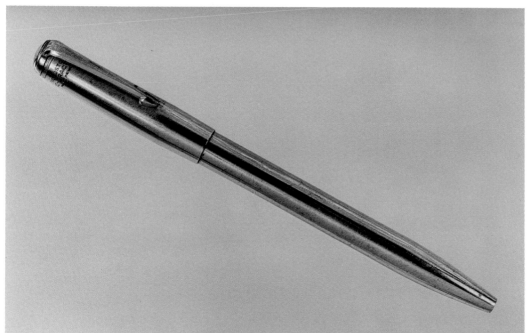

FIELDSTON, ca. 1947. This model is marked "Re-Tract-O" and is cap actuated. Value $20-$25.

GUARANTEED UNTIL 2000 A. D.

We believe the FISHER Cushioned Point PEN to be the finest writing instrument ever made. Behind its design and operation lie years of careful scientific research and production experience.

If for any reason your pen should fail to function properly, send it direct to the Fisher Pen Co. with thirty-five cents to cover handling and postage. Your pen will be promptly repaired and returned to you postage prepaid. Your retailer can supply refill cartridges, but for repairs do not return your pen to the retailer. Return direct to:

FISHER PEN COMPANY
3658 BROADWAY, CHICAGO 13, ILLINOIS
DIVISION OF FISHER-ARMOUR MFG. CO.

FISHER PEN, ca. 1950. One of the first Fisher pens guaranteed for 50 years. Made by the Fisher-Armour Mfg. Co. of Chicago. Value $40-$50.

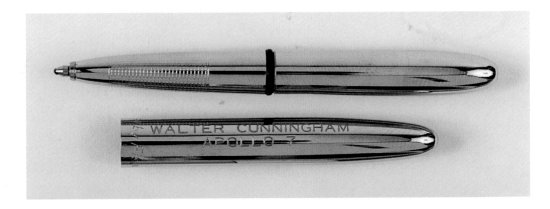

FISHER, ca. 1968. The Fisher Space Pen that went to the moon in 1969, but first flew aboard Apollo 7 in October 1968. Value $20-$40.

FISHER SPACE PEN, 1968. Walter Cunningham's Apollo 7 Fisher Space pen. This was presented to Cunningham, one of the three astronauts aboard Apollo 7, by The Fisher Space Pen Company after the flight. It was purchased from Cunningham's collection at auction. The Fisher used a nitrogen pressurized refill. Apollo 7 was the first space flight where a ball point pen was used. It was also the first flight that was televised live from space. Value $500-$600 (having been Cunningham's pen, otherwise $15-$25).

THE FISHER SPACE PEN

NORMAL PRODUCTION TIME: Imprinted, 30 days. Not imprinted, 15 days
LESS THAN MINIMUM: Not available
SHIPPING WEIGHT: 1 lb. per carton of 12
SPLIT DESTINATION SHIPMENTS: $2.50 each. No extra charge for multiples of 500
INDIVIDUAL ITEM SHIPMENTS: Not available
F.O.B. POINT: Factory in Illinois
PERSONALIZATION: Engraved: $.07 per character; with color-fill $.09 per
    character ($.60 per name, piece minimum). Customer must furnish
    typewritten list of names.
NORMAL PACKAGING: In individual boxes with guarantee slip telling the
    fascinating story behind this remarkable pen
COLORS OF IMPRINTING: Any standard color. Black or blue recommended for
    #395C; white recommended for #727
NORMAL COPY LIMIT: On barrel: 6 lines of 22 characters and spaces each;
    1-3/16" area
EXTRA LINES: Not available
COPY CHANGES: $6.00 each
PROOFS: $6.00 plus minimum quantity unit price
ADDITIONAL INFORMATION: For reproduction of trademarks, logos or special
    type styles, customer must furnish camera-ready black-and-white artwork.

871 20M SC   ASI 5442   Printed in U.S.A.

FISHER SPACE PEN, ca. 1971. The card and two styles of pen are from an advertising kit to sell The Fisher Space Pen with the customer's name imprinted upon it. Value $50-$60 for the kit.

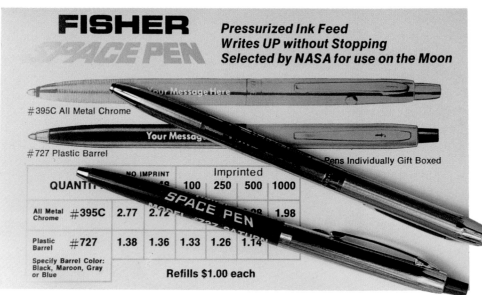

FISHER SPACE PEN

Pressurized Ink Feed
Writes UP without Stopping
Selected by NASA for use on the Moon

#395C All Metal Chrome — *Your Message Here*

#727 Plastic Barrel — *Your Message*

Pens Individually Gift Boxed

QUANTITY	NO IMPRINT		Imprinted			
			100	250	500	1000
All Metal Chrome #395C	2.77	2.72				1.98
Plastic Barrel #727	1.38	1.36	1.33	1.26	1.14	

Specify Barrel Color: Black, Maroon, Gray or Blue

Refills $1.00 each

FISHER SPACE PEN, ca. 1979. The Fisher Space Pen that went to the moon, also flew aboard the first Space Shuttle flight in 1981. This model was available in advance of the Shuttle flight with the commemorative coin. Two variations of coin are shown. Value $25-$35 w/one coin.

FISHER, ca. 1981. The Fisher "Futura" was one of Fisher's attempts to make an "executive" style pen and pencil. Value $25-$30.

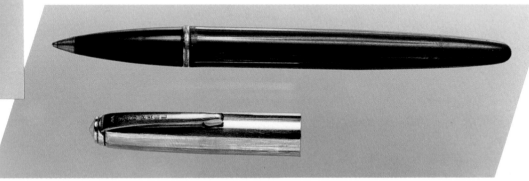

FLO-BALL, 1949. The Flo-Ball dollar pen. Value $6-$9.

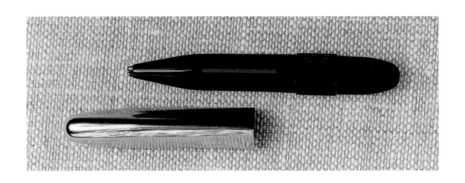

FLO BALL TRITONE, ca. 1953. A small chrome and plastic three color pen only 3.5 inches long. Unusual in that the three colored points are always extended. You turned the pen to the color, facing up, that you wanted to write with. Value $15-$20.

FLO-BALL, 1949. Advertisement for the Flo-Ball dollar pen.

FLO-BALL, 1953. Advertisement for Flo-Ball's Tri Tone and other pens.

FLO-BALL, 1957. A late model retractable Flo-Ball pen. Value $10-$15.

GROB, ca. 1952. Two color nickel plated pen. Possibly made in Germany. Value $20-$25.

GOODMARX, ca. 1953. A simple capped plastic and metal pen with an interesting name. Value $10-$12.

The BALL POINT PEN With The Retractable Point...

Hamilton Ross *Jet flow* BALL PEN

· Guaranteed For Always

The PEN-ULTIMATE...NOW!

Writes For Years Without Refilling —

HAMILTON ROSS, 1947.
Advertisement for the Hamilton Ross "Jet Flow" pen.

HOLLY, ca. 1952. A plastic pen with a chrome plated cap. Its interesting characteristic is the small double slit under the pocket clip that locked the cap into place when the pen was closed. Value $8-$10.

HOLT, ca. 1954. The "Neetline" pen was made by George Holt, Inc. in Providence, Rhode Island. This model has a pen at one end and a pencil at the other, a design made popular in the 1930s. Value $20-$25.

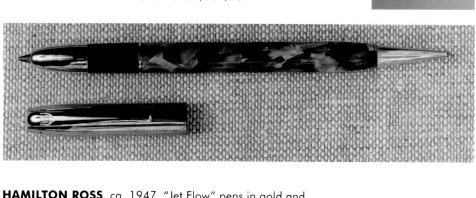

HAMILTON ROSS, ca. 1947. "Jet Flow" pens in gold and burgundy, gold and black, and blue and silver. All are anodized aluminum. A half turn of the cap extends the point. It is believed to be one of the first pens to use the twist mechanism to extend and retract the point. The original cost was $10.00 and the pen was made in Chicago. Value $70-$90.

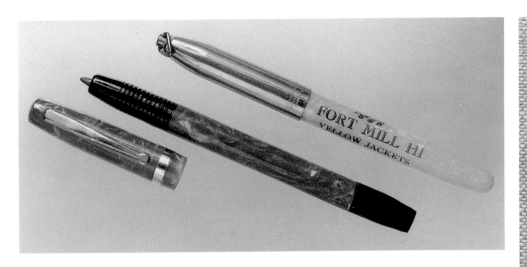

HOLT, ca. 1954. Three "Neetline" pens made by George Holt, Inc. The green one with the plastic cap was made in Crompton, Rhode Island. The yellow one and the green one with a metal cap were made in Providence, Rhode Island. Value $15-$22.

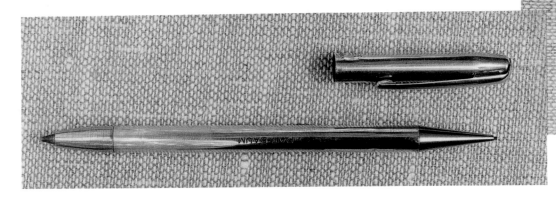

HOLT, ca. 1954. This sterling silver pen/pencil combination was made by George Holt, Inc. in Crompton, Rhode Island. Value $55-$65.

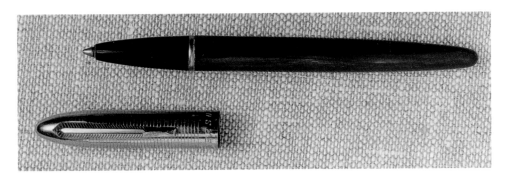

INGERSOL, ca. 1948. A plastic barrel with a metal cap. Ingersol was know for its "Dollar" pens. Value $6-$9.

INGERSOL, ca. 1948. A great Mickey Mouse pen only 3.75 inches long. Mickey appears several times as a decal around the cap. These are very difficult to find in perfect condition and are avidly sought by comic character collectors. Value $95-$120.

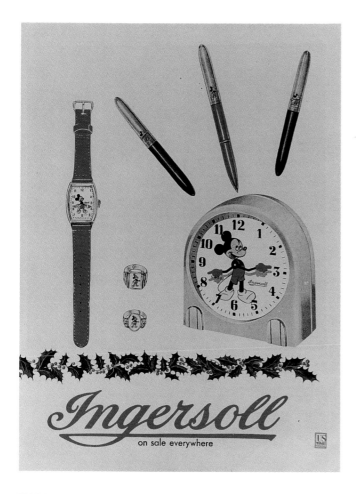

INGERSOL, 1948. Advertisement for Ingersol's Mickey Mouse pens.

KIMBERLY, ca. 1946. A nice early Kimberly, a purse size pen of chrome plated metal. Value $35-$40.

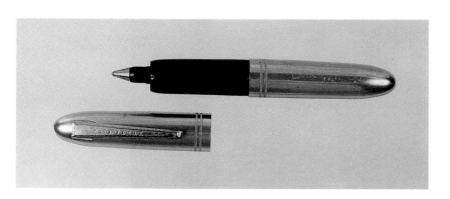

INKOGRAPH, ca. 1950. A short chrome plated pen with the traditional Inkograph look. Instead of a stylographic point, it has a ball point. Value $15-$20.

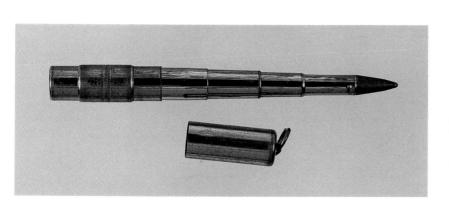

JL, ca. 1956. A tiny pen that telescopes to use. When closed it is only 1.75 inches long. The only marking on the pen says "JL". Value $8-$10.

83

KIMBERLY, ca. 1947. A gray plastic pen that originally cost $12.50, from this maker best known for their shorter purse sized pens. Kimberly was bought by Eversharp about 1948. Value $20-$25.

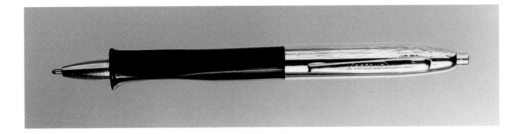

KONTOUR, ca. 1955. A USA made, hand contoured metal and plastic retractable pen. Value $15-$20.

KWIK-KLIK, ca. 1956. A rather unexceptional plastic pen with a gold plated cap, but on closer look, they added a knurled aluminum piece upon which the cap would friction fit rather than use a threaded section. This may have been used to avoid a patent infringement for the screw together section. Value $8-$10.

KWIK RITE, ca. 1948. A pen that is very similar in shape to the Rolls pen. Value $35-$45.

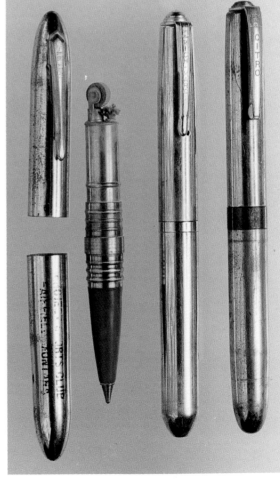

LIFELONG, RICH MARO & CITRO, ca. 1952. Three similar brass pens with plastic inner barrels with different names. Most of these brass pens have no name. The Lifelong was a combination pen/cigarette lighter. The Rich Maro was a single pen and the Citro was a double ended pen with a red ink side and a blue ink side. Value $10-$20 each.

LINDY, ca. 1957. A small (3 inches long closed) "Lady Lindy" ball point in blue and red plastic with a gold filled band. Value $15-$18.

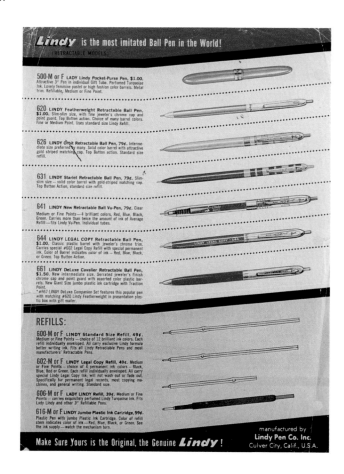

LINDY, ca. 1959. Lindy Pen advertising page from a dealer's catalog showing the different models available.

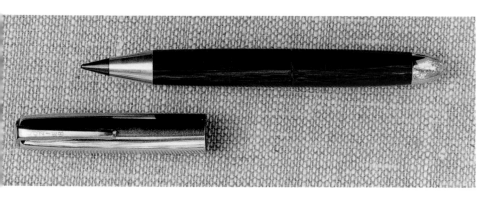

MANSON, ca. 1949. An interesting anodized aluminum pen with a gold plated cap. Value $15-$20.

LOZIER, ca. 1949. An aluminum and plastic pen. Value $15-$20.

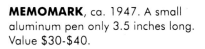

MEMOMARK, ca. 1947. A small aluminum pen only 3.5 inches long. Value $30-$40.

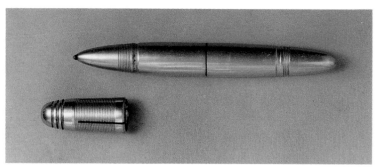

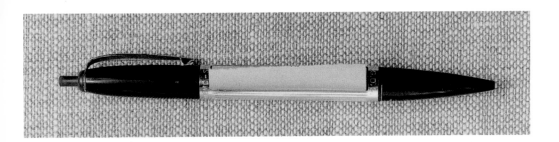

MEMOSTYLO, ca. 1955. An unusual German made plastic and metal pen with a built in roll of memo paper. Marked "BTE S.G.D.G." Value $25-$35.

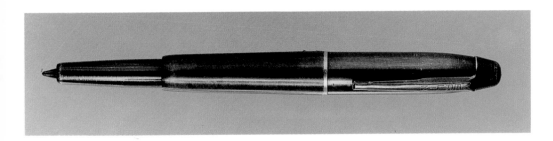

MERLIN, ca. 1947-51 All aluminum, streamline, quality construction. Black ends with dark green, metallic barrel. Highly unusual threaded shroud mechanism to cover point. Early, thick plastic refill. Required return to factory for refill. Rare. Value $75-$80.

MICROPOINT, ca. 1960. A slim button retractable pen. Value $8-$10.

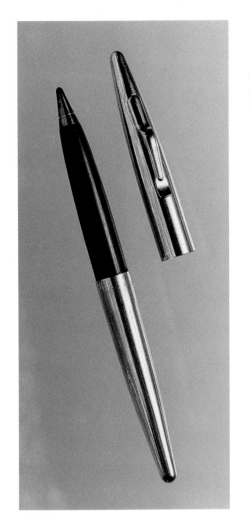

MINUET, ca. 1950. A nicely shaped small aluminum and plastic pen. 4.5 inches long. Value $15-$20.

MINUET, ca. 1950. A Minuet pen with an attached suction cup made to stick on the side of a telephone. 4.5 inches long. Value $15-$20.

MORRISON, ca. 1959. A fancy flower pattern sterling silver overlay Morrison pen. Value $25-$30.

MORRISON, ca. 1959. A fancy sterling silver overlay Morrison pen in its leather cover. Morrison has been making fountain pens since the mid-1920s. Value $20-$25.

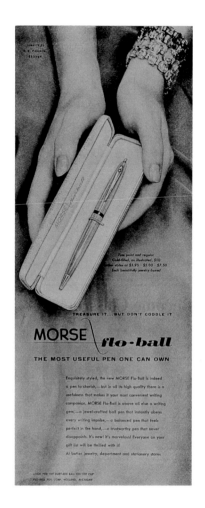

MORSE, 1954. Advertisement for the Morse "Flo-Ball" pen.

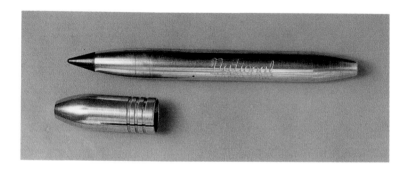

NATIONAL, ca. 1947. A small aluminum pen only 3.75 inches long made by the National Pen & Pencil Company of Los Angeles. Value $30-$40.

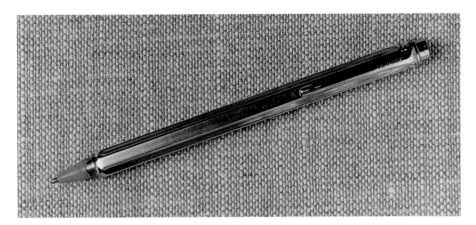

NESOR, ca. 1960. A silver plated pen with a plastic point end. It was made in Japan. Value $10-$15.

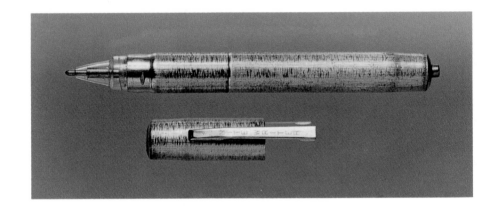

NITE WRITER, ca. 1975. An interesting ball point with a built in flashlight so that you can write at night. Value $10-$15.

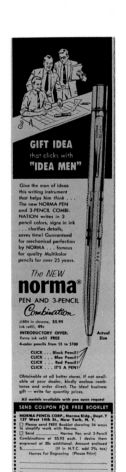

NORMA, 1955. Advertisement for Norma's combination three color pencil and a ball point pen.

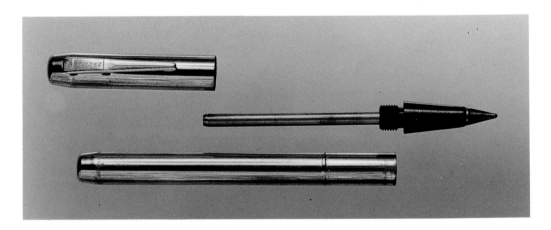

NORMAN, ca. 1948. The Norman pen was made by Normandy, of gold plated brass. Value $20-$35.

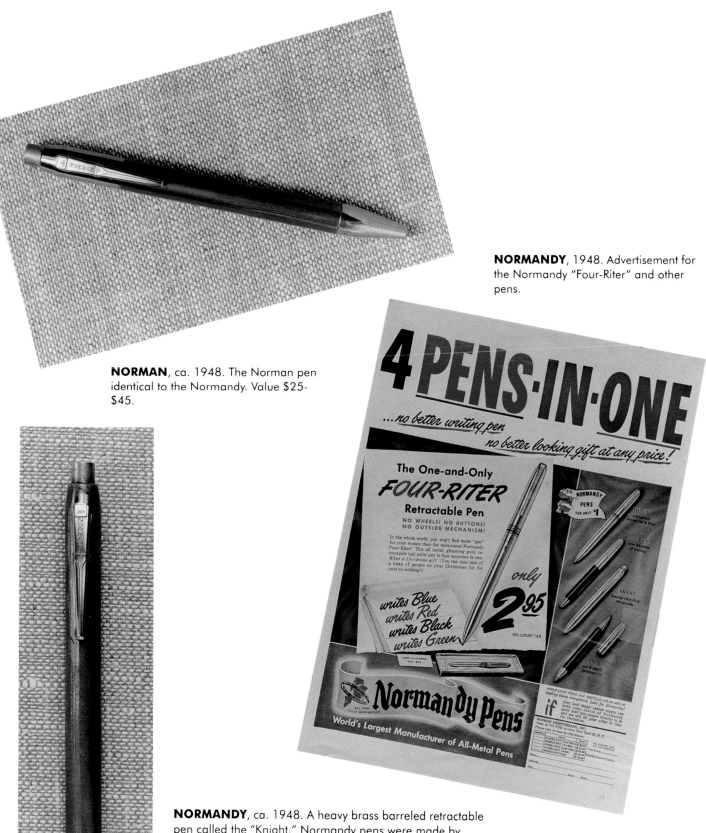

NORMANDY, 1948. Advertisement for the Normandy "Four-Riter" and other pens.

NORMAN, ca. 1948. The Norman pen identical to the Normandy. Value $25-$45.

NORMANDY, ca. 1948. A heavy brass barreled retractable pen called the "Knight." Normandy pens were made by Norman Gerstenzang, 715 Fifth Ave., New York City, who claimed to be the "World's Largest Manufacturer of All-Metal Pens." There were five models of Normandy available—The "Four-Riter" retractable four color pen, the "Two-Rite" retractable pen that wrote blue and red, the "Long John" that supposedly wrote 58 miles, The "Knight" (illustrated), and the "Page" with a pencil at one end and a pen at the other. All pens cost one dollar, postpaid, except the Four-Riter that cost $2.95. Value $25-$45.

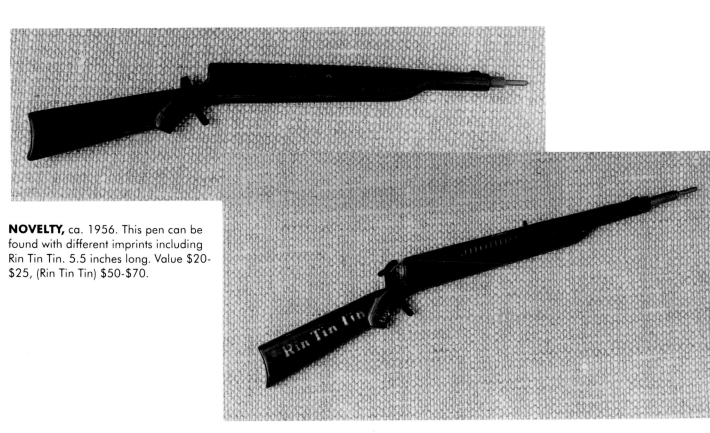

NOVELTY, ca. 1956. This pen can be found with different imprints including Rin Tin Tin. 5.5 inches long. Value $20-$25, (Rin Tin Tin) $50-$70.

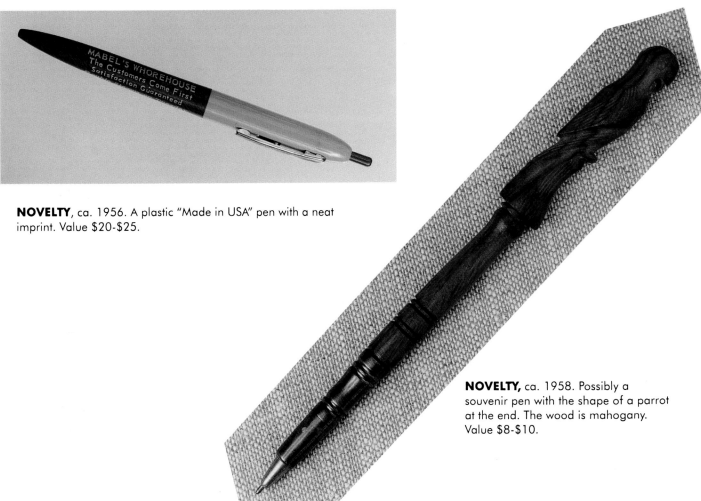

NOVELTY, ca. 1956. A plastic "Made in USA" pen with a neat imprint. Value $20-$25.

NOVELTY, ca. 1958. Possibly a souvenir pen with the shape of a parrot at the end. The wood is mahogany. Value $8-$10.

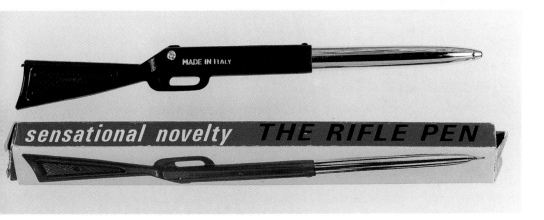

NOVELTY, ca. 1959. An Italian made rifle pen. Value $10-$15.

NOVELTY, ca. 1960. An unmarked souvenir pen from Inverness, Scotland, with the Loch Ness monster floating past the Inverness castle. The point extends when the metal front end is turned. Value $20-$25.

NOVELTY, ca. 1960. Two plastic "Denmark" imprinted "stripper" pens. When the pen is turned over, the girl's bathing suit appears or disappears. This is a double stripper model. It can also be found with only one stripper on the pen. Value $15-$20.

NOVELTY, ca. 1960. A plastic "Made in USA" pen with a viewer at the end and a window to let in light. When the pen is held up to the light, there are 10 photos of naked ladies. This one would be "X" rated. The photos change by turning the barrel. Value $40-$45.

NOVELTY, ca. 1960. A gold plated metal nail pen. Twist the head of the nail and the point moves in or out. Value $7-$9.

NOVELTY, ca. 1960. A gold plated metal hammer pen. Twist the head of the hammer and the point moves in or out. Value $7-$9.

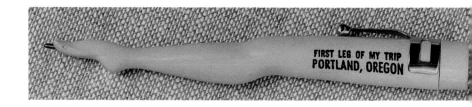

NOVELTY, ca. 1960. A great leg shaped pen in flesh colored plastic. Value $10-$12.

NOVELTY, ca. 1965. A Louisville Slugger. Value $8-$12.

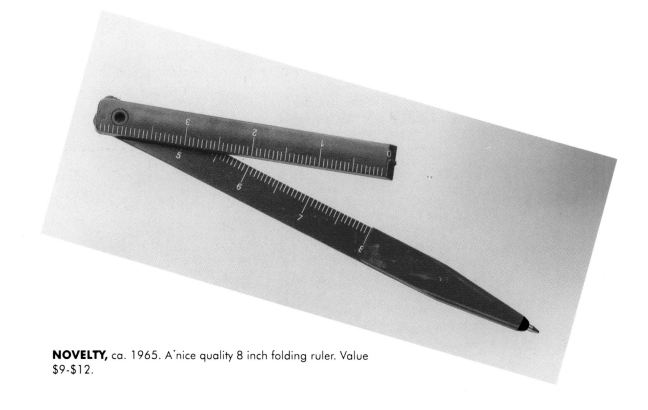

NOVELTY, ca. 1965. A nice quality 8 inch folding ruler. Value $9-$12.

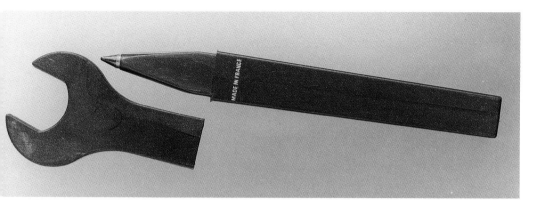

NOVELTY, ca. 1970. A plastic wrench, made in France. Value $4-$7.

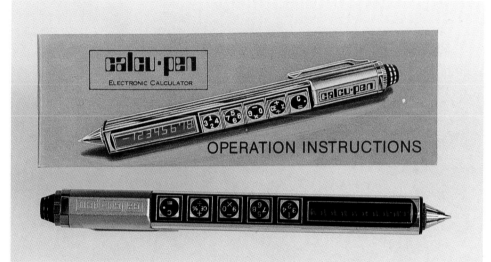

NOVELTY, ca. 1975. A Japanese made calculator pen. Value $65-$75.

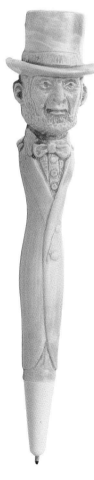

NOVELTY, ca. 1976. A plastic "Great American" pen with Lincoln's head and torso. Made by the Locke Co. of St. Charles, Illinois. Value $20-$25.

ORBIC, 1946. Advertisement for the Eagle Orbic $10.00 pen.

ORBIC, 1946. Advertisement for Eagle's Orbic pen.

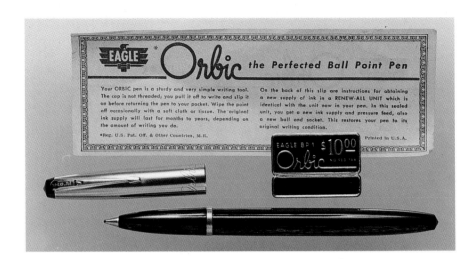

ORBIC, 1946. The Eagle Orbic $10.00 pen. Value $20-$25.

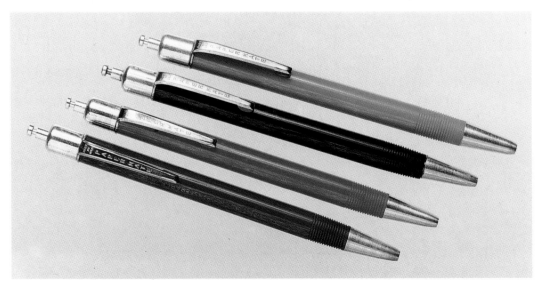

PAPER MATE, ca. 1950-1953 Paper Mate's first model button retractable pens in different colors. Aluminum ends with plastic barrel. Stamped steel clip. These came in a large variety of colors. Note similarity to Blythe. Refill spring held on by a crimp instead of a clamped ring as in the Blythe model. Value $30 to $35.

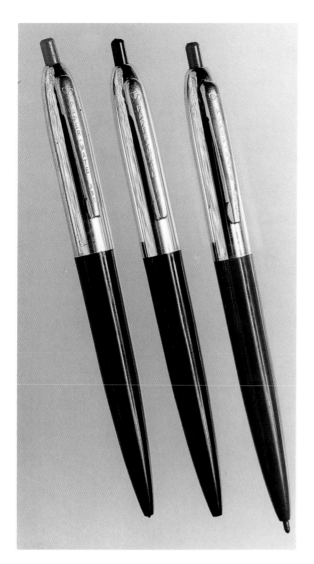

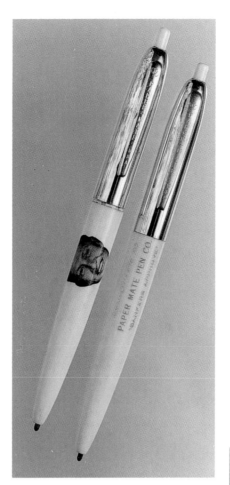

PAPER MATE, ca. 1953. Paper Mate button retractable pens with gold plated caps. Value $20-$25 each.

PAPER MATE, ca. 1953. Paper Mate button retractable pens in different colors. Value $20-$25.

PAPER MATE, ca. 1955. Paper Mate pen button retractable pens available in different "Tu-Tone" color combinations, some with Paper Mate advertising. "Silvered tip," "Widco" ink, one-click positive retractor action. Ads suggested matching Paper Mate colors to your new car's colors. Originally sold for $1.69. Value $20-$25 (with pen company advertising $40-$50).

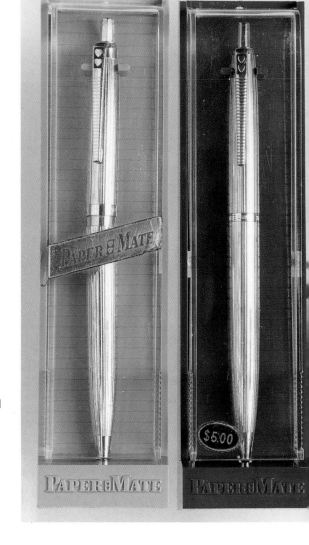

PAPER MATE, ca. 1957. Paper Mate button retractable metal pens with their original packaging. Value $25-$30 each.

PAPER MATE, ca. 1957. The "Capri No. 5" pen. It is gold plated metal with two small diamonds in the clip. Original cost was $50.00. Value $125-$150.

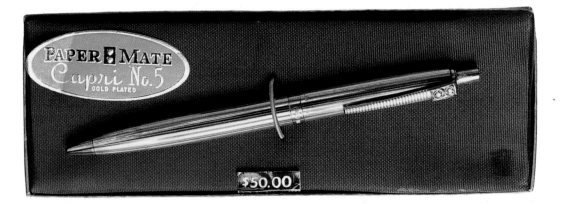

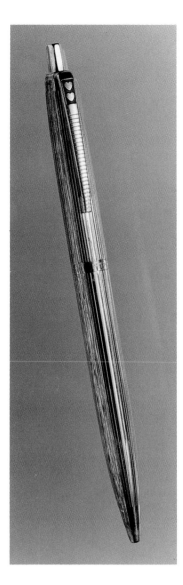

PAPER MATE, ca. 1957. Paper Mate "Capri Mark IV" button retractable, gold plated, metal pen. Value $20-$25.

PAPER MATE, ca. 1957-63. Lady Capri models. "Dark pink" (manufacturer's name for this color) barrel with red star bursts over metallic silver cap, black barrel with gold star bursts over metallic white cap, black with gold star bursts over creme cap, black barrel with gold star burst over gold cap. Very chic, fifty-ish, post-war design. Retractable, button. A single "Piggy-Back" metal refill. Most Paper Mates of this era had two refills, one inserted into the other (hence, "Piggy-Back" appellation and symbol displaying one heart atop another. Concept was that of a spare tank similar to that currently used by some European cartridge fountain pens). Value $30-$40 each.

PAPER MATE, ca. 1957-63. Lady Capri model with its original carry case for the purse, mint in the box along with another not offering the carry case. Value $30-$40.

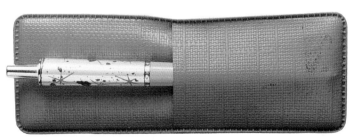

PAPER MATE, ca. 1958. Paper Mate's top of the line 14kt gold "Capri" pen with two diamonds in the clip. The original cost was $100. Value $200-$250.

PAPER MATE, ca. 1958. The "Golden Capri Mark IV" pen. It is gold filled metal with two small diamonds in the clip. It was offered to dealers as a prize for ordering an 11 dozen pen assortment. It was also available for $100. Value $90-$110.

PAPER MATE, ca. 1958. Paper Mate pen button retractable pen with a metal cap. Value $12-$15.

PAPER MATE, ca. 1959. Paper Mate "Holiday" button retractable pen with Paper Mate advertising. Value $9-$12 plain, $35-$40 with pen company advertising.

PAPER MATE, ca. 1959. Paper Mate "Capri III" button retractable pen with Paper Mate advertising. Value $9-$12 plain, $35-$40 with pen company advertising.

PAPER MATE, ca. 1959. The "Ninety-Eight" pen. It is plastic (available in different colors) and chrome with a retractor button above the pocket clip. Original cost was ninety eight cents. It was one of Paper Mate's best sellers. Value $15-$18.

PAPER MATE, ca. 1959. A great Paper Mate "Holiday" pen made to commemorate the 1959 World Series. Value $70-$95.

PAPER MATE, ca. 1960. Paper Mate "98" button retractable pens in different colors. Value $12-$15 each.

PAPER MATE, ca. 1959. Paper Mate "Capri Mark III" button retractable pens in their original packaging. Value $15-$25 each. in original packaging.

PAPER MATE, ca. 1960. Paper Mate Desk pen and base in black plastic. Value $25-$30.

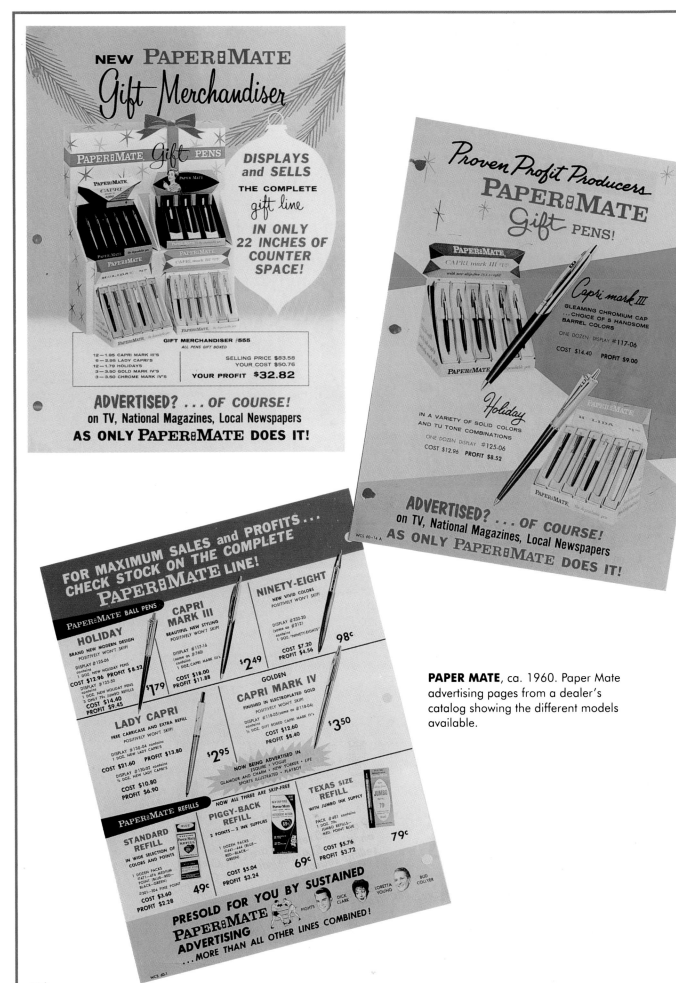

PAPER MATE, ca. 1960. Paper Mate advertising pages from a dealer's catalog showing the different models available.

PAPER MATE, 1960. Advertisement, starring Joe E. Brown, for Paper Mate's pens.

PAPER MATE, ca. 1962. Paper Mate advertising page from a dealer's catalog showing the different models available.

PAPER MATE, ca. 1963. A great Paper Mate "Capri Mark III" pen made to commemorate the 1963 World Series. Value $65-$85.

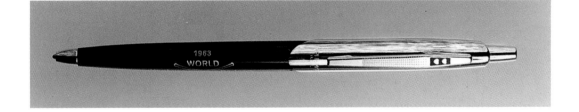

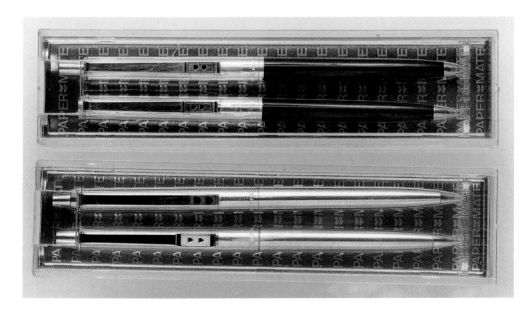

PAPER MATE, ca. 1963. Paper Mate button retractable pens and matching pencils in their original packaging. Value $25-$35 each.

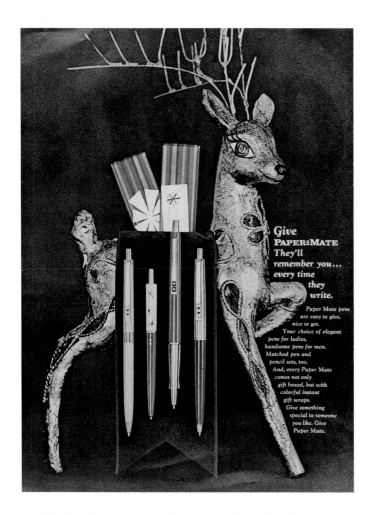

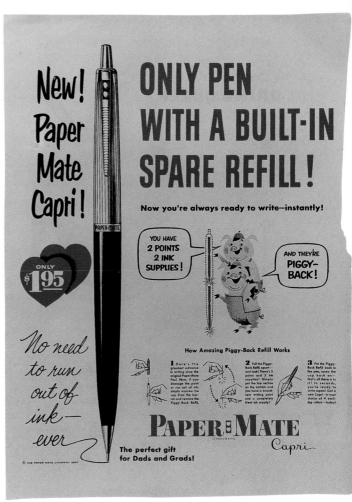

PAPER MATE, 1966. Advertisement for Paper Mate's pens.

PAPER MATE, 1966. Advertisement for Paper Mate's pen with a "piggy back" refill.

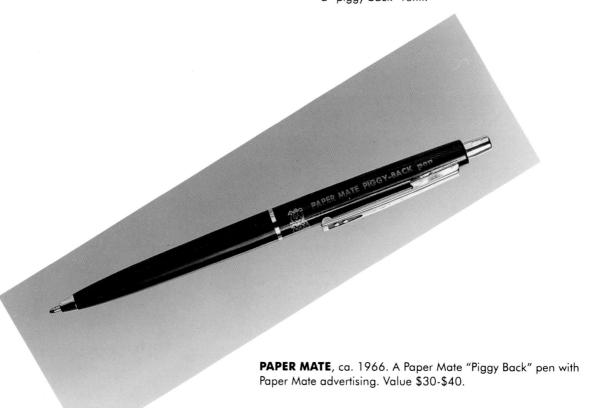

PAPER MATE, ca. 1966. A Paper Mate "Piggy Back" pen with Paper Mate advertising. Value $30-$40.

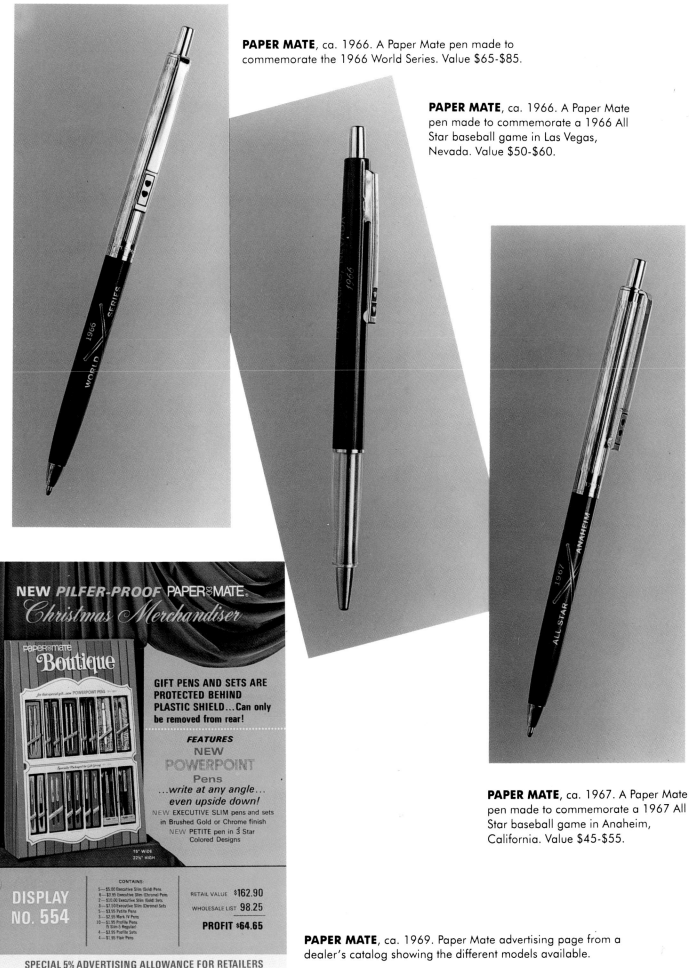

PAPER MATE, ca. 1966. A Paper Mate pen made to commemorate the 1966 World Series. Value $65-$85.

PAPER MATE, ca. 1966. A Paper Mate pen made to commemorate a 1966 All Star baseball game in Las Vegas, Nevada. Value $50-$60.

PAPER MATE, ca. 1967. A Paper Mate pen made to commemorate a 1967 All Star baseball game in Anaheim, California. Value $45-$55.

NEW *PILFER-PROOF* PAPER MATE.
Christmas Merchandiser

paper mate
Boutique

for that special gift...new POWERPOINT PENS

Specially Packaged for Gift Giving

GIFT PENS AND SETS ARE PROTECTED BEHIND PLASTIC SHIELD...Can only be removed from rear!

FEATURES
NEW
POWERPOINT
Pens
...write at any angle...
even upside down!
NEW EXECUTIVE SLIM pens and sets in Brushed Gold or Chrome finish
NEW PETITE pen in 3 Star Colored Designs

15" WIDE
22½" HIGH

DISPLAY NO. 554

CONTAINS:
5—$5.00 Executive Slim (Gold) Pens
6—$3.95 Executive Slim (Chrome) Pens
2—$10.00 Executive Slim (Gold) Sets
3—$7.50 Executive Slim (Chrome) Sets
5—$3.95 Petite Pens
5—$2.95 Mark IV Pens
10—$1.95 Profile Pens
(5 Slim-5 Regular)
4—$3.95 Profile Sets
4—$1.95 Flair Pens

RETAIL VALUE **$162.90**
WHOLESALE LIST **98.25**
PROFIT $64.65

SPECIAL 5% ADVERTISING ALLOWANCE FOR RETAILERS
POWERPOINT CHRISTMAS TELEVISION ADVERTISING
SEE REVERSE SIDE

PAPER MATE, ca. 1969. Paper Mate advertising page from a dealer's catalog showing the different models available.

PAPER MATE, ca. 1974. A Paper Mate pen made to commemorate the 1974 World Series. Value $35-$45.

PAPER MATE, ca. 1974. A Paper Mate souvenir to commemorate its involvement with the World Series. Value $45-$55.

PARKER, Earlier Jotters (1954-1980) have a threaded brass bushing in the cap.

PARKER, Later Jotters (1980-present) have a threaded plastic bushing in the cap.

PARKER, The push button was rounded on top and had no arrow imprint before 1973. From 1973, the top of the button was flattened and the Parker imprint was stamped in it.

PARKER, ca. 1946? The Blue Diamond cap is a 1945-46 vintage piece that goes to a Parker 51 fountain pen. The barrel fits like it was made for the cap. Perhaps it is an early Parker prototype for a ball point pen, or perhaps a homemade variation. Value $35-$50.

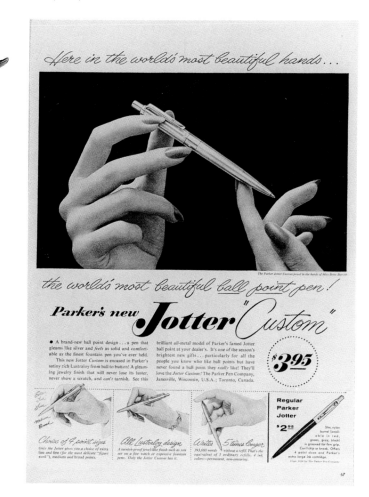

PARKER, 1954. Advertisement for the Parker "Jotter Custom" pen.

PARKER, ca. 1951. Parker's first ball point, the Hopalong Cassidy Ballpen. Value $80-$90.

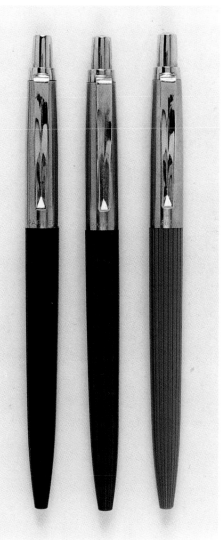

PARKER JOTTER, ca. 1954-56. A group of three first clip style Parker Jotters. The original models had nylon grooved barrels, called a "Grooved Grip," with no tip protector. The cap had a threaded brass bushing into which the barrel screwed. The three colors are black (first year color), dark gray, and light gray (first year color). They originally sold for $2.95. Value $60-$75.

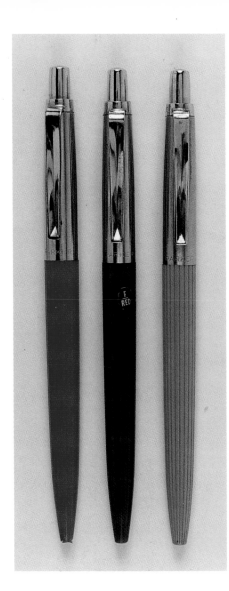

PARKER JOTTER, ca. 1954-56. A group of three nylon bodied first clip style Parker Jotters. The three colors are red (first year color), blue, and orange. Value $60-$75.

PARKER JOTTER, 1954. A transparent first year Jotter demonstrator. Parker used the clear barrel to show that the ink refill rotated with each click of the button and also the huge capacity of the refill unit. Value $250-$275.

PARKER JOTTER, ca. 1954. A gray first year Jotter in its original packaging. Value $75-$85.

PARKER JOTTER, ca. 1954. A difficult to find Jotter "Custom" Jotter in burnished stainless steel. It originally sold for $3.95. Value $85-$100.

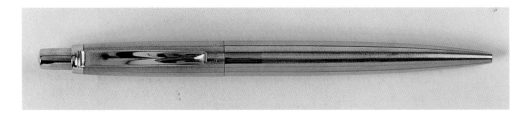

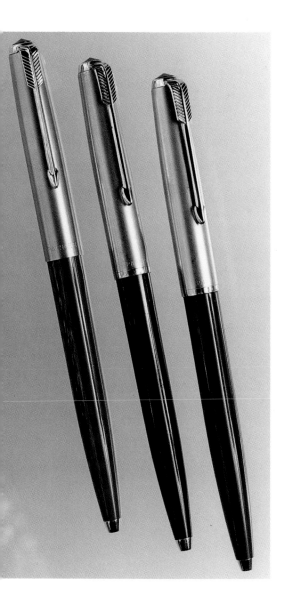

PARKER 51 JOTTER, 1955. The Parker "51" Jotter was an addition to the Parker 51 fountain pen and pencil line. It came with a Lustraloy cap and used the Jotter refill. Originally priced at $5.00. It was renamed the "V.I.P." in 1958. The three colors shown are blue, black, and green. Value $70-90.

PARKER 51 JOTTER, 1955. The Parker "51" Custom Jotter. The gold filled Custom model is difficult to find. Value $125-145.

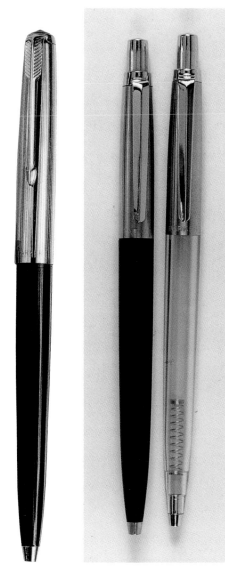

PARKER 51 JOTTER, ca. 1955 and 1957. The Parker "51" Jotter on the left and the "51 Custom" on the right. They are very tough to find. Value $75-100 (51), $125-$145 (51 Custom).

PARKER LABORATORY JOTTER, ca. 1957. In 1957, Parker introduced this stainless steel version of their Jotter pen (with the "21" clip) and called it the "Laboratory Jotter." Tough to find. Value $80-$90.

PARKER "21" JOTTER, ca. 1957. Two "21" models. The first clip of the Jotter had a V shaped indent running down the center. In the "21" model, it had a raised V shape running down the center like the Parker 21 fountain pen. This style clip only lasted a few years. Value (black) $40-$50, demonstrator $125-175.

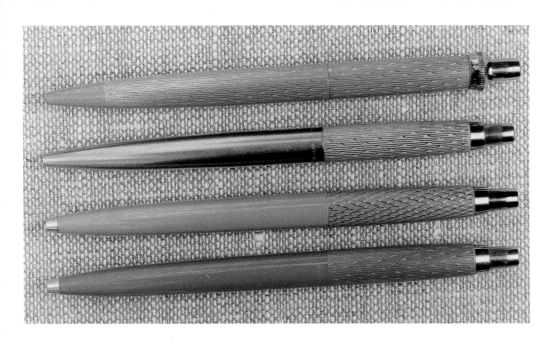

PARKER DEBUTANTE JOTTER, ca. 1957. The Debutante Jotter with an engraved design was available in several colors, finishes and without a clip. The Debutante name became the "Princess" in late 1958. The Princess with plain barrel cost $5.00, with a decorated barrel and cap it cost $7.50 and with a hand engraved floral pattern it cost $10.00. Value $45-$60 each.

PARKER MINIM JOTTER, ca. 1958. The vest or pant's pocket Jotter, called the "Minim," was shorter than the standard models. The gold filled model was $8.75 and a 14kt gold model cost $25.00. The mechanism to keep the pen point extended used a spring metal piece to lock the point in extended position. Value $65-$75 in gold filled metal. Model shown is 14kt, cap and barrel. Value $250-$350.

PARKER DEBUTANTE JOTTER, ca. 1958. The Debutante Jotter with a hand engraved design was available in several colors and finishes. In late 1958, Parker changed the name to the "Princess." Value $60-$70.

PARKER MINIM JOTTER, ca. 1958. The "Minim" was shorter than the standard models and cost $5.00 when new. Value $50-$55 each.

PARKER PRINCESS JOTTER, ca. 1959. The Parker Princess Jotter with a clip is rare. The Princess was introduced in 1958 as the evolution of the 1957 Debutante. It was made for ladies and did not have a pocket clip. The pocket clip model may be a prototype. Value $75-$85.

PARKER, 1959. Advertisement for the Parker "Minim" pen.

PARKER, 1959. Advertisement for the Parker "V.I.P." pen.

PARKER, 1959. Advertisement for the Parker "International" pen.

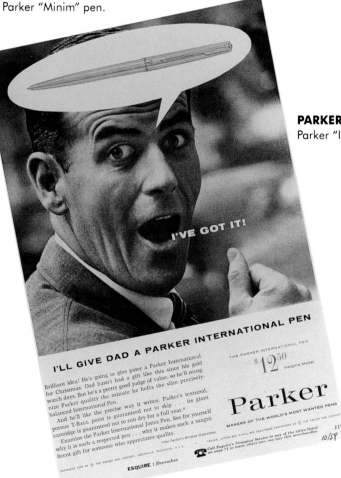

PARKER JOTTER, ca. 1960. A prototype black button Parker Jotter. Parker was constantly trying different materials to expand its popular Jotter line. Many unusual pieces have come out of the Parker design labs. Value $40-$55.

PARKER JOTTER, ca. 1959 and 1962. The Parker "V.I.P." Jotter on the top and the "61" on the bottom. Note that the arrow clips have more feathers than earlier models. Value $75-$85.

PARKER 61 JOTTER, 1962-1971. The 61 Jotter was made to go with the Parker 61 fountain pen and pencil. Value $65-$85.

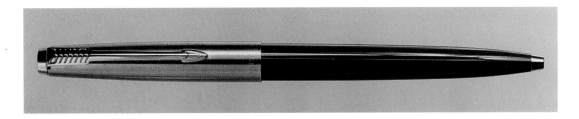

PARKER "45" JOTTER, ca. 1962. The Parker "45" Jotter. It used the Jotter refill and has a 45 fountain pen shape. Value $40-50.

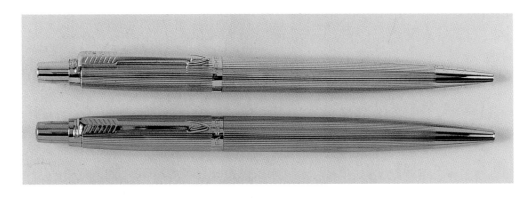

PARKER "45" JOTTER, ca. 1963. Two hard to find lined metal Parker Jotters that would go into a 45 set. They were only made for a year or two. Gold filled on the bottom and chrome plated on the top. Value $60-$80 each.

PARKER JOTTER, ca. 1963. Two hard to find lined metal Parker Jotters. Gold filled caps on a black and on a brown barrel. Value $45-$65 each.

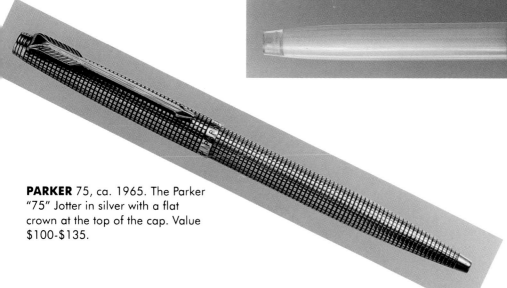

PARKER 75, ca. 1965. The Parker "75" Jotter in silver with a flat crown at the top of the cap. Value $100-$135.

PARKER, ca. 1964. Parker created this Jotter style saccharin (sugar substitute) dispenser. When the white button is pushed, a small plunger comes out the point end and gives one serving of sugar substitute. Very rare. Value $40-$50.

PARKER JOTTER, ca. 1965. The hard to find smaller and shorter Compact Jotters. These were made for women with smaller hands and were sometimes referred to as "girl size". They can be found in a set with a pocket note pad. Green, blue, black, and gray. Shown with a regular sized Parker Jotter. Value $30-$40 each.

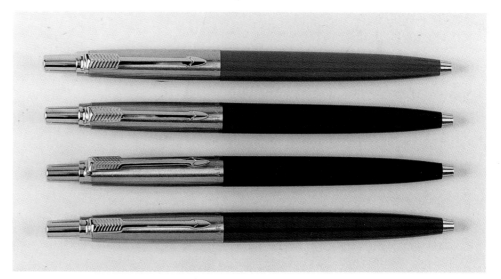

111

PARKER JOTTER, ca. 1965. A Jotter Desk pen in brushed chrome and black. Value $25-$30.

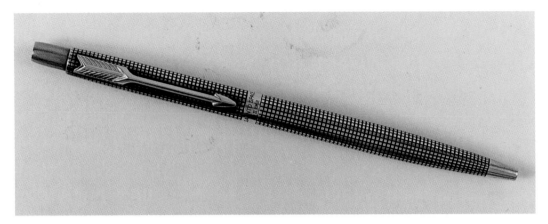

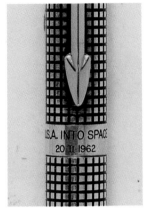

PARKER CLASSIC 75, ca. 1966. A very rare sterling silver pen that incorporates a piece of metal from John Glenn's booster rocket, recovered in Africa, as the push button. The imprint says "U.S.A. into Space, 20 II 1962". There were allegedly 125 of these pens made by Parker for NASA and Government officials. They rarely appear for sale. Value $1,200-$1,300. The Parker Classic 75 fountain pen was introduced in 1963 to celebrate Parker's 75th anniversary and the ball point pen about a year later. The standard Classic 75 in this style is valued at $55-$65.

PARKER CLASSIC 75, ca. 1966. The Parker Classic "75" Jotter in silver. Value $55-$65.

PARKER 75, ca. 1966. The Parker "75" Jotter in a Vermeil (gold plated sterling silver) with a flat crown at the top of the cap. Later models have an indentation in the top of the crown. Value $100-$135.

PARKER TIARA JOTTER, ca. 1967.
The Tiara Jotter was made for a lady's
or girl's hand and had a diamond cut
design on the ring below the button.
Value $40-$50.

PARKER JOTTER, ca. 1969. This was a special pen made to
commemorate Astronaut Wally Schirra's visit to the Parker
factory. Value $40-$45.

PARKER T-1,
1970. The T-1
was a titanium
pen. Parker
produced a T-1
fountain pen to
commemorate
man's landing on
the moon.
Titanium is an
extremely light,
high-tech metal
that does not
tarnish or rust
and is popularly
used in the
aerospace
industry. Working
a pen out of
titanium was too
costly and the
fountain pen was
discontinued after
about a year. The
ball point and felt
tip T-1s were
probably
dropped at about
the same time.
Value $200-
$250.

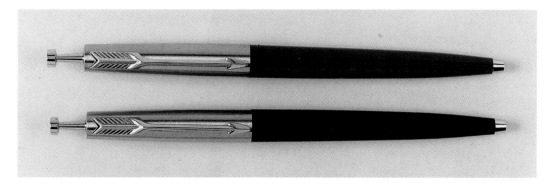

PARKER JOTTER, ca. 1969. Two prototype vase top Parker
Jotters. The two colors are black and green. Value $40-$45
each.

PARKER JOTTER, ca. 1970. A group of three prototype matte finish barreled Jotters.
Parker was forever trying out new variations in color, finish, and style of the Jotter. Most
prototypes were made in the Parker design workshops and come from the collections of
former Parker designers. The colors are purple, blue, and gray. Value $50-$65 each.

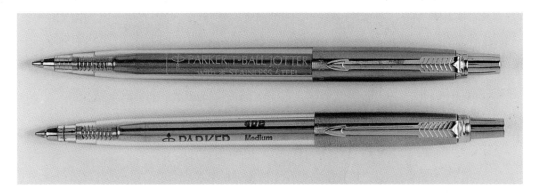

PARKER JOTTER, ca. 1970 and 1980. Two demonstrator clear-barreled Jotters. The top model is earlier and has a brass bushing. The model on the bottom has a plastic bushing. Value (top) $55-$65, (bottom) $45-$50.

PARKER JOTTER, ca. 1971, 1980. Two Window Jotters with Parker advertising. When the button is pushed, the message in the clear window of the pen changes. The message is printed on the refill. One advertises Parker Window Jotters (1971) and the other was presented by Parker to security analysts, financial institutions, and selected press people in 1980. Value $50-$75 each, with Parker advertising.

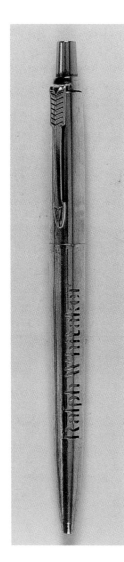

PARKER JOTTER, ca. 1973. A rare Jotter with a complete Sterling Silver overlay and the later style push button. Value $150-$175.

PARKER JOTTER, 1974. A "milestone" pen made to celebrate the production of the 100 millionth Jotter. Value $40-50.

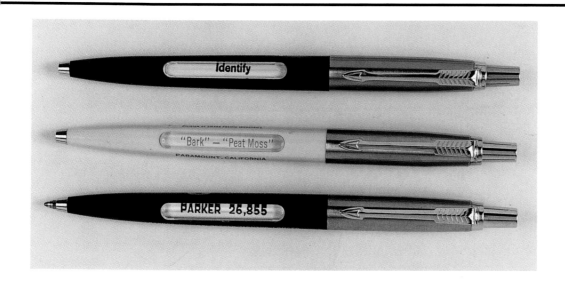

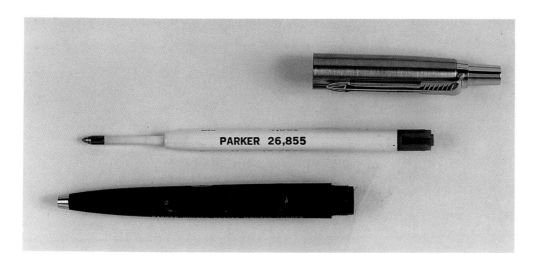

PARKER JOTTER, ca. 1979. Three hard-to-find Window Jotters. The Window models were introduced in 1958. When the button is pushed, the message in the clear window of the pen changes. The message is printed on the refill. Two are especially desirable in that they are Parker Pen Company advertising models. Value (with Parker advertising) $60-$75, other advertising $20-$35.

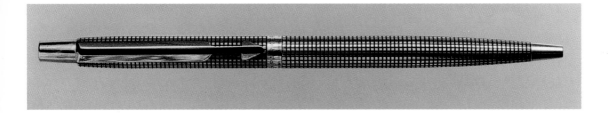

PARKER CLASSIC 75, ca. 1979. This sterling silver model with a long arrow clip may have been made up to see if there was customer interest. Value $75-$100.

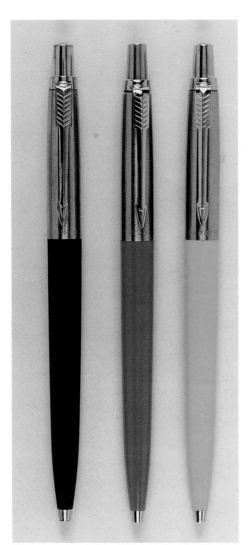

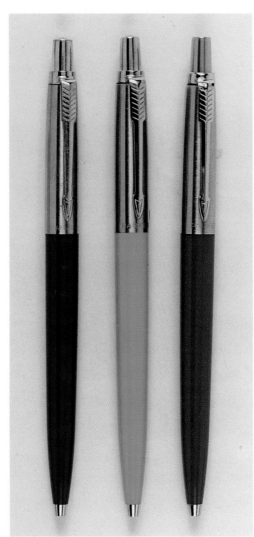

PARKER JOTTER, ca. 1985. A salesman's sample Jotter showing four types of engraving, imprinting, or hot stamping that were available to the customer. Value $55-$65.

PARKER JOTTER, ca. 1980. These unusual colored Parker Jotters were made for the South African market. Colors shown are green, red, yellow, maroon, light blue, and blue. Value $20-$25.

PARKER JOTTER, ca. 1985 and 1995. Presidential model Parker Jotters. The President gives these to visitors and guests of the White House. Value $35-$50.

PARKER JOTTER, 1994. An anniversary pen made to celebrate the 40th anniversary of the Parker Jotter. Value $30-$40.

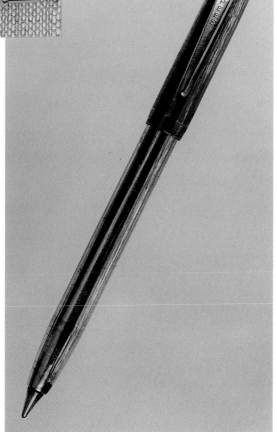

PEN-ETTE, ca. 1964. This pen was made to resemble a lipstick case and was made in Waterbury, Connecticut. Value $8-$10.

PEER, ca. 1948. A brass and aluminum pen that retracts and extends by pushing the cap down and turning it to lock. Value $25-$30.

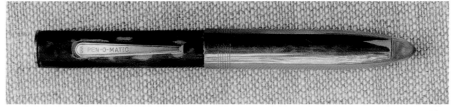

PEN-O-MATIC, ca. 1953. A push on the plastic barrel toward the metal cap made a trap door open and the pen point come out. Value $30-$35.

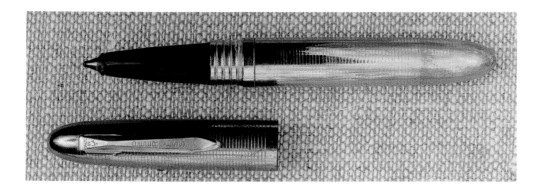

PEERLESS, ca. 1957. A brass and plastic pen with the center area made of turned heavy brass. Value $6-$9.

PELIKAN, ca. 1955. The German made Pelikan ball point, model 455, was made in this striped brown and green tortoise color for only a few years. Value $40-$50.

PENMAN, ca. 1954. A simple black plastic pen with a screw thread cap. Value $6-$9.

PRESTO, ca. 1950. A metal, button retractable pen made of gold plated brass. Value $25-$45.

REDIPEN, ca. 1948-51 Brushed aluminum with black barrel. Permanently installed refill, the cap twists to retract the point, nicely finished. Value $25-$30.

REDIPEN, ca. 1948-51 Gold plated with brown barrel. Permanently installed refill, non-retracting, nicely finished. Value $30-$35.

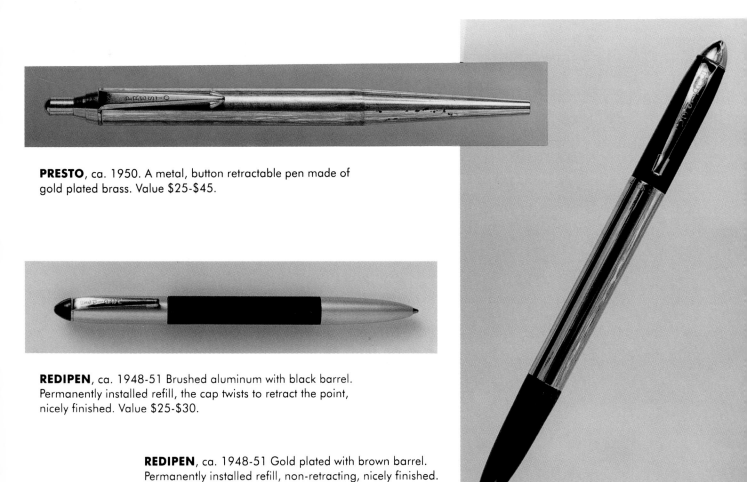

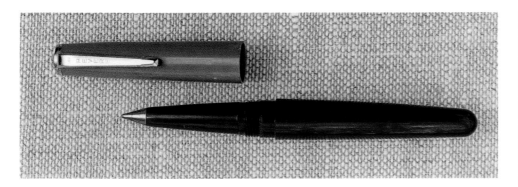

REVERE, ca. 1956. Possibly made by Revere Copper & Brass Company. This pen is made mostly of plastic. Value $6-$9.

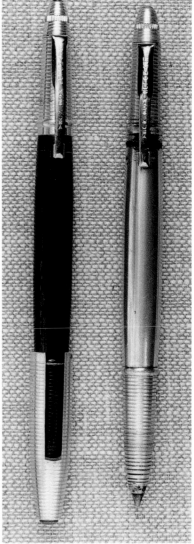

REYNOLDS INTERNATIONAL, ca. 1945. Several examples of the original Reynold's "International" pen with the aluminum cap. They are made of plain, painted, and anodized aluminum. Original cost was $12.50. Value $75-$90 each.

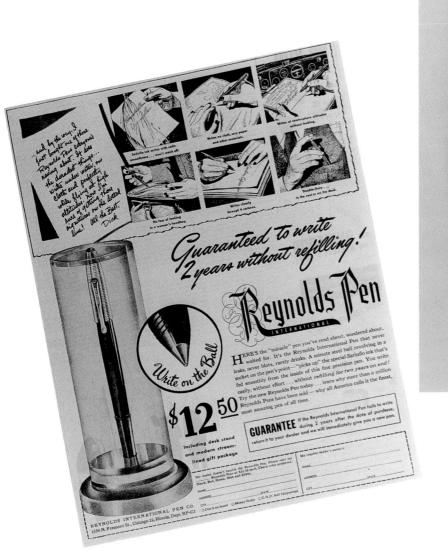

REYNOLDS, 1946. Advertisement for the Reynolds "International" pen.

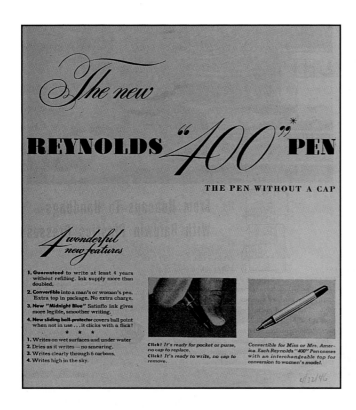

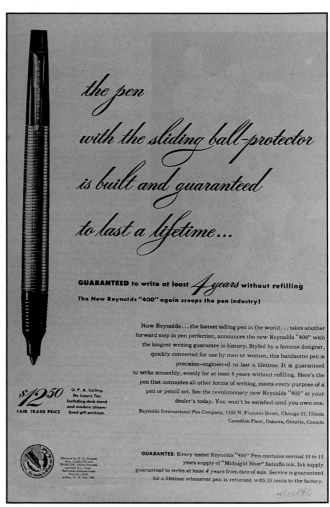

REYNOLDS, 1946. Advertisement for the Reynolds "400" pen.

REYNOLDS, ca. 1946. The Reynolds "400" pen. These are full sized pens in gold anodized or plain aluminum. The ink tube is fixed in place and the aluminum sleeve extends and retracts. Value $50-$65 each.

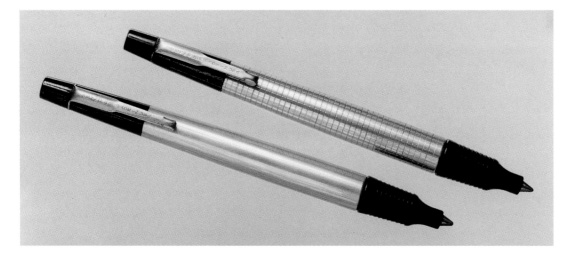

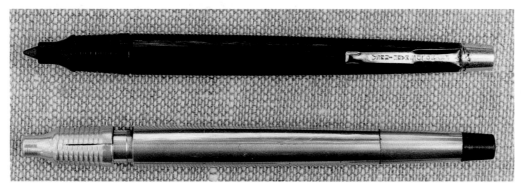

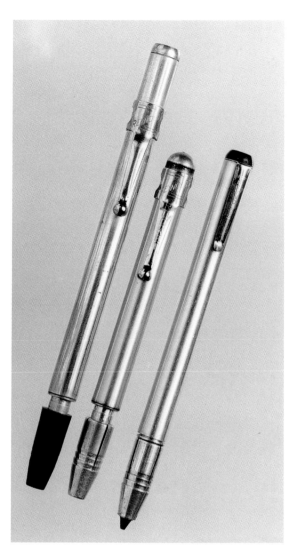
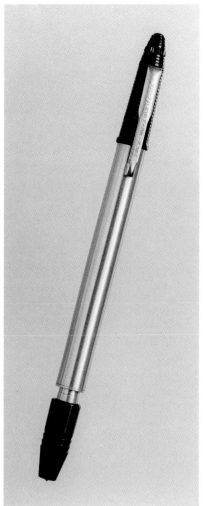
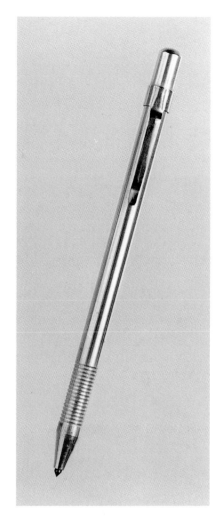

REYNOLDS, ca. 1946. Reynolds "Rocket" pens. Variations in Aluminum. Value $50-$60 each.

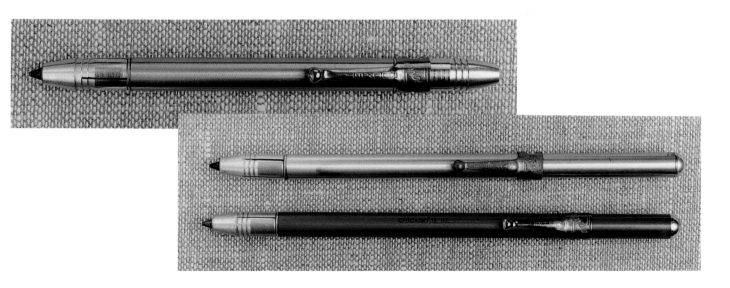

REYNOLDS ROCKET, ca. 1946. Examples of the standard and long (7 inches) Reynold's Rocket pens with the point fixed in place. The aluminum sleeve extends and retracts. It is made of plain and anodized aluminum. Value $40-$50.

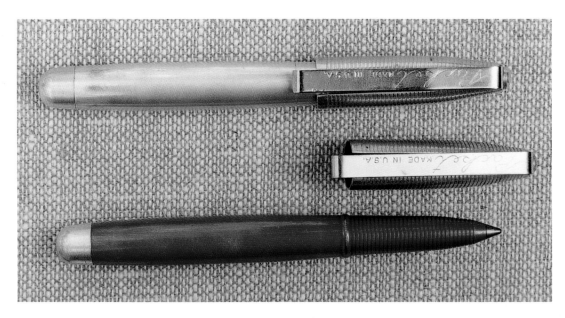

REYNOLDS, ca. 1947. The Reynolds Packet pen. Reynolds produced this smaller companion pen to its Rocket pen. The clips of these do not have Reynold's name on them. Aluminum. Value $40-$45.

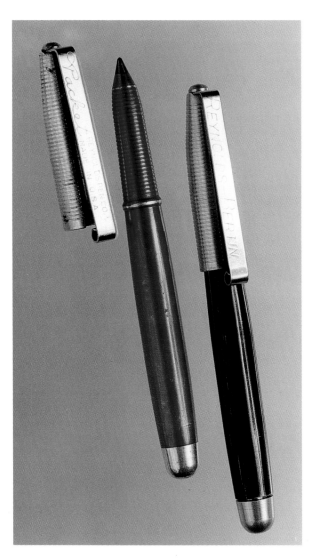

REYNOLDS, ca. 1947. The Reynolds Packet pen. Reynolds produced this smaller companion pen to its Rocket pen. The clips of these have Reynold's name on them. Aluminum. Value $40-$45.

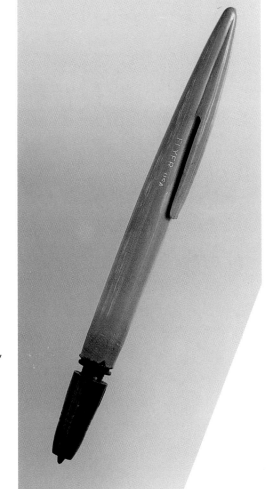

REYNOLDS, ca. 1947. The "Flyer" was Reynolds' attempt to introduce a plastic pen. Value $60-$75.

REYNOLDS, 1995. A 50th anniversary Reynolds reproduction pen.

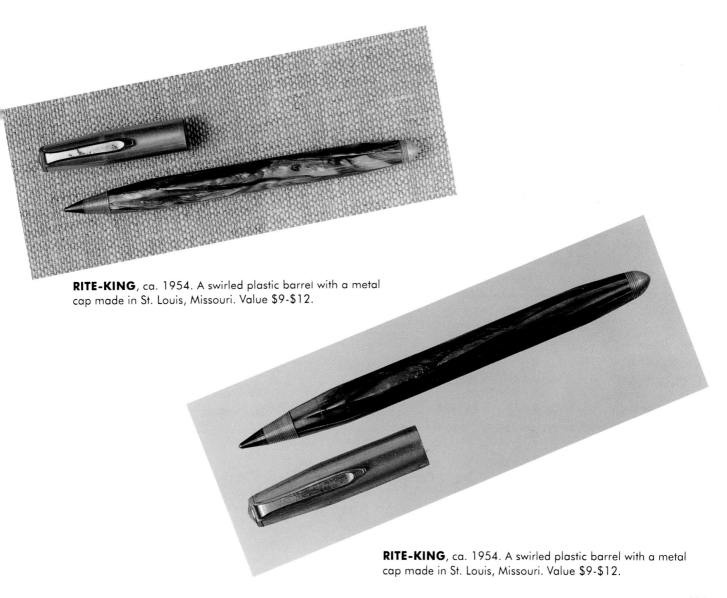

RITE-KING, ca. 1954. A swirled plastic barrel with a metal cap made in St. Louis, Missouri. Value $9-$12.

RITE-KING, ca. 1954. A swirled plastic barrel with a metal cap made in St. Louis, Missouri. Value $9-$12.

RITE-KING, ca. 1955. A plastic pen/pencil combination with great styling. Value $20-$25.

RITEPOINT, ca. 1952. A nicely made plastic pen with metal cap. Value $8-$10.

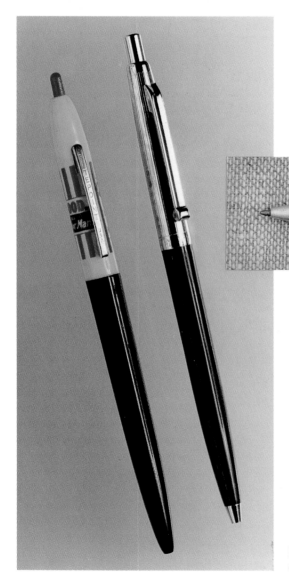

ROCKET, ca. 1952. The Rocket pen was made of thin aluminum and the point extended and retracted by pushing down on the cap. Note: not related to Reynolds. Value $20-$25.

RITEPOINT, ca. 1952-60. Well made pens, often found with advertising on them. Value $8-$12.

ROLBALL, ca. 1949. A metal capped pen with cut out windows in the lower end of the cap. Value $15-$25.

ROLLIT, 1948. Advertisement for Rollit dollar pens.

ROLLIT, 1947. Advertisement for the Rollit Convertible pen.

ROLLIT, ca. 1948. An interesting plastic pen with a metal cap. To use the "Rollit Retractable" pen, the cap was pushed down and the point extended. To retract the point, you pushed the cap back up. Made by the Diversey Machine Works in Chicago. Value $15-$25.

ROLLIT, ca. 1948. An Aluminum and plastic pen that retracts and extends by pushing the cap down and turning it to lock. Value $65-$85.

ROLLS, ca. 1946-47. The Rolls pen, made by Continental, is an early competitor of the Reynolds. Two models in aluminum and anodized aluminum. Value $45-$50.

ROLLS, ca. 1947. The Rolls pen is an early competitor of the Reynolds. Anodized aluminum. Value $45-$50.

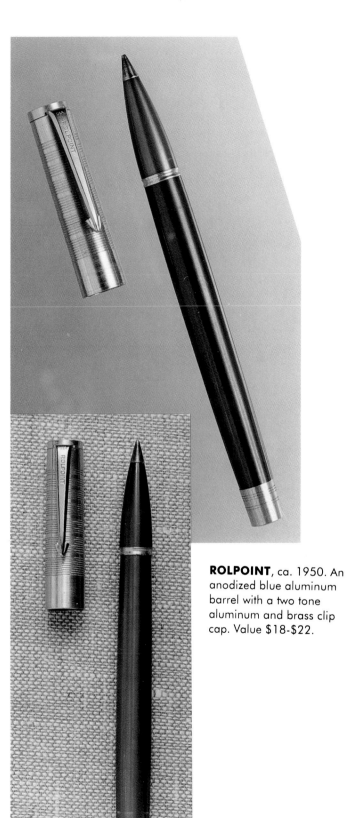

ROMUR, ca. 1955. A simple and inexpensively made three color pen. Value $8-$10.

ROLPOINT, ca. 1950. An anodized blue aluminum barrel with a two tone aluminum and brass clip cap. Value $18-$22.

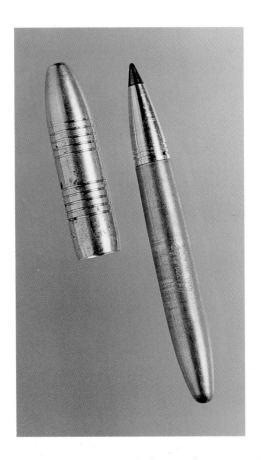

RONNIE, ca. 1947. A small aluminum pen only 4 inches long. Value $30-$35.

SCRIPTO, 1955. Advertisement for Scripto pens.

SCRIPTO, 1956. Advertisement for the Scripto "Feathertone" twenty-nine cent pen.

RONNIE, ca. 1947. A small aluminum pen only 4 inches long. Value $30-$35.

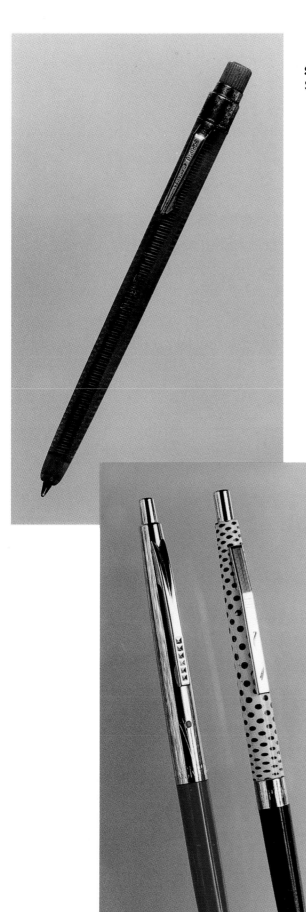

SCRIPTO, ca. 1956. A nice early green plastic stick pen. Value $5-$7.

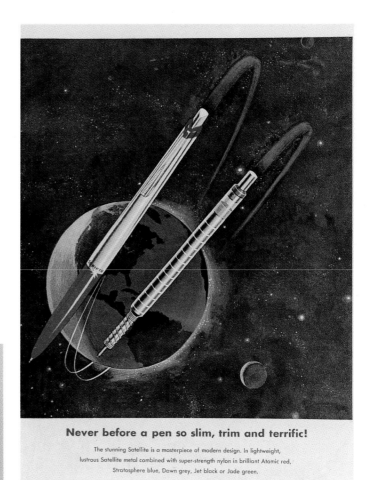

Never before a pen so slim, trim and terrific!

The stunning Satellite is a masterpiece of modern design. In lightweight, lustrous Satellite metal combined with super-strength nylon in brilliant Atomic red, Stratosphere blue, Dawn grey, Jet black or Jade green.

SCRIPTO, 1958. Advertisement for the Scripto "Satellite" pen and refill.

SCRIPTO, 1958. The Scripto "Satellite" pen. Value $12-$18.

SCRIPTO, 1958. Advertisement for the Scripto "Super Dollar" pen.

SCRIPTO, 1964. Advertisement for the Scripto "Tilt-Tip" pen.

SHEAFFER, 1947. Advertisement for Sheaffer's "Stratowriter" pen.

SHEAFFER, 1947. Advertisement for Sheaffer's "Crest Deluxe Threesomes."

SHEAFFER, ca. 1947. A group of "Tuckaway Stratowriters." The short clip models were called "Tuckaway." The second pen from the left is a "Crest Tuckaway Deluxe Stratowriter." The blue pen on the right is the "Valiant Tuckaway." $35-$45 each.

SHEAFFER, ca. 1948. Sheaffer's Crest Deluxe set—a Triumph nibbed fountain pen, a mechanical pencil, and the "Stratowriter" ball point pen in a gold filled trim. The ball point had a small bump at the top of the clip to identify it. Value $150-$200 (set), $35-$45 ball point pen alone.

SHEAFFER, ca. 1948. Sheaffer's Sentinel Deluxe Stratowriter ball point pen in a chrome and gold filled trim. Note the small bump at the top of the clip to identify it as a ball point pen. Value $30-$35.

SHEAFFER, ca. 1948. Sheaffer's "Statesman Stratowriter" ball point pens in three versions. They may be found in sets with Sheaffer's Triumph fountain pens. $35-$45 each.

SHEAFFER, 1948. Advertisement for Sheaffer's ball tip pens.

SHEAFFER, 1949. Three advertisements for Sheaffer's "Micro-Crafted" refills.

SHEAFFER, ca. 1950. Sheaffer's "Valiant Stratowriter" in green and "Saratoga Stratowriter" ball point pen in black. They may be found in sets with Sheaffer's Triumph fountain pens. $35-$45 each.

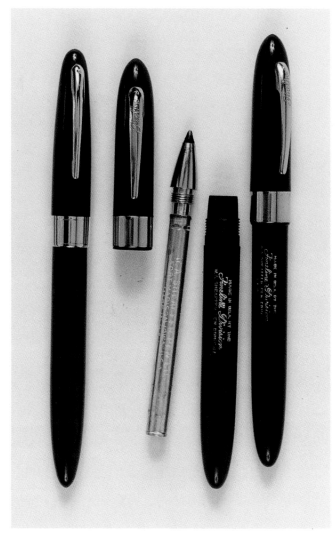

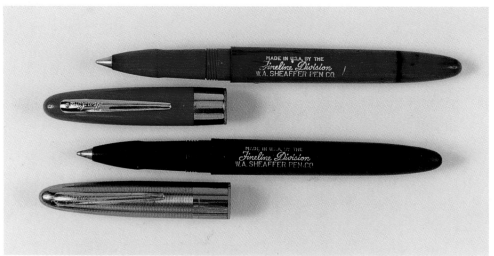

SHEAFFER, ca. 1950-1956. Sheaffer's Fineline division was usually reserved for their lower priced pens. Shown are variations in color—brown, black, maroon, red, and black with gold plated cap; and finish—nickel plated trim and gold filled trim. Value $15-$20.

SHEAFFER, ca. 1950-1956. A group of pens in various colors, cap styles, grip areas, and size variations from Sheaffer's Fineline division. Value $15-$20 each.

SHEAFFER, ca. 1952. A smaller Sheaffer Stratowriter pen, 4 inches long, with a great image of the Sheaffer factory and advertising Sheaffer's open house in August 1952. Value $45-$55.

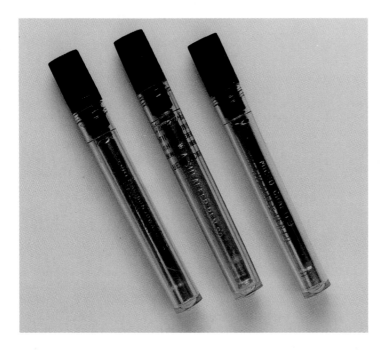

SHEAFFER, ca. 1952. Three Stratowriter refills in their plastic cases. $5-$10 each.

GUARANTEED TO WRITE FIVE TIMES LONGER !

THE BRAND NEW

Fineline "500"

RETRACTABLE BALLPOINT PEN

No other ballpoint gives you ALL these features . . .

RETRACTABLE	WON'T TRANSFER	STARTS INSTANTLY	CHOICE OF COLORS
WON'T SMEAR	WON'T STAIN	DRIES INSTANTLY	BANKER APPROVED
WON'T LEAK	WON'T FADE	SMOOTH WRITING	NO CAP TO LOSE

PLUS

500% more writing mileage Guaranteed

Only Fineline can give you this money-back guarantee!

No other ballpoint can dare compare the capacity of its writing unit with Fineline "500". Here's why: Fineline "500" has a completely new, exclusive type of writing unit. It is fully protected by U.S. patents. It cannot be duplicated. Go to your dealer and have him show you the skinny unit of any other ballpoint alongside Fineline's massive unit. Compare and see for yourself why Fineline "500" writes five times longer. No other ballpoint can write as long because no other ballpoint holds as much ink! So end refill worries today . . . buy a Fineline "500" — it writes smooth and long like a ballpoint pen should!

BUY *Fineline 500* **. . . END REFILL WORRIES TODAY!**

Compare!

GIANT CAPACITY OF FINELINE "500"   SMALL CAPACITY OF ORDINARY BALLPOINTS

Special Introductory Price $**1**95

© 1953, FINELINE, a division of W. A. Sheaffer Pen Company

Fineline **PENS**
• Biggest one-stroke capacity of any pen!
• Points tipped with precious metal!
• Interchangeable point styles!
• Metal or plastic caps; colored barrels!
$**2**10

Fineline **PENCILS**
• "Viewpoint" tip to reduce lead breakage!
• Easy in-and-out lead action!
• Spiral finger grip!
• Lead storage compartment!
$**1**65

SHEAFFER, 1953. Advertisement for the Sheaffer "Fineline 500" pen.

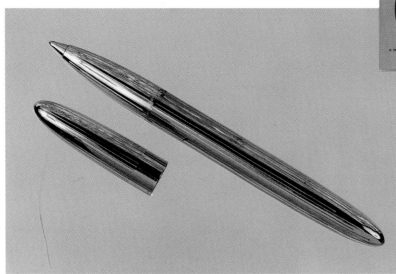

SHEAFFER, ca. 1952. A gold filled metal pen. Value $20-$25.

SHEAFFER, ca. 1954 and 1957. Two Sheaffer pens. One to match the Sentinel Fountain pen (note interesting indented finger grip area) and the earlier one from the Fineline Division. Value $10-$15.

SHEAFFER, ca. 1955. This pen was the prize in 1955 for the finalists of a spelling bee sponsored by the Herald Journal. Value $12-$15.

SHEAFFER DEMONSTRATOR, ca. 1956. A Sheaffer demonstrator, click retractable. Value $60-$70.

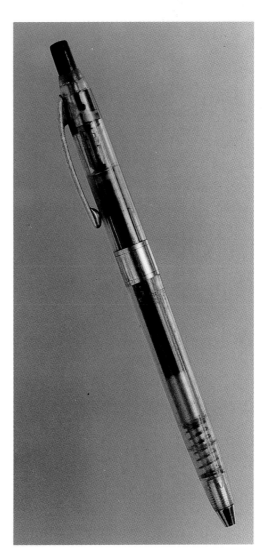

SHEAFFER, 1957. Advertisement for Sheaffer's sterling silver ball point pen.

SHEAFFER, 1957. The Sheaffer "Clicker" ball point pen. Value $15-$20.

SHEAFFER, ca. 1958. A rare pair. Sheaffer touchdown filler "Skripsert" fountain pen and matching ball point. The touchdown filling system in fountain pens was available from 1949 to the 1960s. Skripserts fountain pens, 1958-1964, are usually found as cartridge fillers. Value (set) $120-$150.

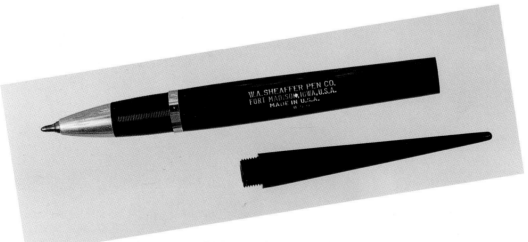

SHEAFFER, ca. 1957. A black plastic Sheaffer desk pen. Value $20-$25.

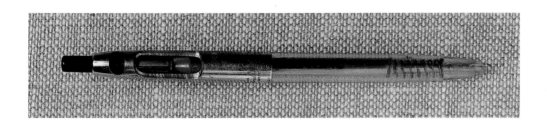

SHEAFFER DEMONSTRATOR, ca. 1958. A Sheaffer Fine Line demonstrator, click retractable. Value $45-$55.

SHEAFFER, ca. 1958. A Sheaffer click retractable with a rectangular button. It uses the multi metal finger-like retractor. Value $15-$20.

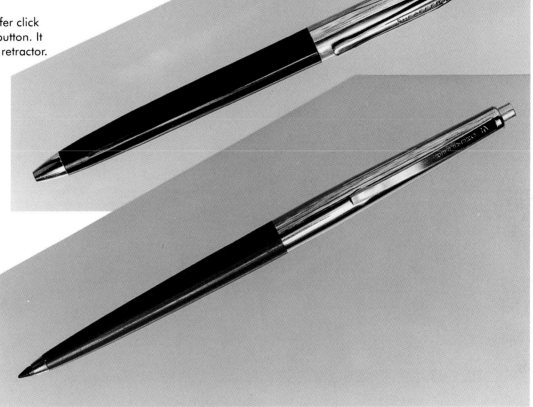

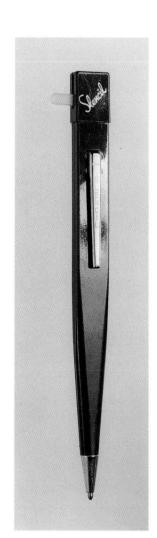

SHEAFFER, ca. 1962. A Sheaffer click retractable with a super smooth action. Value $15-$20.

SLENCIL, ca. 1965. A plastic flattened pen with an interesting retractor lever. Value $9-$12.

SHEAFFER DEMONSTRATOR, ca. 1965. Transparent Sheaffer demonstrators. Value $50-$65.

SOLAR POWERED PEN, ca. 1978. A clear plastic barrel with a cute imprint. Value $7-$10.

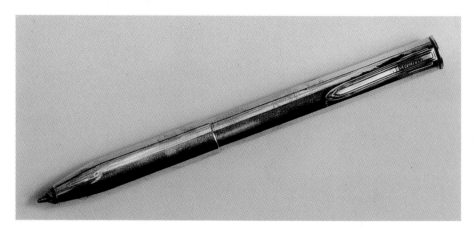

STERLING, ca. 1949. This early pen, made of sterling silver, may not actually be a "Sterling" pen, but that is the name stamped on the clip. The front end slides backward to expose the point and forward to cover the point. The refill may be inserted from the point end. Value $40-$45.

STRATFORD, 1947. Advertisement for Stratford's "Celebrity" pen.

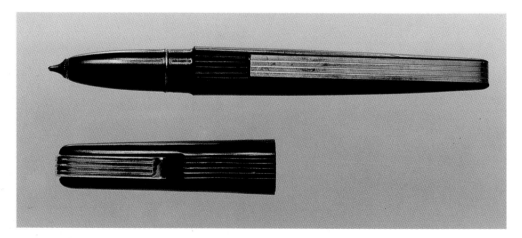

STRATFORD, 1947. The Stratford "Celebrity" pen in plastic and gold plated metal trim. The pen had a flattened cross section so that it would not roll off a table. Stratford had a flair for making futuristic looking pens and is known for its Roy Rogers and rocket shaped fountain pens. Value $20-$25.

STRATFORD, April 1948. Advertisement for Stratford's Name It contest.

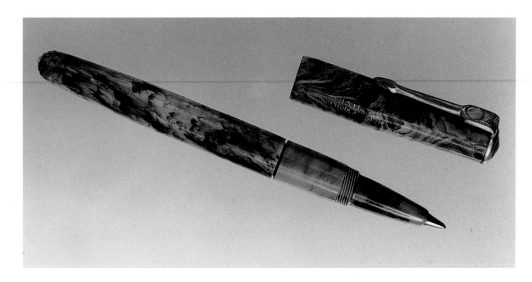

STRATO, ca. 1945. An early plastic pen in a blue/gray marble from the Industria Argentina Company in South America and probably made under the Biro patent. It consists of three separate ink tubes fused together. The barrel uses a reverse thread. Value $150-$200.

STYLEKING, ca. 1947-49 All aluminum, anodized barrel, ribbed end. Brushed, press-fit aluminum cap, pop-riveted steel clip. Factory installed aluminum refill. Blind-cap unscrews for refill replacement by factory. Value $55-$75.

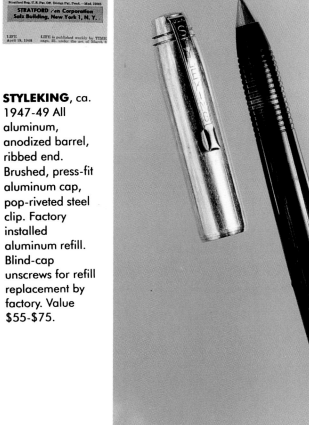

TIFFANY, ca. 1959. A small sterling silver pen, made in Germany, only 4 inches long. Value $50-$55.

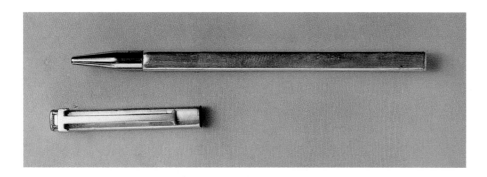

TIFFANY, ca. 1965. A square sterling silver pen with the signature Tiffany "T" clip. Value $40-$45.

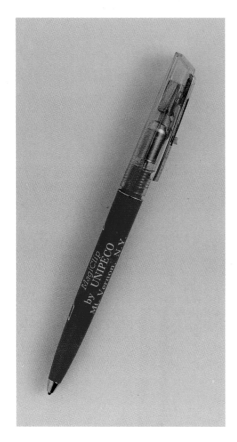

TOWER, ca. 1948. The Tower ball pen has an interesting cap. It is plastic and gold plated metal. It closely resembles the Conqueror pen. Value $10-$15.

UNIPECO, ca. 1955-66. Magiclip model. Plastic demonstrator, clear cap to show mechanism. Made in Mt. Vernon, New York. This mechanism is similar to later Mont Blanc pens. Value $25-$30.

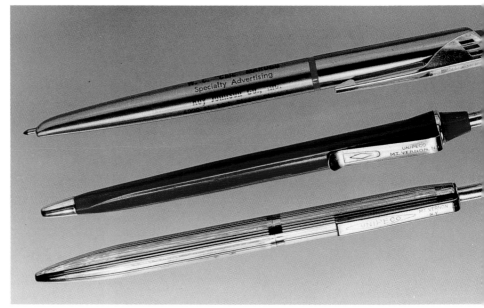

UNIPECO, ca. 1955-66. Three variations of the Unipeco pen made in Mt. Vernon, New York. Value $8-$12.

UNIPECO, ca. 1958. A plastic pen from this maker of advertising pens. Value $6-$8.

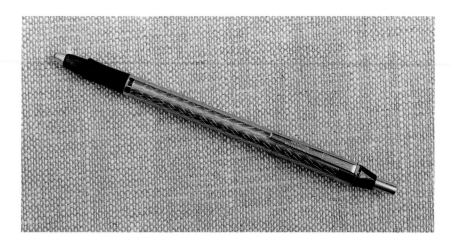

UNIPECO, ca. 1960. An attractive gold plated retractable pen made in Mt. Vernon, New York. Value $8-$10.

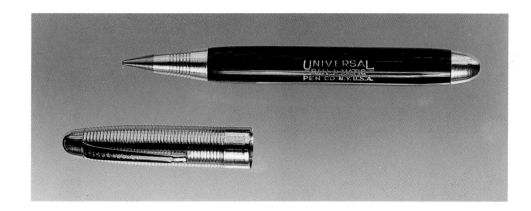

UNIVERSAL, ca. 1947. The Universal "Ball-O-Matic" was a popular pen and many have survived. Value $15-$20.

UNIVERSAL, ca. 1947. The "Buck Ball" pen made by the Ball-O-Matic Corp. of New York. The Universal was a common pen that competed on price with the major pen makers. Value $15-$25.

UNIVERSAL INK-N-TROL, ca. 1949. A plastic barrel with a metal cap. A feature that sets this pen apart from other Universals is the button at the end to help send the ink down to the point. Value $55-$75.

UNIVERSAL, ca. 1949. A metal pen with a retractable point. The point comes out the bottom when the cap is pushed down. Value $12-$15.

UNIVERSAL BUCKBALL, ca. 1950. A black plastic barrel with a metal cap. Value $10-$20.

UNIVERSAL BUCKBALL, ca. 1950. A black plastic barrel with a metal cap. Value $6-$9.

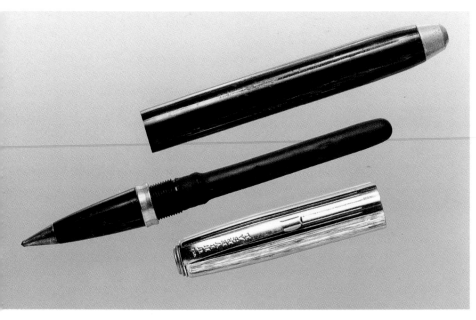

UNIVERSAL BUCKBALL, ca. 1950. A plastic barrel with a metal cap. The feature that sets this pen apart from the standard Buckballs is the fact that the manufacturer covered the ink container with a fountain pen sac to add extra protection to prevent the pen from leaking. Value $15-$25.

UNIVERSAL BUCKBALL, ca. 1952. A black plastic barrel with an unusual ribbed metal cap. Value $15-$25.

UNIVERSAL TWINPOINT, ca. 1952. A very unusual double pointed pen. To move one point in and the other point out, you would unscrew one barrel a few turns, then turn the gold center ring in the direction to extend the point and then tighten up the plastic barrel. Value $25-$35.

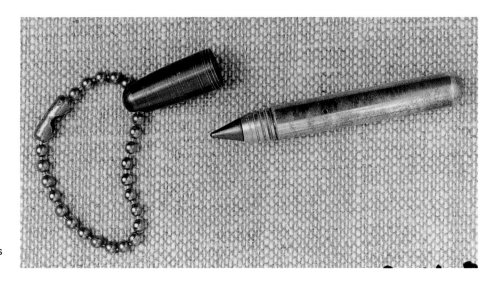

UNKNOWN, ca. 1946. A small key chain pen, possibly a Reynolds, 3 inches long. Value $30-$35.

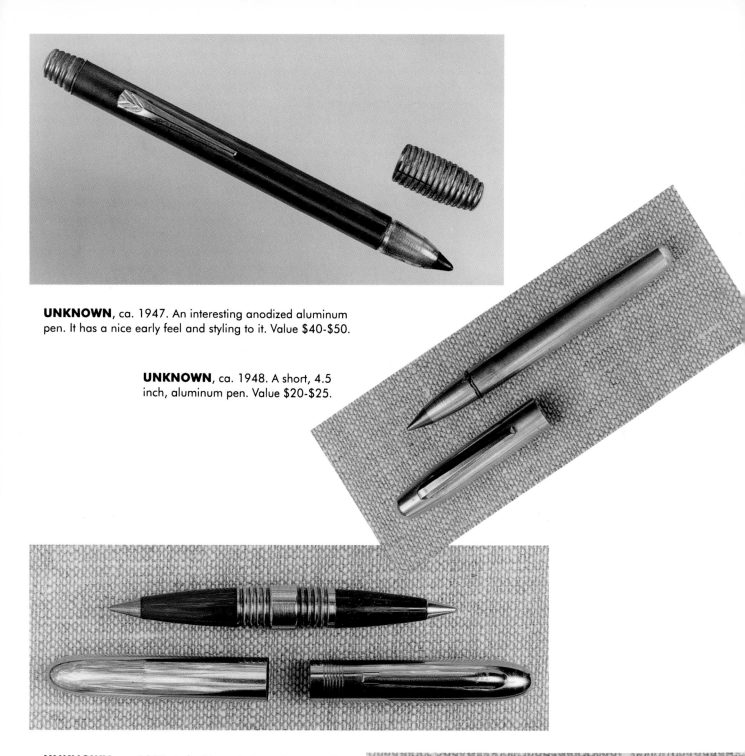

UNKNOWN, ca. 1947. An interesting anodized aluminum pen. It has a nice early feel and styling to it. Value $40-$50.

UNKNOWN, ca. 1948. A short, 4.5 inch, aluminum pen. Value $20-$25.

UNKNOWN, ca. 1950. A double ended pen that wrote in blue ink and red ink. It had a heavy brass center. Value $8-$12.

UNKNOWN, ca. 1951. A small key chain pen 3 inches long. Value $8-$10.

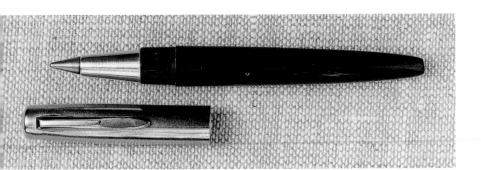

UNKNOWN, ca. 1951. This unknown pen has a familiar clip but no markings. It is nicely made of aluminum and plastic. Value $12-$15.

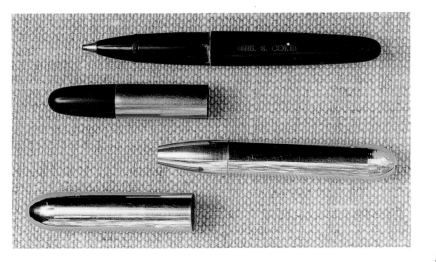

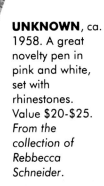

UNKNOWN, ca. 1958. A great novelty pen in pink and white, set with rhinestones. Value $20-$25. *From the collection of Rebbecca Schneider.*

UNKNOWN, ca. 1955. Two small pens, (top to bottom) 4 inches and 3 inches long. Value $8-$10.

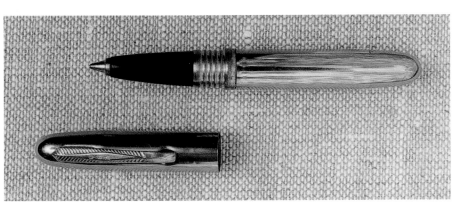

UNKNOWN, ca. 1957. There are quite a few of these unmarked pens with the center area made of turned heavy brass. Value $8-$10.

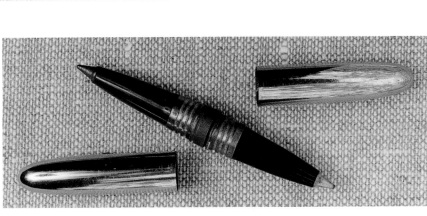

UNKNOWN, ca. 1957. A two color double ended pen with the center area made of turned heavy brass. 4 inches long. Value $10-$15.

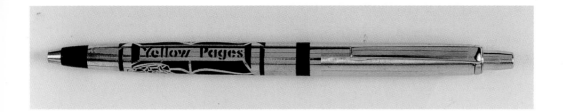

UNKNOWN, ca. 1965. An unusual sterling silver overlaid barrel advertising the Yellow Pages. There is a telephone and a name cut out in the silver. Value $40-$50.

UNKNOWN, 1968. A great metal and plastic desk set for the space race. To the left of the pen is a representation of the top of the Earth with a free floating space capsule. When the pen holder is pressed and released, the capsule spins around the Earth. Value $45-$60.

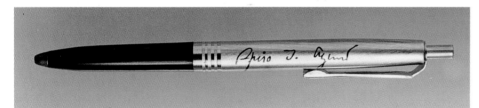

UNKNOWN, ca. 1970. Maryland's Governor, and later Vice President, Spiro Agnew's name appears on the side of this pen. Value $30-$40.

UNKNOWN, ca. 1976. Ball point pen in stainless steel with a built in digital clock. The barrel was twisted to extend the point and the clock was set by depressing the small button at top. This was the pen to have at the birth of electronic miniaturization. Value $10-$15.

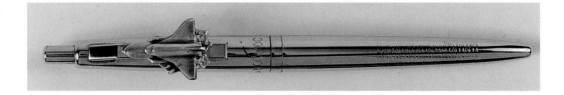

UNKNOWN, 1988. A ball point pen made in the Soviet Union with the Buran Space Shuttle. The Buran, which was a space shuttle look-a-like, never flew. It was abandoned when the Soviet Union broke apart. Value $45-$55.

VENUS, ca. 1957. This Venus plastic pen with metal cap has a small button at the top of the pocket clip that retracts the point. Value $8-$10.

WALDORF, ca. 1949. One of many brass pens made in this style. Value $6-$9.

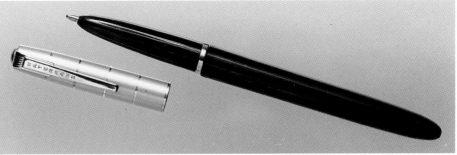

WATERMAN, ca. 1949. Waterman "Crusader" ball point, made to complement the Crusader fountain pen and pencil. Value $20-$25.

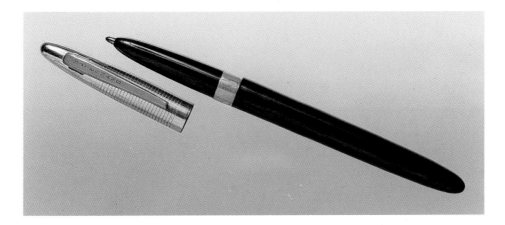

WATERMAN, ca. 1952. One dollar Waterman "Ball Pointer" ball point. Value $15-$20.

WATERMAN, 1952. Waterman's "Ball Pointer" pen. Value
$15-$20.

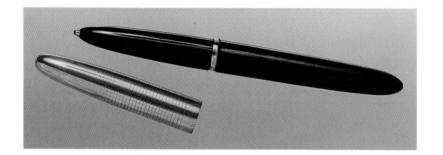

WATERMAN, ca. 1952. The interesting aspect of this pen is
that to remove the cartridge, you unscrew the barrel in a
clockwise fashion. The threads turn opposite to the way that
you would normally unscrew the barrel. Value $20-$25.

**WATERMAN
DEMONSTRATOR**, ca.
1953. A gold plated
"Sapphire Jewel Point"
pen. The side has been cut
away to show the inside of
the pen mechanism. Value
$45-$50.

1952 ad for Waterman Ballpointer.

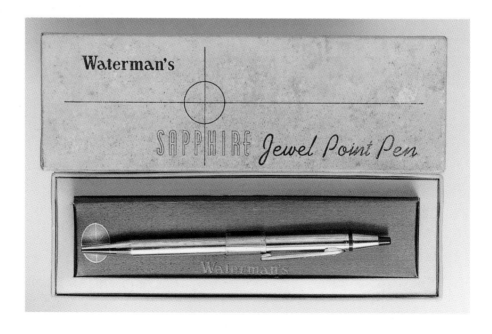

WATERMAN, ca. 1953. A gold plated "Sapphire Jewel Point"
pen. Value $30-$35 mint in the box.

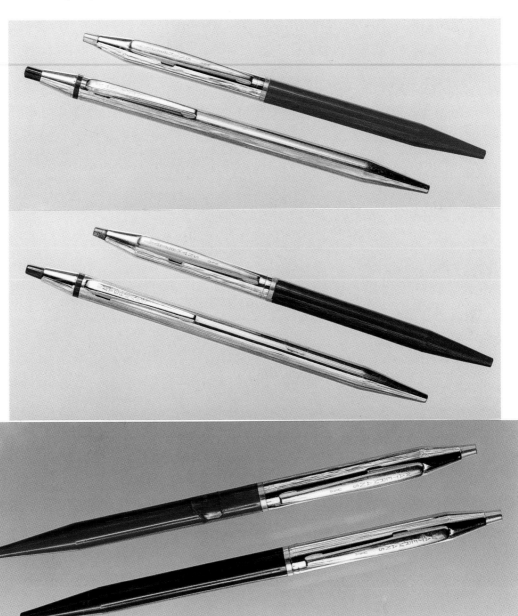

WATERMAN, ca. 1954. Waterman "Sapphire Jewel Point" pen in chrome plated metal. Value $15-$20.

WATERMAN, ca. 1954. Waterman "Sapphire Jewel Point" pens. Value $15-$20.

WATERMAN, ca. 1956. Waterman's pen made in their Seymour, Connecticut, plant. Value $20-$25.

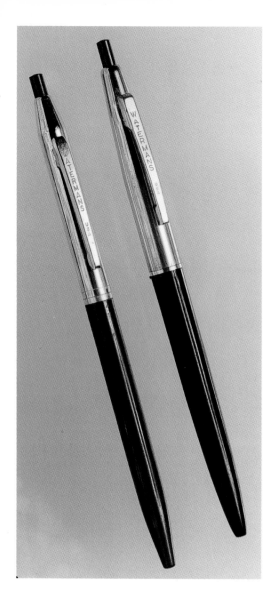

WATERMAN, ca. 1957. Two variations of Waterman retractable pens. The pen on the right is fatter and the area above the pocket clip is less tapered. Value $20-$25 each.

WATERMAN, ca. 1957. The Waterman high quality "CF" ball point, in rust red, was made to complement their CF (cartridge filler) fountain pen and pencil. The cap was twisted to extend the point. The CF line was made in the USA or Canada from 1955 to 1958. In the 1958, Waterman was sold to the French importer of Waterman (BIC). After about 1961, pens bearing the Waterman-BIC name ceased to be made. However, Waterman pens continued to made in France. Value (ball point) $40-$50.

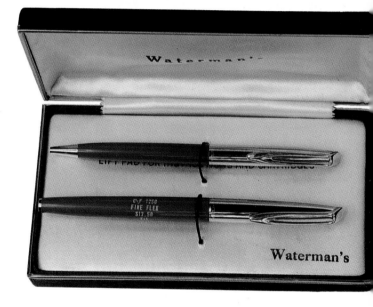

WATERMAN, ca. 1957. The Waterman CF ball point in blue with chrome and gold filled cap and accompanying CF (cartridge filler) fountain pen. Value (ball point) $40-$50.

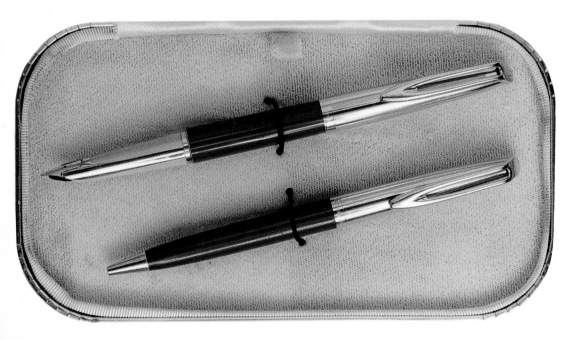

WATERMAN, ca. 1957. The Waterman CF ball point in blue with gold filled cap and accompanying CF (cartridge filler) fountain pen. Value (ball point) $35-$45.

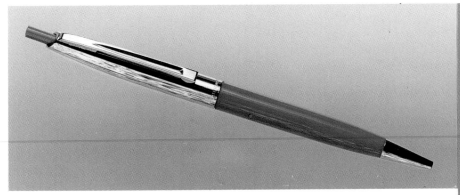

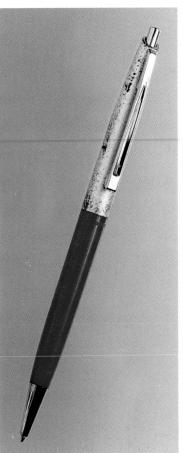

WATERMAN, ca. 1958. Waterman click retractable ball point. Value $18-$25.

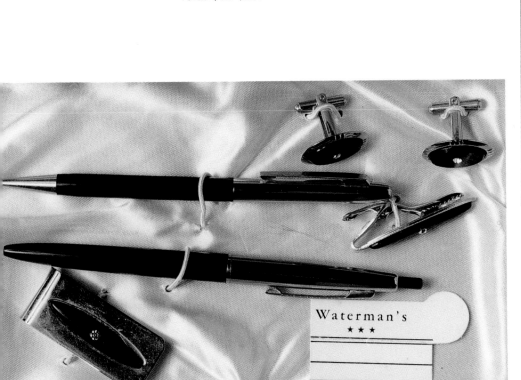

WATERMAN, ca. 1958. Waterman's ensemble came with a pen, pencil, cuff links, tie clip, and money clip. Value $25-$30.

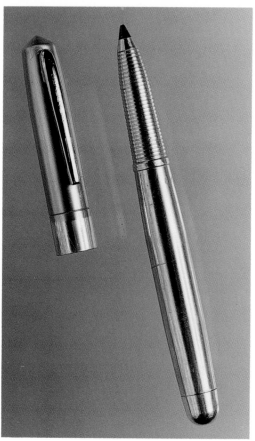

WEAREVER, 1948. An early Wearever aluminum pen. Value $40-$45.

WEAREVER, 1956. Advertisement for Wearever's pens.

WEAREVER, 1955. Advertisement for Wearever's ball pens.

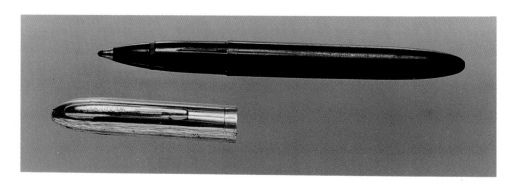

WEAREVER, ca. 1956. A plastic pen with a gold plated cap. Value $8-$10.

WEAREVER, ca. 1957. An anodized blue-green aluminum four color pen with slide levers to move the points in or out. Wearever was made by the David Kahn Company of North Bergen, New Jersey. Original cost was $1.00. Value $15-$20.

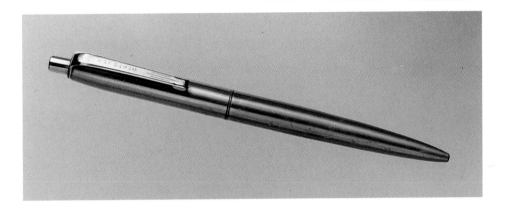

WEAREVER, ca. 1958. A great looking anodized aluminum retractable pen. Value $12-$15.

WEAREVER, ca. 1962. A small (3.5 inches long) plastic retractable pen made for young girls. Value $10-$12.

WECLE, ca. 1991. A Japanese made double ball point pen desk set in black metal whose pens have rubber gripping areas and use the short Lamy refill. Although a late entry into the field of ball point pens, Wecle has made some very innovative looking pens that are as much art as they are fine writing instruments. This style is no longer available. Value $95-$115.

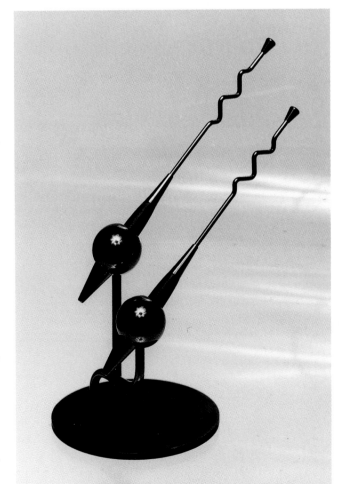

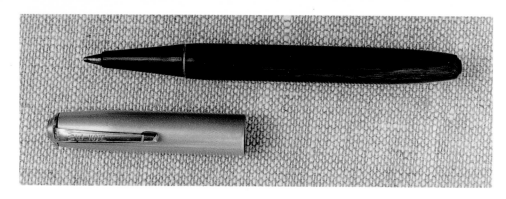

WELSH, ca. 1956. The Welsh Pen Company was located in Providence, Rhode Island. Value $10-$12.

WINDSOR, ca. 1955. A gold plated Windsor pen. Value $8-$10.

WINGMATIC, ca. 1957. A nice quality advertising pen. Value $8-$10.

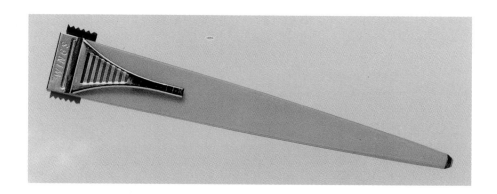

WINGS, ca. 1964. A plastic flattened two color pen with an interesting look. Value $10-$14.

ZANER BLOSER, ca. 1958. The Zaner Bloser College of Writing taught a specific style of writing. They contracted with various makers to produce pens to their specifications. Parker was among the pen makers to make pens for Z-B. Value $15-$20.

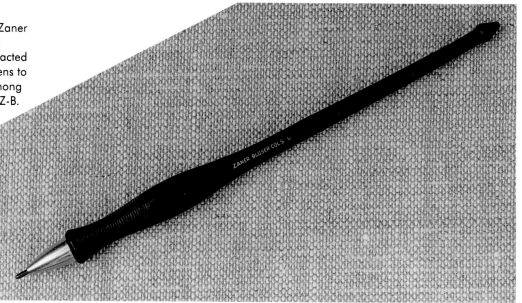

Bibliography

Alexiades, Alex. *The BIC Beginning*. Milford, Connecticut: BIC Corporation, 1990.

Bowen, Glen Benton. *Collectable Fountain Pens*. Gas City, Indiana: LW Book Sales.

"Pen Phenomenon." *Business Week* (December 15, 1945).

"Three More Ball-tip Pens." *Consumers' Research Bulletin* (August 1946): 22-24.

"Six Ball-Point Pens." *Consumer Reports* (June 1946): 150-151.

"Ball Point Pens." *Consumer Reports* (November 1946): 287-290.

"Ball Pen: Something New for Angles and Left Hands." *Consumer Reports* (April 1950): 169.

"Better Ball Point Pens." *Consumer Reports* (November 1950): 473.

"Ball Point Pens." *Consumers Union* (June 1949): 261-263.

"The Ball Pen Story, History of a Success." *The Counselor* (March 1962).

Cross, A.T. *Man's Written Communication, A Pictoral History*. Providence, RI.: n.d.

_____. Corporate histories brochure. n.d.

Diotte, Alfred P. Memo announcing Eversharp relocation to Janesville, and as a Parker division rather than a subsidiary. January 10, 1968.

Erickson, Robert. "Engineering the Ball Point." *PenWorld* vol. 3., no. 1 (Fall 1989).

Eversharp Pen Company. Fountain Ball Introduction, Press release. September 16, 1958.

_____. Forty illustrated, wholesale product fact sheets, promotional material, and price lists. 1946 to 1961.

_____. Miscellaneous press releases. 1958 to 1961.

Fischler, George, and Stuart Schneider. *Fountain Pens & Pencils, The Golden Age Of Writing Instruments*. Atglen, Pennsylvania: Schiffer Publishing, 1989.

"Fountain Pen Scramble." *Fortune* (July 1946).

Frantz, Thomas E. Sheaffer Inc. Letter. September 12, 1995.

_____. Letter, including corporate history. August 2, 1996.

Gillette Company, Corporate Public Relations. Chronology. Corporate history, 92 pages. 1995.

Gillette Company, Stationary Products Group, Santa Monica Manufacturing Center. Patrick Joseph Frawley, Jr. Biographical sheet. n.d.

_____. Paper Mate Product Story. Illustrated, 20-page history. ca. 1961.

_____. Paper Mate Chronology. Listing. ca. 1992.

_____. Paper Mate Fact Sheet. Corporate history, 7 pages. ca. 1971.

Gostony, Henry. "One of a Kind Waterman's." *PenWorld* vol. 4, no. 4 (March/April 1991).

_____. "A Breathtaking view of the Skyline." Parts 1 and 2. *PenWorld* vol. 7, no. 2 (November/December 1993); vol. 7, no. 3 (January/February 1994).

_____. "The Incredible History of Milton Reynolds and His Ball Point Pens." Parts 1-3. *PenWorld* vol. 7, no. 6 (July/August 1994); vol. 8, no. 1 (September/October 1994); vol. 8., no. 2 (November/December 1994).

Grabecher, Kurt. *Meisterstuk for the Art of Writing, a History of the Firm Montblanc*. Hamburg, Germany: Montblanc, Inc.

Harvat, Dennis, Manager Information Technology, Gillette Company, Stationary Products Group (Paper Mate), Santa Monica. Telephone interviews. January to March 1997.

Howe, Dresson. "Ball Point Pen Writes Legacy of Its Inventor." *The Washington Post* (Sunday, November 3, 1985).

"Parker Pen Will Introduce Jotter to European Market." *Janesville Daily Gazette* (Friday, June 4, 1954).

"Parker Announces Five New Series of Products." *Janesville Daily Gazette* (Saturday, September 27, 1958).

"Jotter's Arrow Hits Bulls Eye to Lead Parker Pen Parade." *Janesville Daily Gazette* (Saturday, June 1, 1974).

"Big Project Planned for Beach City." *Los Angeles Times* (Sunday, October 21, 1956).

Milwaukee Journal, *Thirteen Cents Ball Point Pens*

Snubbed by Janesville, (Sunday, November 18, 1956).

"Three New Parker Ball Pens." *Pacific Stationer and Office Outfitter* (July 1954).

Paper Mate Company, Inc. Letter: Patrick Frawley to wholesalers announcing sale of Paper Mate to Gillette. December 28, 1955.

_____. 85 dealer price sheets, product announcements, and illustrations. 1954 to 1971.

Parker Pen Company. Change of Model Name: Executive Line To Be Called VIP Line Bulletin for Parker Distributors, No. 500. April 29, 1959.

_____. Feminine Ball Points To Appear. Press release. September 25, 1958.

_____. General letter No. 14. T-ball information kit. July 17, 1957.

_____. Hopalong Cassidy Ball Point Pens. Press release. 1950.

_____. Jotter Product Sheet. Press release. January 5, 1954.

_____. Position of the Parker Pen Company Regarding Ball Point Pens. Press release. December 16, 1953.

_____. Parker Pen Production Models—Ballpoint Pens 1951-1986. ca. 1986.

_____. Sell the New Parker Jotter Gift Line. Dealer flyer. March, 1959.

_____. Smart Set. Press Release. ca. October, 1954.

_____. Standard Jotter Ballpoint, LL-275 Pencil. Bulletin for Parker Distributors, No. 350. June 1, 1956.

_____. T-ball Fact Sheet. Distributor hand-out. June 18, 1957.

_____. Thirty Millionth Ballpoint. Bulletin for Parker distributors, No. 576 June 16, 1961.

_____. 51 Jotter press release. July 14, 1954.

_____. Compact Jotter press release. February 19, 1965.

_____. Fourteen miscellaneous press releases. January-March, 1954.

_____. Jotter 18-pen counter display press release. January, 1954.

_____. Pardners Set press release. June 7, 1956.

_____. Seven miscellaneous T-ball Jotter press releases. July-September, 1957.

"Jotter Scores High In Market Tests." *Parkergram* (March 1954).

"Jotter Works 1,000,000 Times and More." *Parkergram* (March 1956).

Petroski, Henry. *The Pencil*. New York: Alfred A. Knopf, 1993.

Plewa, Fred. "Early Ball Points." *PenWorld* vol. 3, no. 1 (Fall 1989).

_____. "Reynolds Pen." *PenWorld* vol. 8 no. 1 (September/October 1994).

Roe, Geoff. *Writing Instruments*. England: Manchester Literary & Philosophical Society, 1993.

Rosenberg, Robert Leonard. *The Ventures and Adventures of an Errant Entrepreneur: Milton (Ball-Point) Reynolds*. Seattle: University of Washington, 1971.

Schneider, Stuart. *Collecting And Valuing Early Fountain Pens*. Hudson Valley Graphics, 1980.

Schneider, Stuart, and George Fischler. *The Book of Fountain Pens & Pencils*. Atglen, Pennsylvania: Schiffer Publishing, 1991.

Schneider, Stuart, and George Fischler. *The Illustrated Guide To Antique Writing Instruments*. Atglen, Pennsylvania: Schiffer Publishing, 1994, revised 1997.

Senseman, Ronald S. War Department, Office of the Quartermaster General, Letters to W.A. Sheaffer Company soliciting possible ball point pen production. Washington, D.C. August 10 and November 3, 1944.

Sheaffer, Inc. Twenty-eight ball point pen patents assigned to W.A. Sheaffer Pen Company. 1945 to 1981.

"Background on the Jotter, How Fast Can a Company Move?" *Shoptalker* (January-February 1954).

"Eversharp Operations Relocated from Culver City to Janesville." *Shoptalker* issue 372 (December 19, 1967).

"Eversharp Transfer of Operations to Janesville Completed." *Shoptalker* issue 391 (April 25, 1968).

"One Hundred Millionth Jotter." *Shoptalker* issue 708 (November 18, 1974).

"Parker Pen Enters Ball Point Field." *Southern Stationer & Office Outfitter* (February 1954).

Stocker, J. J. "The Ball Pen, an Industry Products Success Story." *National Stationer* (March 1961).

Wharton, Don. "Mighty Battle of the Pens." *Nation's Business* (November 1946).

Whiteside, Thomas. "Where Are They Now?" *The New Yorker* (February 17, 1951): 39-61.

Index